John O'Farrell's first book was the bestselling memoir *Things Can Only Get Better* (the sequel, *Things Can Only Get Worse*, is coming in Autumn 2017).

He is also the author of five novels: *The Man Who Forgot His Wife*, *May Contain Nuts*, *This Is Your Life*, *The Best a Man Can Get* and, most recently, *There's Only Two David Beckhams*.

He has also written two bestselling history books: *An Utterly Impartial History of Britain* and *An Utterly Exasperated History of Modern Britain*, as well as three collections of journalism from his *Guardian* columns.

His books have been translated into over twenty-five languages and have been adapted for radio and television.

A former comedy scriptwriter for *Spitting Image*, *Room 101*, *Have I Got News For You*, *Murder Most Horrid* and *Chicken Run*, he is founder of the UK's first daily news satire website, *NewsBiscuit*, and more recently co-wrote the Broadway musical *Something Rotten!*

'Very funny and much better than anything he ever wrote for me'
Griff Rhys Jones

'Very funny book . . . about the pity and the misery and the sheer boredom of being a devoted Labour supporter'
Simon Hoggart, *Guardian*

'Very well-written. And very funny'
Big Issue

'This book evokes many of the words not normally associated with political memoir. Charming, self-aware, humble, witty and downright funny. I read it at one sitting'
Nick Hancock

'Hilarious'
Gerald Kaufman, *Daily Telegraph*

'*Things Can Only Get Better* is really about growing up, but growing up in the Labour Party at a time when it was going through convulsive change. It is a hilarious read . . . a very funny account of O'Farrell's odyssey from left-wing innocence to a mature acceptance of New Labour'
Mirror

'The whingeing memoirs of a snivelling leftie. The man should be shot'
Jack Dee

'Political activists will have their own recollections of those wasted, mean years, but few will achieve the wit of this candid personal tale of hacking through Thatcherism . . . wickedly funny'
Gary Kent, *Tribune*

'The funniest book I have read for two and a half years'
Arthur Smith

BY JOHN O'FARRELL

FICTION

The Best a Man Can Get
This is Your Life
May Contain Nuts
The Man Who Forgot His Wife
There's Only Two David Beckhams

NON-FICTION

Things Can Only Get Better
Global Village Idiot
I Blame the Scapegoats
I Have a Bream
An Utterly Impartial History of Britain
An Utterly Exasperated History of Modern Britain
Isle of Wight to get Ceefax (editor)
Things Can Only Get Worse

THINGS
CAN ONLY
GET BETTER

Eighteen Miserable Years
in the Life of a Labour Supporter
1979–1997

JOHN O'FARRELL

BLACK SWAN

TRANSWORLD PUBLISHERS
61–63 Uxbridge Road, London W5 5SA
www.penguin.co.uk

Transworld is part of the Penguin Random House group of companies
whose addresses can be found at global.penguinrandomhouse.com

First published in Great Britain in 1998 by Doubleday
an imprint of Transworld Publishers
Black Swan edition published 1999
Black Swan edition reissued 2017

A CIP catalogue record for this book
is available from the British Library.

ISBN
9781784163211

Typeset in 11/13pt Melior by Phoenix Typesetting, Ilkley, West Yorkshire.
Printed and bound by Clays Ltd, Bungay, Suffolk

Penguin Random House is committed to a sustainable future for
our business, our readers and our planet. This book is made from
Forest Stewardship Council® certified paper.

3 5 7 9 10 8 6 4 2

To my mother and father

Acknowledgements

With thanks to the mainstay of Queenstown ward Labour Party during my years there, especially Phil Green, Eileen Hogan, Libby Ridgeway and Liz Tomlinson, and to all the people at Battersea Labour Party, especially Alf Dubs, Ann Creighton, Fiona Mactaggart and Martin Linton. I would also very much like to thank Georgia Garrett, Bill Scott-Kerr, Mark Burton, Pete Sinclair, Pat O'Farrell and, most of all, my wife Jackie.

Author's note

I have tried to be as accurate as possible in this book and have checked facts wherever I could, but I apologise now if I have overlooked any mistakes. On the key points I am sure my memory serves me correctly:

1) Mrs Thatcher was in power during the 1980s.
2) I did not like her very much.

J. O'F

Where there is discord ...

General Election – 3 May 1979

Maidenhead. The slag heaps and the dirt. The rattle of the giant wheel at the pit head. The faces of the coal-miners as they trudged up the cobbled streets back from Cookham colliery, their white teeth and eyes gleaming as the noises of the brass band echoed through the Thames Valley. My father was a pit deputy at Littlewick Green colliery, and led the famous picket at Henley-on-Thames coke works back in the strike of '72. The Labour Party was in my blood. They didn't count the Labour votes in Maidenhead, they weighed them.

If only it could have been thus. But the real reason that they didn't count the Labour votes in Maidenhead was because there weren't any. You were considered subversive if you only mowed your lawn once a week. To be fair, there were *two* Labour votes in Maidenhead, but in all likelihood both my parents' ballot papers would have been helpfully put into the Conservative pile because the nice people at the count would have presumed that somebody must have crossed the wrong box by mistake. Maybe if there had been a home counties coalfield my dad would have got a job as a miner, but instead he had to make do with being an anti-quarian book dealer. Maidenhead was a comfy town and we lived in the comfy part of Maidenhead.

Why was I so privileged? It just wasn't fair. Why couldn't I be horribly disadvantaged and espouse left-wing views with the anger and accent that came from years of capitalist oppression? When the word 'Tory' came out of my mouth it just sounded like I was one. On my first student demonstration, the crowd from Salford University could shout 'Education for the Masses, Not the Tory Ruling Classes' and it rhymed. Masses and classes! But when I joined in, everyone looked round to see who was this posh git shouting 'Education for the Masses, Not the Tory Ruling Claaaaaasses'. Maybe if I'd joined the Socialist Workers Party I could have gone to the specialist voice-training classes they organise where paper sellers are taught to shout 'SOcialiss Worker'. But it wasn't just the accent. Every definite opinion I attempted to make petered out halfway through as I realised I ought to consider the other side of the argu-ment, until the end of my sentence ended up contradicting the beginning. If I had had to do what Lenin did in 1917 I would have said, 'Um, I suppose we could possibly perhaps seize control of the state, maybe? In the name of the workers, as it were – sort of on their behalf ... is that a good idea? On the other hand perhaps we ought to just run that idea past the Mensheviks – we don't want to upset anyone. Best stay here then I suppose, yes.' The middle classes of England are in a permanent state of embarrassment as it is. To be left-wing and embarrassed about the very

14

fact that I was middle-class took embarrassment into a new dimension.

I was not old enough to vote when Margaret Thatcher came to power, but it was the fourth election in which I cared about the result.

I had wanted Labour to win in 1970 because my dad did, just as I had wanted Dana to win the Eurovision Song Contest because my dad did.

In 1974 I went with him when he went to the polling station and was rather impressed to see a policeman standing there. My dad voted Labour and no arrests were made.

My parents were political in very different ways – my father pored over the politics pages of the *Guardian* and could tell you who was the minister for defence procurement (which is probably more than most prime ministers could do), while my mother was active in Oxfam and Amnesty International. On one Amnesty flag day my dad managed to combine his style of politics with hers by sitting in a pub and reading the *New Statesman* while putting ten-pence pieces into the collection tin that he was supposed to be shaking in the High Street. Unlike my older brother I cared enough to stay up to watch the election results in February 1974. The failure of the Heath government had been discernible even to an eleven-year-old boy: television ending at ten o'clock, shopping by candlelight, and – therefore – a marked increase in shoplifting in W. H. Smith's in Maidenhead High Street by the said eleven-year-old boy.

In February 1974 we had a school mock election in which I voted Labour, to howls of derision from the two prefects whose job it was to make sure that no one was

15

intimidated at the polls. I accepted the universal hostility to Labour as a cross I had to bear, like having acne or a stupid name; my political allegiance was not something I could change. At a pre-election rally I remember one senior prefect taking the stand for the Conservatives and shouting at the climax of his speech that, if Labour got in, Russian tanks would be rolling down Whitehall within five years. This person was so superior to me in age, authority, status and, I had presumed, intellect, that it was quite a shock to hear him talk such arrant rubbish. What was more bizarre was the way the room erupted into cheers of enthusiastic agreement and applause. Were *all* these older boys mad, or was it me?

Labour did get in and no Russian tanks were seen in Whitehall, although the reality was apparently almost as bad, as any Conservative will tell you. In the run-up to the 1997 general election a wave of letters to the newspapers reminded us all just how terrible life was under Labour in the 'Winter of Discontent'. Each contained the same key phrases. Rather than saying, 'A wage dispute between council workers and their employers, many of them Conservative councils, led to a strike by dustmen', it was compulsory to say, 'Rubbish piled up in the streets.' Labour didn't negotiate a loan from the International Monetary Fund and subsequently impose some rather right-wing policies to control inflation. What Labour did was go 'cap-in-hand to the IMF'.

Because Conservative politicians repeated these phrases so often, they became the acceptable way to refer to the episodes. If an interviewer was grilling a Labour politician he wouldn't say, 'But isn't there a fear that we may see a return to the days when a brief strike by grave-diggers delayed some funerals?', he would say, 'Isn't there a fear that we may see a return to the days when *we couldn't even bury the dead*!'

For eighteen years we Labour supporters had to endure this terrible shame: 'Look at what happened under the last Labour government.' I did once see a Conservative minister on *Newsnight* saying to a Liberal MP on the panel, and I swear that this is true: 'Well I think our record stands up very well when we look at what happened under the last Liberal government.' What? Was he criticising a member of the 1990s Liberal Democrats for the fact that the assassination of Archduke Ferdinand plunged Europe into the most terrible war the world had ever seen? The fact that the Conservatives were allowed to build up this myth about the Winter of Discontent was partly Labour's fault for failing to put the events of 1978/9 into some sort of perspective with everything that happened in the following eighteen years. If the Britain of 1997 had been transported back to 1979 we would have thought ourselves in paradise. Except, perhaps, for having to queue up in your lunch-hour to get cash from the bank and having to buy both the *Radio Times* and the *TV Times* to get the television listings, Britain was clearly a much happier place before eighteen years of Conservative government put 3 million on the dole, beggars on the streets and Carol Thatcher on *Loose Ends*.

Of course in 1979 not even Margaret Thatcher would have had the self-confidence to predict that the Conservatives would remain in power for eighteen years. The result of the 1979 election – much like the assassination of Archduke Ferdinand – is much more depressing when you look at everything that followed it. I had expected the Conservatives to win, and they did, but Labour would win next time. In that very year I was doing an O Level in British Government and they taught us that power in Britain operated like the swing of a pendulum: Tory, Labour, Tory, Labour ... How could they give me such a false sense of security? These were textbooks on British Government and there it was, printed on the page in black and white: 'Power operates like the swing of a pendulum.' Not one of them had a little note to say, *except for the period when* you *first become actively involved in politics, when your lot will be out of power till your hair's falling out and you're spending your Sunday mornings dragging your kids round the garden centre.*

Between the Labour landslide of 1945 and the watershed election of 1979, the two main political parties had taken turns to run the country within generally agreed parameters. They both accepted that the state had to take an active role running essential services like education, health and transport, and they both believed in solving problems through negotiation rather than confrontation. Then in the mid-1970s along came Mrs Thatcher who suddenly blew away all the accepted conventions. She was the first punk politician.

Margaret Thatcher had come to my attention in strange circumstances in 1975. We lived in an imposing house by the river – the sort of address that makes a policeman suddenly let go of your lapels when he hears it. But the Thames had no such respect and in February 1975 it burst its banks, surrounding our house completely. The paper boy was obviously too lazy to swim through 300 yards of freezing cold floodwater (that's just how bad things were under Labour) and so I volunteered to set off to get Maidenhead's only copy of the *Guardian* in a pair of waist-high rubber wading boots. I distinctly remember stopping and standing in the floodwater to read a story on the front page about the possibility that Margaret Thatcher could beat Willie Whitelaw for the leadership of the Tory Party. I reported this to my dad who laughed and said, 'Margaret Thatcher? Don't be ridiculous.' Like the bubonic plague and stone cladding, no one took her seriously until it was too late. Her first act as leader was to appear before the cameras and do a V for victory sign the wrong way round. She was smiling and telling the British people to fuck off at the same time. It was something we would have to get used to.

Politics was never an interest particularly shared by my schoolmates. We did not stand around in the playground exchanging bubblegum stickers featuring members of the cabinet saying, 'I'll swap you Tony Crosland for Barbara Castle.' We did not argue about the best possible line-up for the cabinet.

'What is Sunny Jim doing putting Roy Mason in Northern Ireland ...'
    'Oh, come on, he's got Owen in Defence, Healey has got to stay at number 11 – he's got no option.'

We didn't cut pictures of Shirley Williams out of *Smash Hits* and stick them above our beds. The ownership of an Anti-Nazi League badge was about the only trendy thing about my teenage politics. It was red and yellow with little black bits on it and matched my face perfectly. I asked the teacher who told me to take it off, 'How can you *not* be anti-Nazi?'

Generally speaking the rest of the school were either instinctively Conservative or completely uninterested in politics or both, much like the British people really.

Contrary to popular belief, there are few people as reactionary as teenagers. I do remember cringing at the adulation with which a boy my age was received at the Tory Party conference in 1977, and thought he was such a prat that he would surely disappear for ever more. But this of course was the Conservative Party, so maybe I should have guessed that they were applauding the next Tory leader but one.

The collapse of the Labour government, i.e., their defeat in a motion of confidence, happened the day after my seventeenth birthday (a birthday I shared with the prime minister, Jim Callaghan, apropos of nothing). His government lost by one vote. One Labour MP, Sir Alfred Broughton, claimed that he was too ill to attend the vote, and just to prove a point he died a few days later.

In 1979 another mock election was to be held in the school and this time I wasn't a five-foot first-former with a squeaky voice and a squashed Aztec bar in my blazer pocket, I was a sixth-former. I had status. I had an Adam's apple and a chair in assembly. When the deputy headmaster announced that he was looking for candidates I was naturally at first reluctant. But then I consulted with my constituency association and was persuaded that for the good of the party I should allow my name to go forward for the first ballot. Which translates roughly as 'Limelight! Power! Gimme, gimme, gimme!' My entry into politics was driven by nothing more worthy than vanity. How unlike a real politician.

The selection went like this: anybody interested in standing as a candidate in the school general election was to go to room B12 at one o'clock. There were several boys interested in representing Labour. Those that were not sixth-formers were quickly told to get out and stop wasting everybody's time. That left me and one other boy. We tossed a coin. I won. But then he raised a mild objection that I hadn't tossed it properly and had dropped it when I tried to catch it. So we tossed again and I won again. Thus I was selected. It was only later in life that I was to realise that this was actually quite a well-organised and fair selection meeting as far as the Labour Party goes. So there it was – out of a school of over a thousand boys I had the job of representing the government of the day.

I went down to W. H. Smith and bought a Labour manifesto which proved most useful. Not for its contents particularly, but for the picture of a red rosette on the back cover, which I cut out and stuck on top of my Ian Dury and the Blockheads badge so that wherever I walked I could be stopped and engaged in earnest political discussion. This was the rather naive ideal. The level of discourse never really rose much above 'Oi, Labour! Wanker!' or 'Oi, Labour! Greeny!' and a cocktail of spit and catarrh would drop from the bridge between the old school building and the science block. And all of that was actually quite cultured criticism compared to the hostility of one of the PE teachers. The slogan on my carefully cut out rosette read something like 'The Labour Way is the Better Way' but unfortunately some of the boys with learning difficulties misread this as 'Please throw a wet tennis ball at me as hard as you can'. The whole exercise was supposed to be a lesson in how adult politics works. People fired pellets at me, shouted insults and occasionally threatened violence, so from that point of view it was a great success.

The Tory candidate was a classmate of mine called Nigel who was probably selected for the Tories on the grounds that he was called Nigel. I remember that his dad owned a grocery store and I think he felt this bestowed upon him the attributes of Margaret Thatcher. Fortunately for him it didn't. But the candidate who caught the imagination of the school was Tom Gill, who stood for the Pupils' Alliance for Liberation. He was a thoroughly decent, principled and sincere bloke on his way to Oxbridge who never took any of the privileges that sixth-formers were permitted. While any normal A Level student went straight into the tuck shop, Tom would queue up for ten minutes behind all the first-years (who obviously thought he was completely mad). He did it because he believed it was right and fair, and he didn't care that people laughed at him. Looking back I wish I'd never sung 'Ra-Ra-Rasputin' when he cycled into school wearing a big furry hat.

Pretty early on he looked like a front-runner. He combined a popular subversive message with a flamboyant way of promoting it – the exact opposite of Labour, now I think about it. He walked around wearing a sandwich board promising to take pupils' grievances directly to the headmaster, a pledge no one else could match, and as his popularity grew it looked as if my vote was getting caught in a classic Conservative/Pupils' Alliance for Liberation squeeze.

Labour's campaign in the rest of the country was not going much better. I later read in the diaries of Tony Benn that when the election was declared the cabinet spent the following few days locked in smoked-filled rooms arguing about the wording of the manifesto. It struck me that the need for a manifesto in an election campaign was something that a political party might have possibly foreseen. Perhaps at some point in 1978 somebody had raised this at a meeting of Labour's National Executive Committee and Jim Callaghan had said, 'Oh no, let's wait until the election is declared.' So while Margaret Thatcher was whizzing around the country snipping pound notes in two to illustrate the value of 'the Labour pound' (which is actually an offence but one for which she has still not been arrested), half the Labour front bench were nowhere to be seen because they were locked away until three in the morning arguing over the wording of their wage-bargaining policy. Should it be termed 'fair deal free bargaining' or 'fair deal collective wage bargaining' – this was the challenge for Labour's finest in the last days of March 1979. If anyone is interested the latter won the day, but somehow this event failed to set the election campaign alight for Labour. For some reason, the *Sun* didn't lead with *'Phwoar!* Fair Deal Collective Wage Bargaining it is!'

Meanwhile, Margaret Thatcher's photocalls in factories and supermarkets were on every front page. She was confident enough to be photographed holding up a rather terrified calf somewhere in Suffolk. She visited a chocolate factory in Birmingham and had to put on a white coat and hat, as did her entire entourage of Tory MPs, giving us a surreal preview of the lunatics who were about to take over the asylum.

'Where do you export your chocolate to?' she asked a factory worker.

'A lot of it goes to Africa.'

'Oh, doesn't it melt?'

With this sort of grasp on African affairs the forthcoming talks on Rhodesia looked set to pass off very smoothly indeed. She attended a rally of Conservative trade unionists, at which Pete Murray introduced Vince Hill and Lulu to sing 'Hello Maggie, well hello Maggie, it's so great to see you on the way to Number 10'. At which point I began a mental list of all the hateful celebrities who helped the Conservatives. The issues that she hammered on about were the unions, income tax cuts, the unions, Labour militants, the unions, law and order, the unions, and immigration and the unions.

Although the general expectation was that the Conservatives were going to win, there were a few straws of hope to which Labour supporters could cling. One poll in the *Daily Mirror* on 14 April had Labour ahead by 3 per cent in the marginals but the next day a poll in the *Observer* had Labour 16 points behind. Jim Callaghan was consistently more popular than Margaret Thatcher but the Tories led on every issue except the Health Service. Labour definitely trailed in the ratings for 'Ability to bury the dead' and 'Least likely to go cap-in-hand to the IMF'.

The night before I was due to speak to the masses of Desborough School at the specially arranged election meeting, I was sitting in my bedroom copying out the best bits from the manifesto. My dad came up to tell me that there was a poll giving Labour a lead of 0.7 per cent. It was 36 hours till election day, and I thought that there was still a possibility that Labour might just do it. This was a sensation I was foolishly to allow myself to feel during every election for the next couple of decades.

On 2 May came the climax of the school campaign – the debate in the sports hall. By now the Pupils' Alliance for Liberation was looking unstoppable. The various head-cases and gang leaders in the different years had decided that this was the cool party to support and had lined up their troops to heckle and boo anyone who opposed their leader. It really was the strangest alliance – an intellectual sixth-former in Hush Puppies and a grey suit (when we were still supposed to wear school uniform) carried aloft by these frankly rather terrifying mods and skinheads. But then I suppose Geoffrey Howe and Norman Tebbit were in the same cabinet together.

When I stood up to make my speech I knew I did not have the mob on my side. The booing and catcalling was louder than my voice and I pathetically attempted to quieten the mob while I recited lots of lines I had learnt the night before. A few people seemed to take in the point that the profits from North Sea oil should go to Britain and not the American multinationals, and then I said, 'Under a Conservative government, the rich will get richer and the poor will get poorer!' and attempted a sort of stabbing gesture with my index finger that I had seen Len Murray do on the news. Suddenly, from one of the candidates' chairs behind me, came solitary but very enthusiastic applause. 'Hear, hear!' shouted a lone voice. I turned around assuming the intervention was ironic, that I was being heckled, but it was Tom Gill, the man who was heading for a landslide victory, genuinely applauding my point. I had been prepared for every-thing except positive heckling from my rivals and the rest of my speech fizzled out under the howls of the fourth-formers who could see that I had completely lost it.

Out of a possible twelve hundred I polled 35 votes. Labour Gain Maidenhead it was not. I came fourth or possibly fifth; a friend of mine stood for the Apathy Party ('Lie Down and Be Counted') and may have pipped me for fourth place. However, I got my deposit back, which was more than can be said for the Plaid Cymru candidate who made the early tactical mistake of standing in a school that was not in Wales.

As he handed me back my crinkled pound note on the morning of 4 May the deputy headmaster said, 'Well, the school seemed to go the same way as the rest of the country.' What did he mean? A landslide victory for the Pupils' Alliance for Liberation? If only Margaret Thatcher's most damaging policies had been the abolition of school uniform and the right for fifth-formers to park their mopeds in the bike sheds, then the country would not have been in the terrible mess it was in by 1997.

Most people remember Margaret Thatcher's speech on the steps of Downing Street: 'Where there is discord, may we bring harmony, where there is error, may we bring truth, where there is doubt, may we bring faith, where there is despair, may we bring hope ...' It's one of those pieces of footage that you think you saw at the time even if you didn't because it has been played so many times since. It usually features as the preface to 'London's Burning' by The Clash over footage of the Brixton riots. It was a victorious battle cry to remind us exactly what kind of person we had just handed the keys of Downing Street to. It said, 'You don't like me because I am a ghastly, strident, un-self-aware, right-wing, preachy, mean-spirited bigot. Well I've won – so let me remind you just how ghastly I really am. There! And there's nothing you can do about it.'

She won with a record post-war swing of 5 per cent, gaining a majority of 44 over all the other parties. It was a larger Conservative victory than anyone had predicted. A few months afterwards I saw lying around the house a pamphlet that had been sent to my father from the Fabian Society. Its title was 'Can Labour Win Again?' I thought, How ludicrous! Of course Labour can win again – Mrs Thatcher is clearly unbearable, people will realise this and Labour will be re-elected.

I was seventeen years old – I had to live that many years again and more before it was to happen.

Best foot forward

Labour Leadership Election
– 4 and 10 November 1980

When I left home to go to university I was fairly confident of my politics. I had grown up in a home with basic left-wing values and, at the age of eighteen, I had it all worked out. Labour were good, Tories were bad and the act of sponsoring a child in Africa absolved me of a fraction of the guilt I felt at being so privileged. I made the mistake of telling one school friend about this act of charity and he just couldn't get his head around it: 'Yes, but sponsoring him to do *what*?' I think he imagined that children in the Third World only got Action Aid's money if they swam 100 lengths of their local swimming pools with their pyjamas on.

My parents had always encouraged me to care about the outside world. When I was about eight one of my Christmas presents was to have a donkey sponsored in my name. I had been rather hoping that the final present on Christmas Day would be an Action Man or a machine-gun, but instead I just looked at this certificate which told me that somewhere in a field in Wiltshire was a retired donkey that was being cared for with the money that would have been spent on my Christmas present.

'Can we have it in the garden?' I asked optimistically.

'No, dear, he's a very old donkey, he can't travel all the way here. But we can go and see him.' If I had known the meaning of the word 'bemused' that is what I would have said I felt.

So one day we all got in the car and set off on the long journey to the donkey sanctuary. As on most long journeys I vomited out of the car window and the Morris Traveller was adorned with its usual 'go-faster sick' along the side. I became irritable and impatient and when we arrived I was certainly not in the mood to admire a half-dead old nag. I had been hoping for some Disney-type donkey that would frolic around the field playfully on recognising its benefactor. But this specimen was obviously at the cheaper end of the sponsored donkey range: one year only – guaranteed not to survive till next Christmas. It was like the abused horses that used to get rescued in *Follyfoot*: its head hung low, patches of fur were missing and you could see its ribs sticking out. I burst into tears. 'I hate it!' I bawled. I wanted to rescue healthy happy donkeys, not horrible ugly ones like this. I had an ice-cream shoved in my hand and then it was off to look at some important old rocks called Stonehenge that seemed about as impressive as a manky old donkey. But perhaps somewhere at the back of my brain the idea of helping those worse off than yourself took root.

I would help at Oxfam's summer fête without questioning why my mother was Chair of the local Oxfam group, and I would march against the Greek colonels with my dad without wondering why my friends from school were not going on demonstrations at the age of five. As I got older I started gradually to put the pieces together: that my dad shouting at Ted Heath on the news was philosophically connected to the fact that he didn't want to go to Spain on holiday while Franco was alive and that this was all part of the same ethos that had me helping to carry raffia-work table mats into the Oxfam shop on a Sunday morning and shaking tins for Amnesty International on rainy Saturdays. By the time I was thirteen I cared enough about things to have a fight with another boy in my class who supported the National Front. (When I say 'fight' we stood nose to nose for few minutes shoving each other and saying, 'Yeah? ... Yeah!' but for me it was Cable Street '36 all over again.)

That is not to say that my political education was inevitable. My brother grew up in exactly the same environment but somehow politics and most of the outside world managed to pass him by. He achieved the monumental feat of attending Chelsea Art College in 1977 without ever becoming aware of punk. Many people were shocked by the scale of Callaghan's defeat in 1979. My brother was just shocked to learn that Harold Wilson had not been prime minister for the last three years.

But I, on the other hand, knew my stuff. While other boys could name the 1966 World Cup winning team, I could name every prime minister this century, with the year that they were elected. I knew the difference between the legislative and the executive, I knew that Britain had an unwritten constitution and I knew that Keith Joseph was completely bonkers. Labour supporters like me were the goodies, Conservative supporters like Pete Murray and Lulu were the baddies. Simple.

And then suddenly it all got a lot more complicated. On 6 October 1980 I set off for Exeter University in my Ford Escort weighed down with David Bowie records and some carefully selected Athena posters of Impressionist paintings. I stopped for a hitch-hiker as I got on the motorway at Maidenhead. 'Which way are you going?' I asked him.

'I don't care – I've been in Maidenhead thirty minutes and I'm getting out now.'

'Oh. I've been here eighteen years and I'm getting out now.'

He turned out to be a former Exeter student and warned me that the place was packed with public school Tory boys who had failed their Oxbridge entrance exams. This turned out to be true, although in my immediate circle of new friends I suddenly realised that the posh right-wing one appeared to be me. Damn! Why did I bring my car?

Whereas at school everyone had been to the right of me, at university all my fellow students were to the left of me. I was the young eighteen-year-old who had spent the summer broadening my mind by playing Space Invaders in The Hand and Flowers every night, while my new contemporaries were 19- or 20-year-olds who had had a year off, inter-railing round Europe, hitching across India or experiencing socialist heaven in a kibbutz.

The kibbutz, I was informed, was how socialism would work. As far as I could make out, socialist society involved getting up very, very early, picking grapefruit all day and having it off with various Jewish girls from New York or north London. Only the last bit really

31

appealed. But for someone whose most left-wing experience was a holiday in Yugoslavia when I was nine, I humbly accepted that I was ignorant on the subject of Living Marxism. How Stalin had carried out his five-year plan without getting lots of middle-class students to pick grapefruit for nothing remained a mystery.

As well as travelling, the people who had had a year off had also had proper jobs. They had worked in squalid kitchens or sat in front of conveyor belts in a factory; some of the really lucky ones had experienced bona fide oppression. They could show the scar where a piece of farm machinery had gashed their arm, they could play 'The Times They are a-Changing' on their guitar, they could roll a joint without using a Pritt Stick.

'When we got to this African village the people were so warm and welcoming – and though they had so little, they still shared it with us.'

'Yeah, but you have to be careful – we got detained in Beijing and we were inside this police station for six hours, just for taking photographs.'

What could I contribute to these conversations? 'When you've fired seventeen shots, that's when the little flying saucer comes across the top of the screen, and that's worth five hundred points.'

Not only did they have an extra year's worth of experience to radicalise them, they had also had a whole extra year away from their parents. Any political discussions still found me carrying much of my parents' moderate political baggage with me. 'Get rid of the Queen?' I would exclaim in horror. Before I had even finished the word 'queen' I realised I had almost blown my cover and would quickly attempt to steer the outrage in my voice into a sort of emphatic agreement. 'Get rid of the whole lot of them, you mean!' Such deft moves were required on a daily basis.

The week I arrived at university, the Labour Party held its annual conference at Blackpool, and with Jim Callaghan hinting that he might soon be standing down as Labour Party leader the debate over the succession escalated. There was me thinking that Jim Callaghan had been one of the good guys, when it turned out he was just a TOR-y. The word 'Tory' had its own pronunciation back then – the 'Tor' part lasted about three seconds. Merlyn Rees? TOR-y! Denis Healey? TOR-y! David Owen? TOR-y! Whenever a Labour politician's name was mentioned I would pause to see which way the wind was blowing. 'Yeah, I wonder what would happen if they had Tony Benn as leader?' I volunteered before pausing to see where he fitted into the scheme of things . . .

'Tony Benn?'

'TOR-y?' I asked nervously.

'Tony Benn – a Tory – what are you talking about?'

'No – I was going to say, the TOR-ies wouldn't like that would they, if Tony Benn was leader?'

'Oh – yeah, Tony Benn should be leader, definitely.'

So there it was; a politician I had heard of who wasn't a Tory. I bought a book of his speeches from the second-hand bookshop. And when I stuck the book in the side pocket of my jacket, it always just so happened that the title of the book was facing outwards.

In truth I was never cut out to be a genuine subversive. The true measure of radicalism for my generation was the time it took you to get all your hair cut off between 1976 and 1978. Authentic revolutionaries chopped off their locks in one fell swoop, preferably with blunt scissors, on the night that the Sex Pistols blurted out every known swear word on the *Tonight* programme. My long, greasy hair was gradually trimmed back from my shoulders over a period of twelve cautious reforming months, until bit by bit my ears were revealed to the world from where they had been hiding ever since Rod Stewart first swung his microphone stand on *Top of the Pops*. I pretended to be a rebel in order to conform.

The jump from Callaghan to Benn was a relatively short one. I pitied the poor students whose parents were Conservatives; they had a far steeper learning curve than me. Scornful laughter would greet the clichés that they carelessly trotted out. 'Maybe my father *is* very rich, but he did earn every penny himself,' or 'There's an old lady in my parents' road who has a six-bedroom house, and her rates bill is astronomical.' Not only had this particular girl obviously repeated an example of injustice that her father had repeated from Margaret Thatcher, she had also revealed that her parents lived in a road where the houses had six bedrooms. A classic error on two fronts. Within a year she would have stopped shaving her armpits and started saying she came from Notting Hill instead of Kensington.

Whenever people asked me where I was from, I mumbled 'Maidenhead' in such a dismissive mockney accent that they would say, 'Oh, in Somerset? So you're a local then.'

'No, Maidenhead, not Minehead.'

'What school did you go to?'

'Desborough,' I would say, and then add 'Comprehensive' as if it was part of the school's name even though it wasn't. I didn't want anyone thinking it was some minor public school that they hadn't heard of. I may have grown up in a large house by the

34

river, but because my parents had divided it into two when they bought it, I could describe it as 'semi-detached'. Of course such petty affectations would be beneath my favourite in the race for the Labour Party leadership – Anthony Wedgwood Benn. Sorry – 'Tony Benn'.

In fact the whole Labour Party were conducting themselves with all the maturity and political sophistication of left-wing students in freshers' week. The first week of October 1980 saw the most internecine, destructive, self-indulgent Labour Party conference in living memory. Activists felt more passionately about the right of the Constituency General Management Committees to put their MPs out of a job than they did about the fact that Margaret Thatcher was rapidly putting 3 million ordinary people out of theirs. As someone who had been following the internal affairs of the Labour Party for only a year or so I thought that this was the usual way in which party business was conducted. Looking back I can only assume that these were the days before Labour's conferences were meticulously stage-managed, because if there was a committee in charge of it all I would have liked to have witnessed the planning meeting.

> 'Right, everyone, on Monday we've time-tabled the slow handclap over the appeal for unity – and make sure we've got angry delegates shouting down former ministers in time for the six o'clock news. Tuesday, we've arranged for booing and general heckling, and then the chair will switch off the microphone when a couple of delegates are getting too insulting, just for good measure.'

35

'I'm not quite clear what's happening on Wednesday.'

'That's the whole idea. We thought it would be good to have a day of just general confusion – no one being quite sure what a particular composite motion stood for and then not being clear if it had been passed or not.'

'Yes, that would look good. Let's get Shirley Williams to say at that point that we have already lost the next election.'

The annual general conference is there to debate and resolve policy on the great issues of the day. In this instance, after a week of arguing, the party finally agreed on one thing. That it would meet again in January and start all over again. Why should we limit ourselves to one disastrous showcase of Labour wrangling when we could have a second one five months later? Like a couple rowing in front of the kids, Labour said, 'Look, we'll talk about this tomorrow.' And then they proceeded to row in front of the kids the next day as well.

Jim Callaghan's favoured successor was Denis Healey, but with all the timing that he had shown in failing to call an election in 1978 when Labour still could have won it, Jim clung on to the leadership until the autumn of 1980. Callaghan resigned, he said, to make way for someone younger, which was ironic considering who succeeded him. During the month of October there was some talk of Michael Foot being a caretaker leader. As it turned out, a real caretaker would have been about as effective. But Foot's candidature quickly gained momentum as he was seized upon as the 'Stop Healey' candidate. The left wing of the party

associated Healey with the events of 1976 when, as chancellor, he had apparently taken off his cap, put it in his hand and gone round to see the IMF.

In 1964 Kruschev was toppled on the very day that Harold Wilson became prime minister. My father had spoken about how everyone had tried to take in both events at once. Now all in one day Reagan was the American president and the first ballot of the Labour leadership had Foot looking almost certain to win. I desperately wanted Reagan to lose and Foot to win. It was as if some cosmic trade-off was being exacted. In retrospect it might have been better if I had opted for a Democrat in the White House and Healey leading the Labour Party. Or, perhaps more politically interesting, Michael Foot becoming American president and Reagan leader of the Labour Party. All October I had pored over every piece of political analysis in the papers, studying the form and worrying about the outcome. The papers' conclusion that Foot's impending coronation was bad for the Labour Party was put down to that catch-all dismissal of unpleasant tidings – 'media bias'. As far as I was concerned, Foot was the left's candidate so it had to be good news. That was why the right-wing media tried to say Labour were in trouble – it showed how scared they were of what he stood for. When his ascension was confirmed in the second ballot a week later, my fellow students and I drank a happy toast to this victory for socialism. I looked across to the Tory students on the other side of the university bar and they seemed to be celebrating something too. Perhaps it was someone's birthday, I thought. And so the battle lines were drawn for the Eighties. They had Reagan and Thatcher; and we had Michael Foot. Pah! What chance did they stand?

Jobs not bombs

American Presidential Election
– 4 November 1980

Although the election of Reagan is remembered as a foregone conclusion, there were times in the campaign when Jimmy Carter crept back into the lead. I realise now that this is an old trick by pollsters to get my hopes up and keep me interested in the election. In the end Carter won only six states out of fifty. I remember an American student in our halls of residence screaming and ranting from her window at the result, throwing her stars and stripes out, and generally behaving in a way that we had all wanted to when Thatcher had got in, but couldn't because we were all so British and reserved. Because he was such a ridiculous person to be the most powerful man in the world it was difficult to take him seriously. Perhaps all the jokes were a defence mechanism against the horrific reality that this rather simple bigot had his shaky finger over the nuclear button. Jimmy Carter, as president of the United States, had obviously automatically been a bad guy, but Ronald

Reagan was just not on the scale. The night he was elected I went to an End-of-the-World Party.

By this stage I had learnt to measure the unacceptability of various politicians by the way that the people who knew about these things pronounced their names. Jimmy Carter's name was just 'Jimmy Carter'. Richard Nixon's name had always been spoken with a sort of resigned dismissiveness which said, 'Well, we all know what he's up to!', and everyone would tut and look skywards. 'Gerald Ford!' was uttered with a sort of contemptuous amusement that said, 'Fancy him making it all the way to President.' But when Ronald Reagan won the Republican nomination everyone went, 'RONALD REAGAN!?' A pronunciation that combined incredulity with blind panic. It was a tone that I had not heard since Margaret Thatcher became leader of the Conservative Party.

Reagan and Thatcher soon developed a 'special relationship'. It was 'special' in the sense that the US got to put all their missiles in our countryside, making us the prime target, and we didn't get anything back at all. The deployment of Cruise missiles had actually been agreed between Jimmy Carter and Jim Callaghan, but we were not going to let minor inconveniences like facts get in the way of whom we blamed for the growing arms race. Reagan and Thatcher were horse-persons of the apocalypse. Unpoliticised students had the poster of the tennis player scratching her bum. Those of us who had seen the light had the *Gone With the Wind* poster that featured Margaret Thatcher in Reagan's arms as a mushroom cloud exploded behind them.

Although I always supported the Labour Party, following every depressing poll and buying *New Socialist* and *Marxism Today* when most other

39

students' rooms were stacked up with copies of the *NME*, I still wasn't a member. Joining the party did not really occur to me; I was not interested in student politics and in my first year felt too detached from the city of Exeter to join the party there. The movement that really consumed me in the wake of Reagan's election was the Campaign for Nuclear Disarmament.

The election of Ronald Reagan did wonders for CND. The membership secretary must have rubbed his hands with glee as the arms race spiralled out of control. Before Reagan was sworn in a demonstration attracted 50,000 people to Trafalgar Square, the highest turnout for two decades. Within a couple of years five times that many people would be marching through London and the other cities of Europe. (Though not on the same day, as Michael Heseltine shrewdly pointed out. According to him we were all catching flights to Bonn and Paris and joining the marches there.)

Perhaps it was the simplicity of CND's message that attracted me. Perhaps it was political fashion. But for anyone who wanted to listen I would lecture on why Britain did not need nuclear weapons, how they were so expensive and how they made us less safe because we became a target. But much as I agreed with everything that CND stood for, I could not help cringing at the way they chose to put their message across. When the CIA sat around in Washington noticing that the peace movement was burgeoning and wondering how they might contain it, they must have come up with all sorts of options. Assassinations? Too risky. Arresting the leaders on trumped-up fraud charges? Too complicated. Until some colonel working late one night in the Pentagon had a brilliant idea, a way to make CND look ludicrous and keep it on the fringe of European politics for a decade.

'So what's your idea, colonel?'
'Face-painting, sir.'
'Face-painting?'
'Yes, sir. And circus arts. Face-painting and circus arts, sir.'
'Go on . . .'
'Well, sir, we send our agents to infiltrate the demonstrations armed with some face paints, a unicycle and basic juggling skills. They get shown on the news, and everyone says, "CND – what a bunch of middle-class twats!"'.
'That's an excellent idea, colonel. Better take some annoying whistles and floppy missile costumes for good measure.'

Somewhere between the Aldermaston marches of the 1960s and the demos of the 1980s CND must have hired the worst PR consultants in the world. The *Daily Mail* called the Greenham women 'woolly heads in woolly hats' – a jibe that struck a chord with the millions of people who were not used to having their arguments on defence strategy put to them by people in clown costumes. In the blackest days of the Second World War, when Churchill said, 'If we fail, then civilisation will be thrown back into the Dark Ages,' the country knew what he meant. The seriousness of his message would not have been particularly helped by his then putting on a luminous skeleton costume and throwing himself to the floor by means of an illustration.

I felt so passionately about the rightness of CND's

41

message. I was just depressed that we always came across as so insufferably naff. I remember the publicity for one demonstration: 'If you are on the green route, please wear green, if you are on the red route please wear red, and if you are on the blue route please wear blue.' The idea, I think, was that as the three marches came into Hyde Park, there would be a fantastic explosion of colour that would send out a vivid message about the colourful life that could be lived in a world without nuclear weapons. The reality was that a load of people wandered into the park and then tried to listen to the speeches but couldn't hear them because the police helicopter was hovering directly over the PA system (hired for the afternoon from Gary's Roadshow Disco). Then they milled around for a bit longer, bought an ice-cream and pushed little Jemimah and Jonathan home in their pushchairs, telling them to stop crying and explaining that there wasn't going to be a puppet show on the stage, it was just speeches from Michael Foot and Neil Kinnock.

Did the march organisers really think that the coach carrying the Durham NUM was going to arrive with 50 miners dressed in bright red with glittery scarlet deeley-boppers springing around on their heads for good measure? Would the Ex-Servicemen's CND look best dressed up in red, blue or green? Perhaps there was a meeting between someone from CND and the Chairman of Ex-Servicemen's CND at which the old soldier said:

'Well – we'd rather march without the stilts, if you don't mind.'

'OK, OK – how about dressing up to represent the different seasons?'

'Um – well, I'll put it to the chaps – um – by

the way, what are we supposed to do with
these face paints?'

In one demonstration the idea was for us all to link
hands between Greenham Common and Burghfield via
Aldermaston. Men were not allowed near the Greenham
end of the chain where I'd planned to meet some
friends, so I found myself wandering down this road
somewhere in the middle of the Berkshire countryside,
marvelling at just how many 2CVs there were with
Atomkraft? Nein Danke stickers in the back window.
The message came down that it was time for us all to
link up, so I held the hand of a bearded man from
Stevenage with a cagoule, and then kept hold of it for
about ten minutes. The problem was neither of us was
particularly sure when we should *stop* holding hands.
The small talk never got much beyond 'I expect there'll
be a message in a minute', 'Do you think we can let go
yet?' and 'Hmmm, not sure ... wouldn't want to break
the chain ...'
    My father joined Ex-Servicemen's CND and wanted to
wear his medals from the Second World War. They'd
been stolen in a burglary many years before, but I
managed to track down replacements at a special medal
fair that they have near London Bridge where strange
men browse over Nazi insignia. I went to the trouble of
tracking them down precisely so he could wear them on
CND marches. And when the day came I was proud that
my dad had medals that showed he'd served in the
war, but that he would only wear them in the cause of
anti-militarism.
    Unfortunately, he kept slipping behind into the midst
of a group of women in green boilersuits who were
blowing whistles and banging drums and their leader

43

told him: 'Excuse me – you're in the women-only section of this march.' 'Oh I'm terribly sorry, I do beg your pardon,' he said in his faded Irish accent with the sort of genuine politeness and humility that only old people can carry off sincerely. We marched a bit more and he stopped to look up at a statue of Canning or someone and suddenly this woman barked at him: 'Excuse me, can you keep *out* of the women-only section of the march *please*!' 'Oh, I am sorry, have I done it again ...' and I was saying to myself, Don't let him call her 'Miss', or 'Dear', '... I'll move up a bit, dear.'

Going with one's parents on demonstrations is asking for embarrassment. Another CND demo and another gimmick – this time it was a mass 'die-in' where we all had to lie down in the road to illustrate what a nuclear holocaust would look like. I am not sure if the Delegation of Hiroshima Survivors felt that this was a particularly poignant moment – having thousands of English people all lying down and making the same joke about it being 'nice to have a bit of a lie-down after all that walking'. But like the people who allow holocausts to happen, we all obeyed orders. On this particular demonstration I was with my mother only (my father was presumably in hiding from 'Women Against The Bomb And Polite Old Irishmen'). We were marching through Kensington when the siren went, and Mum and I lay down side by side. People came out of their shops to look at us. Including, as bad luck would have it, my mother's hairdresser.

'Hello, Michael!' she shouted loudly, as fellow demonstrators looked around. 'Mum – shut up,' I whispered, regressing instantly into embarrassed-teenager mode. Michael peered into the crowd and saw

44

Mrs O'Farrell and her golden retriever Fudge lying in Kensington Church Street doing a rather unconvincing impression of a nuclear holocaust.

'I'm coming in this afternoon for a demi-perm, Michael.'

'A demi-perm? I've just got you down for a cut and set.'

'No – a demi-perm, I changed it. I spoke to Louise this morning ...'

The Class War contingent were eyeing me, suspecting I might be linked to this person. I pretended I didn't know her.

'No – it says cut and set in the book.'

'Oh, that's ridiculous – John, take Fudge's lead – I'm going to find Louise,' and I took charge of the golden retriever while Mum sorted out that afternoon's hair-dressing appointment in Kensington. At that point it felt as if a real nuclear holocaust might have been preferable.

What was so annoying about my mum and dad coming on marches was that they always had such a good time. If the route of the march passed a pub, they would happily go inside to enjoy a couple of pints, then decide to have lunch in the restaurant before rejoining the demonstration. And they would cheerfully inform the rather snooty waiter that they wouldn't have a pudding because they had to get back on the march. This is my day for spitting blood at the establishment and Mum is asking me if I want to share a Châteaubriand.

Both my parents were committed to the anti-nuclear movement. My mum would make meals for the women of Greenham Common and explain to the campaigners sitting round the camp fires that the beef stroganoff needed to be eaten that day because it had fresh cream in it, and that the vegetarian dishes were marked with a big 'V' in yellow highlighter pen on the lids. Every time she had a dinner party she would make double portions – one salmon en croûte for their friends, who all voted Conservative, and another for the Greenham women.

Despite all the painful post-hippy woolly-hatted naffness of so much of it, the CND marches were a source of pride to me. The numbers of people taking part were impressive. I knew what 100,000 people looked like – I'd been to Knebworth to see Led Zeppelin, to Wembley to see The Who and to Slough Tech to see John Otway. There were at least two hundred thousand in Hyde Park on several of the demonstrations I went on and it felt uplifting and exhilarating to be surrounded by so many people who felt the same way as you. There was a moment as you entered the park when the scale of it all just hit you. In every direction thousands and thousands of people – 'Look over there, there's a whole new march coming in ... and look over there, there's thousands coming up Park Lane' – and the tannoy would announce that there were still people who hadn't set off from the Embankment yet, and a huge cheer would go up. And you'd jump up on a litter bin or a bench and look around and just marvel at how many people cared enough to come from all over the country to stand in a field and say, 'I'm here because it's important. There were plenty of other things I could have been doing but this is more important. So I got up depressingly early, paid to have a very long, uncomfortable coach journey down the motorway, got caught in a contra-flow, spent an hour in traffic in London, then waited two hours holding my banner before the march set off, walked to Hyde Park, tried to listen to the speeches but couldn't because the police helicopter was hovering directly above the PA again, milled about a bit, and then spent a very long time going home.' And all sorts of people felt strongly enough to do this. Old people, students, trade unionists, doctors, middle-class people, working-class people, people with kids, people with dogs, banners that said 'Plymouth CND' or 'Barrow-in-Furness CND', 'Swansea CND' and 'Norwich CND'; and you thought that if all these people cared enough to come here today, then there had to be hope for the world.

Later you'd watch the report of the demonstration on the news and it would be the third item and they'd show eight seconds of footage of the march, three seconds of some punks with purple mohicans and conclude with five seconds on the solitary bloke who stood at the entrance to Hyde Park Corner with a banner saying 'CND – Kremlin's friends'. Two hundred and fifty thousand of us, and one of him, and he gets the punch-line. Well *I* say there were 250,000 of us; the police estimates usually put the number of people marching at 'seventeen'. Later on the bloke with the 'Kremlin' sign must have come into a bit of money, or got a grant from the Ministry of Defence or something, because at every CND demo, a light aircraft would fly around trailing a banner saying 'CND – Kremlin's April Fools' or something similar, prompting catcalls and strong language from the stage which no one could hear because he was flying directly over the PA system.

Apart from the demonstrations, my opposition to nuclear weapons meant doing very little apart from permanently wearing a CND badge and going to the occasional CND jumble sale, where members had

47

donated any of their clothes that weren't quite scruffy enough. But all the women I knew had an exciting, direct way to get involved – Greenham Common.

I have to admit I privately felt rather jealous of the women I knew who went to the peace camp. Both the women who lived in our student house spent time there, but although this was something that I felt as strongly about as they did, I was not able to join in. Of course women were perfectly within their rights to have a women-only peace camp and the very minor sense of exclusion I felt was an education in how women must have felt for centuries. But dammit I wanted to go to Greenham and invade the base and be on the news and sleep in a tent and wear fingerless gloves and be arrested and come back to Exeter and tell everyone all about it. But for a change all the heroes were women. Why did I have to be part of the only movement, at the only time in history, when it was a disadvantage to be a man?

This frustration boiled over the night that the Cruise missiles actually arrived in Britain. Many of my female friends went straight to Greenham and no doubt sang 'You Can't Kill the Spirit' till they were blue in the face. (If the devil has all the best tunes, then God must have been on our side.) Unable to think where my presence might best make itself felt, I went to the pub with a friend of mine. We decided we would make our own protest – we would go around the town centre spraying the walls with anti-nuclear messages. Today, in my mid-thirties, I don't make this admission with any sense of pride. I hate graffiti and vandalism, and there could have been a thousand better ways of venting my rather self-conscious anger. But hey, I was young, and if you don't spray all over the walls of Barclays Bank when you're young then when do you do it? Certainly not ten years later when I was enquiring about endowment mortgages.

My friend was as determined as me. We would definitely do it there and then. 'Well, hang on, let's have another pint first.' Several pints later he pointed out that we didn't have any spray cans. 'I've got one back at the house. It was there when we moved in,' I announced cheerily. Suddenly there was no getting out of this, and he wasn't as determined as me. But I had convinced myself of the merits of the plan and one hour later, with quite a lot of beer coursing through my veins, I found myself alone, walking down Exeter High Street just after closing time, spraying 'Jobs Not Bombs' on the walls of carefully selected buildings. The Territorial Army Centre – they definitely deserved one. Lloyds Bank deserved one. I wasn't absolutely certain that they were connected with the arms trade, but they had charged me twenty quid twice on the same bounced cheque so there was no debate. All the other banks got one, along with the odd multi-storey car park and bus shelter. The Oxfam Shop was obviously excused.

I had boasted about this piece of urban terrorism before I had set off, and I confirmed that the job was done when I got home. My comrades were suitably impressed at my drink-induced courage. The next morning they came back from the town centre unable to suppress their laughter.

'What? What?'

'Excellent punctuation, John!'

What?

'Jobs – comma – Not Bombs – full stop.'

'What?'

'Jobs – comma – Not Bombs – full stop.' And they laughed some more.

49

And I went and had a look round the town centre and they were right. I had sprayed 'Jobs – comma – Not Bombs – full stop'. The comma and the full stop said: 'I hope this is all right, and sorry about your wall and everything, but would it be OK if we had some jobs rather than all those bombs?' And among the left-wing students of Exeter University I wasn't Che Guevara who had sprayed the truth all over the capitalist banks. I was that bloke who had sprayed 'Jobs comma Not Bombs full stop'.

My chance to emulate the women of Greenham came with RAF Molesworth in Cambridgeshire, the second site selected for Cruise missiles. My local CND group were to take part in a major protest that would stop all building work on the base. There had been an embryonic peace camp at Molesworth as well, but in one of the British army's most brilliant strategic victories a dozen tank divisions, backed up by 10,000 marines with full air cover, led heroically by Michael Heseltine in a flak jacket, had successfully evicted seven hippies and a goat.

The government clearly did not want another Greenham Common on its hands, so our protest was expected to meet with some stiff resistance. The weekend beforehand I attended a Non-Violent Direct Action Workshop. Quite how they managed to take up a whole weekend with a 'non-violent direct action workshop' I do not know, but I seem to remember a lot of sitting cross-legged on the floor discussing what each one of us felt we had got out of the role play we had just done. I had attempted at one point to sit casually on the edge of a table for one of the discussions but I was told I was 'breaking the strength of the circle', so I reluctantly sat on the floor and tried to fold my gangly legs into the impossible yoga position that everyone else managed to make look so comfortable. I never quite understood why a world without bombs also had to mean a world without chairs. And why did rejecting Cruise also require us to reject white bread, shaving or having any sort of dress sense?

On the Monday morning at about six a.m., with snow starting to fall, we queued beside the coach in our waterproofs like troops who had finally been given the order to mobilise. We had done all our training – this was the real thing. One long journey later we got off the coach and were directed towards the gates by CND stewards, where we dutifully sat in the snow. All day. The builders had been given the day off. The police were going to make no attempt to move us, they were just going to let us sit in the snow. All day. This was an outrageous piece of provocative behaviour on the part of the Cambridgeshire police. A total failure to do their duty as police officers, which was to arrest us, manhandle us into vans, and tell us that 'we did not have to say anything but anything we did say et cetera' – all scenarios that we were prepared for and knew how to respond to. I had spent an entire weekend learning how to go all floppy when two policemen try to drag you away. I had learnt what offences I could be charged with, and which were criminal offences and which were civil offences. I had in my pocket the telephone number of a special CND lawyer I was to ring with my one permitted phone call. All for nothing.

'Well, aren't you going to arrest us then?' we'd ask.

'Oh no – you're fine there. Carry on with your protest.'

'But we're obstructing a public highway. It's a breach of the peace.'

'Well, no one's trying to get into the site, so you're fine where you are. Bit of a cold day for it, isn't it?'

'Bloody fascists!'

The police were laughing at us because they thought it was hilarious. And the trouble was that they were right.

Although all the hippy antics of the middle-class alternative left did not seem to be striking terror into the industrial military complex, they were making inroads into the Labour Party. I remember punching the air with delight when the Labour conference voted to adopt Unilateral Nuclear Disarmament. I really believed that before long Britain would have a Labour government that would enact this commitment. Billions of pounds released to spend on hospitals, education, training and infrastructure – and an end to Britain as a first-strike nuclear target. CND had set out to put nuclear disarmament onto the political agenda and had succeeded brilliantly. But the result was that the party that adopted their policy became unelectable in the eyes of the British voters for two successive general elections and CND's aims were further from being realised than ever.

If we had understood the politics of the 1980s more fully we would have shifted the whole argument away from the immorality of risking the destruction of the entire planet and more towards how much nuclear weapons were costing the average C2 voter. 'Let's get rid of the bomb and give everybody seven hundred and forty quid – cash in hand. Seven hundred and forty big ones – what do you say?' Instead of talking in vague terms about nuclear winters and four-minute warnings we should have said, 'Look, it's a straight swap. You can either keep Trident or you can have a brand new video recorder with remote control and thirty-day memory. What's it to be?' Ronald Reagan wouldn't have stood a chance.

Political animals

Labour Party Deputy Leadership Election
– 27 September 1981

In January 1981 the Labour Party held a special conference in an attempt to lose the remaining voters it had failed to alienate the previous autumn. The Wembley conference produced a confusing and unsatisfactory system for electing the party leader, with the union block vote being portrayed by the media as the greatest threat to democracy in Britain since Oswald Mosley. The standard joke was that when the leader of the TGWU put his hand up for tea in Labour Party meetings the chair said, 'Right, that's five million teas with two sugars.'

Of course all these years later we forget just how much the country had lived in fear of The Unions. Gangs of union militants would roam the countryside, poisoning wells, tipping over milk pails and burning haystacks before returning to 10 Downing Street for beer and sandwiches to decide upon their next innocent victims. When I was in the sixth form we used to have a weekly discussion period where the entire year would sit in the

54

common room with Mr Stanley, the Churchillian head of upper school, who would lead a rather self-conscious debate on the great issues of the day. It usually would begin by a boy asking something like, 'Sir, what do you think of the unions bringing the country to its knees?' And Mr Stanley would give a wry sadistic smile and say, 'John – perhaps you would like to answer this one.'

With stuttering ineptitude I would then attempt to defend the British trades union movement, about which I knew very little, in an atmosphere as hostile as the Monday Club on beggar-baiting night. Rather than contradict me, Mr Stanley knew that he could damage me far more by just allowing me to keep on talking and talking while various prefects sadly shook their heads at my misguided foolishness. And then another boy would pipe up that his uncle had had a small business until the unions had moved in and organised a strike that no one had wanted and everyone had ending up losing their jobs.

And, Paxman-like, Mr Stanley would say, 'Well, John, how do you defend that?'

'I don't know, I mean, um, we don't know all the facts, um ...'

'He's just told you them.' Mr Stanley was careful to remain neutral throughout any political discussion.

'Um, well, er, obviously there are some individual cases where the unions may have gone too far, I mean certain members might have exceeded their powers, but, erm, if this is the case then clearly the best party to curb the power of the unions must be, er, Labour.'

A few more lifelong Conservatives were created and the debate was allowed to move on to the next innocuous subject for discussion – 'Public flogging – too good for single mothers?'

55

*   *   *

But as far as I was concerned the unions were champions of the proletariat, with lots of people in them who were not only left-wing but working-class as well – an irresistible combination. In the summer of 1981 I got a temporary job as part of a team cleaning out a factory and the woman at the job agency said to me in very apologetic and sombre tones, 'To work at this factory I'm afraid you do have to join the Transport and General Workers Union.' I nearly kissed her full on the lips.

'Really?' I said, barely suppressing my joy. 'No problem.' Inside I was jumping up and down with excitement. 'Is that for life?' I asked optimistically.

'No, just for the two weeks that you're working there.'

'Oh.'

As the union block vote was established at Wembley the SDP was born. The Gang of Four spontaneously reacted to the outcome of the special conference by issuing a statement that they must have written and duplicated in record time. 'The Limehouse Declaration' set out the aims of the Council for Social Democracy. I can't remember exactly what these were, but presumably something along these lines:

1) To keep Thatcher in power for ever by dividing the opposition, and

2) To make themselves look increasingly ridiculous by falling out with the Liberals and shrinking to a laughable rump of four MPs in five years' time.

Frankly if I was able to stay in the Labour Party while it ceased opposing privatisation, ceased to support unilateral nuclear disarmament, ceased voting against the Prevention of Terrorism Act and went back on just about every policy I believed in to get itself elected in

56

1997, then I think that Shirley Williams could have put up with a few people from the unions who had northern accents and took sugar in their tea.

But Labour's problems weren't just on the right. The other consequence of Wembley was Tony Benn's decision to challenge for the Labour Party's deputy leadership. Tony Benn described the battle that followed as 'a healing process'. I suppose we should just be grateful that he never became a doctor. 'The Party's Over!' proclaimed one newspaper headline as the Labour Party tore itself apart that summer. The more Labour MPs jumped the sinking ship to join the SDP, the greater were Benn's chances of winning. Although I wanted him to win, I wanted Labour to replace Mrs Thatcher far more. I was not yet a member of the party and could take no part in the contest. But as an observer I felt like one of those girlfriends who stand on the edge of fights in pub car parks shouting, 'Leave it, Gary! Stop it, all of you! It's not worth it!'

In July there were riots all over Britain. No effective protest to rising unemployment was coming from the infighting Labour Party – it seemed as if the petrol bombs were the only voice the growing underclass had left. As far as this nineteen-year-old was concerned the most effective opposition to Her Majesty's Government came from The Specials who with impeccable timing got to number one with 'Ghost Town' just as Toxteth and Brixton were burning to the ground. 'It's *so* true ...' I would say every time they reached the line about 'Government leaving the youth on the shelf'. And I went out and bought the single with the money the government was giving me to muck about at university for three years.

* * *

The trouble with the left during this period was that we were so deeply unattractive. The media coined phrases like 'Hard Left' or 'Militant Left', but 'Very, Very Boring Left' would have been more accurate. It wasn't the left-wing-ness in itself that was the problem, it was the excessively bad-tempered and humourless way in which the left argued its corner, which makes me cringe when I remember it. We had somehow got it into our heads that a period in opposition meant that we were now opposed to *everything*.

I remember going to see the pantomime *Dick Whittington* that year with some younger relations and I steadfastly refused to laugh throughout. While my nephew and niece were joyfully shouting, 'He's behind you!', I was tutting and looking skywards. During the interval my parents asked me what I thought of it. I sneered and said that it was typical of the bourgeois theatre to peddle the 'rags to riches' myth because this, by implication, suggested that the poor were to blame for their own predicament. The embarrassed pause was only broken by my confused six-year-old nephew asking his mum, '*Why* doesn't Uncle John like it?' In reality there was not much difference between me and all the other kids there. They were booing all the baddies on the stage and I was booing all the baddies buying gin and tonics in the interval.

My poor parents took the brunt of my painful non-stop rage, perhaps because the real root of it was my battle to break away from them. Although I had physically moved out, I was still taking my emotional washing home, and part of proving my independence was rejecting everything my parents thought was normal or acceptable. Of course if I had really wanted

58

to rebel against them I should have been a Conservative. 'You remind me of me when I was your age' my dad told me, to my extreme annoyance. On another occasion I was walking with my mum in some London park and in an attempt to make conversation she pointed out all the beautiful flowerbeds. Instead of nodding and asking what sort of flowers they were (as I would now), I snorted that I preferred natural landscapes – not regimented, ordered rows of flowers planted by the council when that money could have been better spent on creating jobs or building houses.

'Oh, I agree, dear ... but aren't those begonias lovely?'

Somehow I had got it into my head that *flowers* were right-wing. Not only flowers, but gardening *per se*. All sorts of things that you would not normally expect to have political attributes were right-wing by virtue of being vaguely decadent, frivolous, self-indulgent or just slightly posh. Fish knives, ladies' hats, power steering, wellington boots, the county of Surrey, Donald Duck, conservatories, waxed raincoats and any girl's name that ended in the letter 'a'. All of these were worthy of a contemptuous tut. Dinner parties were obviously right-wing. Apart from being right-wing in themselves they featured a number of right-wing guest appearances such as wine, suits and mangetouts. And concepts like dessert wine and profiteroles were just off the political scale. One of the people I lived with in Exeter decided that *smiling* was right-wing. He pretended to be miserable as a sort of political statement throughout the early 1980s. And hair was another luxury he refused to indulge in: he had a utilitarian number-one cut all over. Randle was from Rochdale and could make you feel right-wing just by repeating your ludicrous pronunciation of words like 'bath' and 'grass'. His girlfriend was from Croydon but spoke with a broad Lancashire accent after they'd been together six months.

While we condemned anyone who did not share our view of the world as 'fascists', we had developed a special fascism of our own, which excluded and condemned people because of what they believed in. Voltaire said, 'I do not agree with what you say but I would die for your right to say it.' We said, 'I do not agree with what you say, so you are not allowed to say it 'cos you're a fascist.' Not only were we constantly vigilant for slips of the tongue by our parents or less politicised students, we would also jump on any comrades that we felt stepped outside the unwritten code in any minor way.

'You eat tuna?' shrieked someone round at my house who was doing a moral inspection of my food cupboards.

'Er – yeah, it's not South African is it?' I asked before I was given a lecture on the cruel murder of dolphins in Japanese tuna nets. On another occasion I let my cynical guard slip and recommended the film *Educating Rita* to a couple of friends. They came back furious about how patronising it was in its portrayal of the working classes and I was left feeling foolish and embarrassed.

I shared a house with five other English or Drama students and as we fed each other's socialism our fervour and certainty grew. The house was organised on a co-operative basis with all food bills and expenses shared equally. The men were quite disappointed when the women declined our kind offer to pay towards their tampons as part of the household expenses. With our ideology came a severe puritan lifestyle that spurned such luxuries as eating in restaurants, enjoying Christmas or buying new clothes. Despite its military overtones, army surplus clothing was *de rigueur* for its austere practicality. You would never have been able to get me onto a dance floor when I was nineteen as I would never consider doing anything as self-indulgent as dancing. Unless of course the DJ put on 'Stand Down Margaret' by The Beat, at which point I would dance really emphatically just to show how much I agreed with the sentiments of the song. The feminist women I knew had developed a very strange and deliberately graceless dance which involved stamping their right foot while bringing their right fist up and down and then repeating the action with their left side. They looked a bit like Indian chiefs in spaghetti westerns, only with Doc Martens on.

My attitude to my feminist colleagues was generally one of tacit submission. To the guilt I felt about my class was added the guilt I was made to feel about my gender. And somewhere along the way it seemed that sex itself had become politically suspect. There was a brave attempt by some men to argue that virginity followed by monogamy was the straitjacket of a patriarchal society and that women must allow their own sexual expression to come to the fore and therefore have sex with them right away. But it was to little avail. If men were shouted down for being sexist when they used the word 'postman', then asking if there was any chance of a quick shag seemed like a bit of a non-starter.

On one occasion a woman came back to my house after a party, and not wanting to appear too pushy I said she was welcome to sleep on the sofa. This was someone I had known for some time and whose strong feminist views I had always supported. She accepted my offer and I lay alone in bed worrying that socialists might actually die out from lack of procreation. But 20 minutes later my bedroom door creaked open and she climbed into my bed. She informed me that she couldn't sleep in the front room 'because the clock ticked so loudly'. Aha! Hooray for feminism – the women take the initiative! If ever there was a thinly disguised code for 'Let's have it off!' this was it, and I responded in the way I thought was expected of me.

'Do you mind not touching me!' she barked. 'God! Why do men always presume that women want sex with them? It's just typical!'

'Oh. Right. Yes I'm sorry ...' I stuttered, '... you're quite right. It was very sexist of me. I'm sorry.'

'God – you're all the same. You can't think of women in any other terms, can you?'

'It's just that when you ... No, you're quite right, I'm sorry.'

And then I attempted to go to sleep beside her in a casual sort of *just because you're in my bed and I've got no pants on, doesn't mean I expect to have sex with you* kind of way.

The next morning when she had gone I couldn't help feeling a slight sense of injustice at being cast as the predatory sexist male. When a man is looking for signals that a woman might be interested in him, her climbing into his bed in her underwear might reasonably be interpreted as minor encouragement. But not in the world of the new puritans. Eve tempted me with the apple and then told me it was South African.

The historical gap between the sexual revolution and the arrival of AIDS was a comparatively short one and I was lucky enough to be young during those years. But tragically I was so right-on that I got *sex* confused with

62

sexism and so my list of carnal conquests during the 1980s is probably shorter than Michael Foot's.

There is something perverse in the fact that the task of making the world a happier place required us to stop having fun. I was opposed to all forms of art that had no worthy political message, opposed to sport as an irrelevant distraction, and against most other forms of leisure on the grounds that they probably involved having to make small talk with Tories somewhere along the line. But although we were dedicated to making the world a better place, we never actually did anything constructive to help this happen. Just believing was all that was required. Nobody actually benefited from our political awareness except perhaps one very lucky battery chicken.

In the way that socially disadvantaged children are taken in by well-meaning liberal families who have seen them advertised in the back of the *Guardian,* our student household adopted a battery chicken. This was something of a spontaneous decision taken while we were driving through the Devon countryside one day. We passed a hand-painted sign which read 'Chickens For Sale — Alive or Dead' and for some reason we thought that a battery chicken would make a good addition to our household. We pulled in and entered a horrific surreal aircraft hangar of a chicken prison, where thousands of bald, mad chickens were screaming at the tops of their voices. Hundreds of bare heads stuck out between the bars, all of them pleading 'Pick me!' Pick me!' On the available bits of wood between the tiny cages the proprietor had stuck up colour centrefolds from pornographic magazines, the ratio being about ten naked chickens to every naked woman. We didn't invite him to dinner. When we announced that we would like to buy a chicken he opened a cage and with his tattooed tree-trunk arms pulled out a terrified bird, saying in a thick Devon accent, 'Do you want me to kill it or do you want to do it later – keep it fresh, like.'

'Oh no!' we swooned. 'Don't kill it – we're going to have it as a pet.'

He looked us up and down to check that we hadn't landed from another planet and thrust this very confused chicken into our hands. Out of 2,000 chickens, God had looked down and picked out one very lucky hen who was going to chicken paradise where she would have her own little coop, a big overgrown garden to run around in, and five students to feed her all the wholemeal bread and lentils that she could eat.

We took her home and put her out the back where she hid under a hedge for three days. No amount of counselling could coax her out; clearly we had an agoraphobic chicken. But gradually she started to flap her wings, scratch and peck the ground and discover what being a chicken was all about. A few feathers started to grow, her comb started to turn red and by the end of the summer she had blossomed into a big fat spoilt only-child of a chicken. But still we worried about her welfare. She was not laying eggs, despite having a lovingly converted chest of drawers full of straw to sit in. We fed her well and she would often supplement her diet by picking at the Sainsbury's roast chicken carcasses that she found inside the bin liners by the back door. I think it was at about this time we all went vegetarian.

Maybe she was lonely, we decided. It was then we made the mistake of getting more hens to keep her company. Not toughened school-of-hard-knocks battery chickens, but three free-range airy-fairy middle-class chickens. These soft woolly-liberal hens had never met any chickens off the council estate before and were in for a bit of a shock. The three of them would stand nervously together at the bottom of the garden while the fat skinhead of a battery chicken came charging down the garden steps at 40 miles an hour to peck them all in the head before looking around, pleased with herself, and going back up to the top of the garden daring them to come near.

The other chickens made a sort of 'tut' noise to each other after she had gone, but lived in perpetual fear of imminent duffing up. Even my dog was scared of this thug of a chicken after being forced off its bowl in the middle of dinnertime. It was not so much a pecking order as a Grievous Bodily Harm order.

This was British society in a microcosm, I decided. The things that bred violence and crime were the same for humans as battery chickens. Exploitation, poor housing, frustration, having to lay eggs every day – oh, no, not that last one. The indignity and alienation that our battery chicken had been through were no different to the deprivations that caused so many of mankind's social problems. I surmised that if the people of the world had the human equivalent of what these lucky free-range hens had had, then we could all live together in a happy non-violent egg-laying paradise. All political discussions would inevitably end up with my earnest battery-chicken allegory, and then somebody else would say, 'Well I think you can taste the difference in free-range eggs.'

'Oh yes – it's worth paying the little bit extra just for that ... Especially the corn-fed ones.'

And the people who had only been half listening

would say, 'How come we're suddenly talking about bloody eggs again?'

Politics ran through everything. Any conversation would be diverted on to the problems of capitalism and the rightness of the left's cause. Some young men are obsessed with a football team, some are obsessed with a rock group; I was obsessed with socialism. I got a copy of *Das Kapital* out of the library and made great progress with it – almost reaching the fourth page. My every waking thought was coloured red. When a couple of drunken Devon boys wanted to fight me and Rochdale Randle in Exeter town centre one afternoon, I rather pathetically said, 'You shouldn't be hitting me – you should attack the government.' At that point they would have been justified in beating me to a pulp. Fortunately we managed to escape unhurt and I now realise that I should have perhaps avoided the subject of politics. But I think at the time I didn't know how to talk about anything else.

We all believed, or rather, we *knew* that socialism would solve everything and that any particular individual who happened to be to the right of us was responsible for all the world's problems and therefore we hated them. As far as I can remember just about everyone I knew on the left was like this. Angry, negative and totally un-self-aware. And Tony Benn's leadership challenge gave the British left the chance to vent its ugly spleen in public. At regular intervals the news would feature Benn supporters booing Denis Healey, pelting him with missiles and picketing his meetings. They seemed to hate him more than they hated Margaret Thatcher. What's more they didn't care what the TV cameras saw. At least when I carried an

SWP banner I had the good grace to tear off the words 'Socialist Workers Party' from across the top, but these people had no shame. The Labour Party rank and file regarded its leadership in the same way that I regarded my parents, and would not miss an opportunity to embarrass them. Surprisingly the British public did not fall in love with us.

Although I cringe when I remember my venomous posturing in the early 1980s, I am also haunted by the possibility that perhaps a little too much anger has dissipated between now and then. I am left with the frightening thought that if a time machine took me back to meet my former self, I would loathe and detest what I have become. Fortunately I am not alone in this. Just as there are special support groups for survivors of harsh boarding schools, or those who have come through painful divorces or bereavements, so there is a therapy group for survivors like me. The society is known by the acronym IWELWITE, which stands for 'I Was Embarrassingly Left-Wing In The Eighties'. We meet regularly in fashionable restaurants in Islington and Holland Park and take turns to talk through how we are coping with the new world in which we find ourselves. I stand up and say, 'My name is John O'Farrell – I was embarrassingly left-wing in the Eighties,' and then I will go on to share with the group the vague unease I feel about giving money to Rupert Murdoch to pay for Sky Sports. The other survivors will give me a sympathetic nod and then someone will pipe up, 'But did you see Shearer's goal on Monday night? No way was he off-side . . .', and I'll know that that lucky person is completely cured. Then another member will speak. They believe in state education but there are no good primary schools in their area, so the expensive prep school is the only option. We nod and say that's OK, we understand, the mess the Tories left our schools in is forcing all of us to make some very difficult choices. We are all very understanding and sympathetic to each other – in direct contrast to the cries of 'Fascist!' we would have shrieked at one another all those years ago. We might eventually get on to discussing some of the campaigns we are involved in at the moment. The person on my left is in a battle with the council over planning permission for their kitchen extension and the person on my right is petitioning their street to get residents' parking – so at least some of that old campaigning radicalism is still there.

People who were embarrassingly left-wing in the eighties still bare the soul-tortured scars of those years. If we buy a *Big Issue* we carry it on the outside of our briefcase in case we meet another vendor who might not believe us when we say we have already bought one. We buy over-priced dusters at our front door and hope the vendor hasn't etched a special mark that denotes 'sucker' on our front gate. We drive around with a carboot-load of bottles to take to the bottle bank some time, thereby using far more petrol than we would otherwise have done. Some of the people who were embarrassingly left-wing in the Eighties now have an awful lot of money, but obviously you won't see them driving round in a Rolls-Royce or a Porsche. A Saab maybe, or an Audi, which is as flash as their conscience will allow them to be. A new Peugeot costing £15,000 is somehow more acceptable than a second-hand BMW costing £10,000.

You would never know to meet these reasonable people now that back in 1981 they spat blood at each other and became sworn enemies on minor points of contention about the Labour Party constitution. Indeed many of them are now MPs ready to lecture the party on discipline and responsibility.

Denis Healey held on to the deputy party leadership 'by the hair of his eyebrow' as he put it. A crucial abstention by Neil Kinnock and his followers denied Tony Benn victory by a fraction of one per cent. 'Careerist twat!' shouted Rochdale Randle at the next CND demo when Kinnock got up onto the platform to speak. I was at my parents' house when the news of Healey's victory broke.

'Thank God!' said my father. 'There's still some sanity left in the world.' I pretended to be disappointed but I think I knew that a victory for Benn might have fatally damaged our election chances. Because, ridiculous as it seems now, I still thought Labour were going to form the next government. We had allowed ourselves to indulge in all this posturing secure in the knowledge that, while we might not be flavour of the month, Mrs Thatcher was about as popular as a swarm of killer bees and she would soon be history. Nothing, we thought, was going to transform her popularity overnight – at least nothing short of her single-handedly winning a war. And that wasn't about to happen was it?

Gotcha

English County Council Elections – 6 May 1982

The first time I ever voted was a very special day. For a week my polling card had been pinned to the kitchen noticeboard at a sort of mock casual angle and its details read and re-read with eager anticipation. When Thursday came I went through my normal morning routine, not hurrying or skipping anything. I had worked out that if I finished my breakfast around half past eight and then washed up the previous night's dishes, it would still leave me just over eleven and a half hours in which to walk the 100 yards to the polling station before it closed. Bags of time.

My dad told me that his father had always put on his best suit to go and vote and now I understood why. I pinned a CND badge onto my lapel to make my sympathies plain and walked purposefully down to the polling station clutching my card. I passed a friend on the other side of the road and I happened to catch his eye.

'I'm just going off to vote!' I called out. 'Right now

actually. Going to vote. Voting Labour. Got my polling card. Just going down there now.'

I followed the signs marked 'Polling Station' that looked like props from a 1950s British film and went inside all ready to give a big smile to the Labour teller and a cold glare to the Conservative. But none of the three parties was anywhere to be seen. There were no fanfares or welcoming committees. There was no banner saying, 'The Council would like to welcome John O'Farrell who is voting for the first time today'.

And so I just handed over my polling card, put a cross next to the Labour candidate, folded it and popped it in the ballot box. That was it. There must be more to it than that, I thought. Couldn't they count it, there and then maybe? But no, that really was it. It was like the first time I ever had sex – I was pleased to have done it, but it was all over far too quickly.

For years I had wanted to make my voice heard. And then I made one little mark on a piece of paper and it was over for another couple of years. I still feel short-changed every time I vote. The trouble with democracy is that everyone's vote is equal. There's me voting Labour with a passion that nearly snapped the lead in the pencil and that counts as one vote. And then a floating voter goes 'eeny-meeny-miny-mo' in the polling booth next to me and cancels out my choice with a random cross next to the Conservative. I thought it would be far more democratic if people's votes took into account how strongly they felt about their support for their particular party. As long as that party was Labour, obviously.

When voting in an election such as this one it is important to be clear why you are opting for a particular candidate. We were electing a councillor to represent

71

our ward on the local council. So obviously the decisive factor governing who we voted for was that person's attitude to a small war which was taking place 8,000 miles away in the South Atlantic.

The local elections of 6 May took place a few days after the sinking of the *Belgrano* and HMS *Sheffield*. Consequently the quality of local councillors, Labour or otherwise, counted for nothing as the Conservatives made unexpected gains in the surreal atmosphere of self-conscious jingoism that gripped the country that summer.

My first reaction to the invasion of the Falkland Islands on 2 April had been shock, although not the shock of most people I talked to who seemed to think the Argentine army had landed somewhere in the Western Hebrides. Unlike normal people who do not sit up in bed at night reading atlases, I did at least know where the Falklands were, and also that Argentina lay claim to them. I had also once known someone who had grown up in the Falklands. He had said it was a pretty desolate and dismal place compared to Maidenhead – which by my reckoning made the Falklands very bleak indeed.

On the Saturday after the invasion I drove from Maidenhead to Exeter and the entire length of the motorway was packed with convoys of army trucks. Nobody had yet announced it, but the British army was mobilising. I hadn't realised that we had that many soldiers. My car had a big CND sticker just above my tax disc, and the squaddies looking out of the back of the lorries would point it out to each other and offer their opinion of me in basic sign language. And I would overtake them with a fixed stare that suggested I simply had not noticed them. If I really couldn't see or hear dozens

72

of squaddies leaning out of the back of their lorries shouting, 'Wanker!' then frankly I shouldn't have been on the road. The motorway service station was packed out with them; loud, excited and even more cocksure than usual. They knew that their moment had come, that everyone was looking at them, that dads were pointing them out to their kids saying that they were going off to fight the Argies. They were like Millwall fans on an awayday. In the toilets there were more soldiers than there were urinals. All I will say is that I decided not to wash my hands in the sink. And how unfortunate – it appeared that my CND badge must have fallen off in the car. I don't know whether I was scared of events getting out of control in the South Atlantic, or a pack of squaddies getting out of control in Gordano service station, but somehow I just felt very vulnerable.

Coupled with this numb fear was the excitement of the political crisis into which the government had been plunged. During my cautious journey past the lorry-loads of witty soldiers I listened to the emergency debate in the House of Commons broadcast live on the radio. The government were in disarray and hearing Mrs Thatcher struggling at the dispatch box and being severely criticised from all sides was better than having the radio play my all-time top 100 singles. The signal on my car radio was weak, and consequently the baying voices from the House of Commons would occasionally merge with a Welsh-language radio station that was broadcasting from the other side of the Bristol Channel. At one moment Enoch Powell was saying, 'Now we shall see what sort of metal the Iron Lady is really made of . . .' and then as if to reiterate his point he would seem to add 'Mae llu o fargeinion i'w cael nawr yn Allied Carpets.'

73

It was generally felt that the government had given the green light to Argentina by announcing the withdrawal of a patrol vessel in the area shortly beforehand. The government was also accused of failing to spot a number of little tell-tale signs that an invasion was about to happen, only slightly less obvious than a telegram from Galtieri saying, 'We're going to invade the Falklands stop Hope that's OK stop'. Britain had been humiliated because of the incompetence of the Conservative government. Perfect, I thought – Thatcher will be gone by Christmas.

But as the task force sailed southwards and the American-led search for a negotiated settlement continued, I gradually realised that because a diplomatic compromise would still leave Margaret Thatcher fatally damaged this was not an outcome she was going to settle for. Only victory in a war could save her political skin, so this was the policy that Britain was doomed to pursue. I could not understand why no one was explaining this grim reality to the British public. All the commentators discussed the possibilities of 'joint sovereignty', reiterating that the task force was there to add strength to our negotiating hand and that there probably would still be a diplomatic solution. But if they had been honest with us they would have admitted this was all just a smokescreen. John Cole should have simply stood outside Number 10 and told the nation straight: 'Margaret Thatcher knows that if she wants to win the next election she has to be seen to give the Argies a right good kicking, so quite frankly all these negotiations are a load of old bollocks.' But he never said this, even if he knew it. When the news came through that an Argentine cruiser had been sunk outside the exclusion zone on orders from Downing Street, I was both depressed and unsurprised. She had lit the blue touchpaper and would not have to retire.

It just wasn't fair. Why did Margaret Thatcher have to go to war against a fascist dictatorship? Why couldn't we have a straightforward goodies and baddies war, where Margaret Thatcher was the baddie and the People's Democratic Socialist Republic of Narnia were the goodies? My father's generation had had Spain. Unelected fascists versus popular socialist republicans; all completely straightforward. And back at home he could rail against the Tory back-benchers and the *Catholic Herald* and the *Daily Express* for their support of Franco. We had to have the most right-wing British prime minister ever versus someone more right-wing than her. To complicate the morality even further, the Conservative government had not provoked the war by invading anywhere, they were just responding to aggression, while Argentina was reclaiming land that she clearly had a better claim to, though we knew Galtieri was only doing this to save his own bankrupt brutal regime. I was so confused.

I settled on the uncomfortable and convoluted position of wanting Great Britain to lose a war for the good of Great Britain. As far as I was concerned another term for the Conservatives would be much worse for the country than losing some windswept colony and a bit of international prestige. Margaret Thatcher should withdraw her forces immediately because only then would the British people really start to turn against Margaret Thatcher. For some reason she never saw the logic of this argument. Demanding a British withdrawal was of course not a view that I could argue loudly in public. One pub we drank in had a large picture of 'Our Boys' pinned above the till and the atmosphere of an

SAS bootroom. Any discussion of opposition to the war was pursued with anxious glances to left and right as if we were resistance fighters in an unconvincing BBC wartime drama. So the more emphatically I made my point, the quieter my voice became.

'All I'm saying is that if I was in charge of the army, I would deliberately lose the war.'

'John, you're whispering, I can't hear a bloody word, what did you say?'

'I said, "If I was a British general I would ..."' (hand covers mouth, half coughing to disguise words) '"... deliberately lose the war."'

'Deliberately lose the war?'

A group of rather intimidating tattooed locals standing by the bar were glancing our way, looking like they had swallowed a dangerous mix of lager and *Sun* editorials, and we suddenly remembered an urgent appointment at another pub.

Obviously this revolutionary defeatism was not an argument that Michael Foot, despite all his pacifist instincts, was able to take up with a great deal of fervour. To oppose the war, he was advised, would risk annihilation at the next election (lucky he didn't go down that road then). The Labour Party was forced to pretend rather half-heartedly that it supported the use of military force while optimistically suggesting that perhaps one or two of them might be invited to join the war cabinet in return for their invaluable support. I don't think the cabinet heard the rest of the answerphone message as they were laughing too much. But while the Labour leadership ostensibly supported the war, many of the rank and file on the left did not. Friends that I later made in the Labour Party said that the war had split activists directly along class lines: working-class members in favour and middle-class members against. On reflection the same split happened in my family: Dad who put HP sauce on his chops was in favour, Mum who put mint sauce on hers was against. My brother just said, 'What war?'

But what were we, the army-trouser-wearing pacifists, supposed to do about this complex political situation? Demonstrate in the streets? Join the Argentine International Brigade? Or just sit around in our student house and get stoned? Rochdale Randle, he who disapproved of smiling and hair, disapproved of the ritual smoking of cannabis even more. So much so that we felt compelled to disappear into my bedroom to do it. After my cumbersome old record deck had got through both sides of *The Velvet Underground Featuring Nico* there came a firm knock at the door. Randle's very, very, very serious face said through the smoke, 'John, the police are downstairs and they want to talk to you.'

Left-wing paranoia is bad enough without the aid of cannabis, but for a stoned leftie to be told in the middle of a war that the police want him – well, this was it, I'd never see my friends or family again. My loyal comrades hid under the bed and in the cupboard in case the police searched my room. It would have had to be a pretty sharp copper to notice anything unusual about the giggling and shushing noises coming from inside the wardrobe.

Two young policemen in uniform stood at the door and a chill ran down my spine. What could this mean? Had I spoken out too brazenly about my opposition to the war? Had they spotted the cannabis plants growing on my roof and now come to catch me smoking them? Or had they been hired by my English tutor as a last-ditch attempt to get me to hand in that essay on the Romantic Poets?

'Are you John O'Farrell?'

Stoned as I was, I worked out the answer to this one. 'Yes.'

'Are you the owner of a Ford Escort registration number TLT 44M?'

'Ah, thank God for that. Yes, I am,' I said with a great surge of relief that probably revealed I was guilty of any number of offences. A driving offence, I thought; they'd never search my bedroom for a driving offence, not even under Thatcher. They proceeded to ask me about a burglary that had taken place near my parents' house the previous weekend. My car had been parked there and someone had taken its number. They were satisfied with my explanation, and just when I thought I had successfully conducted a conversation with half a plant's worth of grass spinning round my head, they suddenly caught me off guard.

'Have you heard?'

'Heard what?'

'The bastards have got one of ours. HMS *Sheffield*.'

'Sorry?'

'Got hit by an Exocet.'

There followed a long pause while they waited for me to ask for more details and I tried not to look too glazed.

'I'm sorry, I haven't the faintest idea what you're talking about.'

'The Argies. They've sunk one of our frigates. Bastards.'

'Oh, that! The Falklands, right, yeah ... oh dear, that's a shame. Sunk? Oh dear.' And then a pause during which I could not think of anything else to say. I suddenly had the sensation that I had been talking to

78

them on the doorstep for about half an hour and must have seemed very rude not to have invited them in. 'Um … Sorry, sorry, do you want to come in for a cup of tea?'

They looked me up and down and I felt as if I was wearing a big T-shirt with the message, 'Stoned Student – Waste of Taxpayers' Money'.

Fortunately they didn't stay, and within half an hour I had coaxed the last of my petrified friends out from under the bed. Rochdale Randle asked me what the police were going on about and I told him that they'd wanted me to know that the *Sheffield* had gone down. He looked a bit puzzled and said, 'Wednesday or United?'

No two groups of people could have been further apart. A pair of patriotic policemen and a bunch of unshaven left-wing anti-authoritarian students. If the police had told us that smoking cannabis was suddenly legal, we probably would have lost interest in it. It had never occurred to them that I might actually be against the war. I was British, ergo, they thought, I supported the British army. But my hatred of Mrs Thatcher tainted the way I looked at everything. Later in the summer I breathed a sigh of relief when England drew 0–0 with Spain and were knocked out of the World Cup. It was quite bad enough having Thatcher welcome home a victorious army without her going to the airport to meet a World Cup winning team as well. And when more serious items of bad news were reported I forgot about the suffering or the poverty that they represented and saw them as another good slap in the face of the government: 'Great! Unemployment is up! Crime's doubled – fantastic! I mean obviously it's terrible that unemployment is up, with all the suffering and misery that that entails, but what I'm saying is that these figures vindicate what we have been saying – that unemployment was bound to rise from these policies and this has proved that she is wrong and will help people to see that they should not re-elect her. Fingers crossed, it might go over three million in time for the local elections.' I was sitting in the gallery at the 1985 Labour conference when the dot matrix information board ran the headline, 'Unemployment Reaches 3.2 Million – Highest Figure Ever', and a frisson of excitement went through the hall at this excellent news and its perfect timing. We had confused Margaret Thatcher the person with Great Britain the country. But then I suppose she started it.

The Falklands victory when it came was very much her victory. Crowds outside Downing Street sang 'For She's a Jolly Good Fellow' and 'God Save the Queen' and Mrs Thatcher presumed both songs referred to her. Bunting appeared on a house in our road and the television news was filled with contrived street parties and squaddies sharing cups of tea with liberated islanders. Even the Princess of Wales joined in and produced a son and heir to the throne in the week of the victory. It was like living through a bad dream. I was against the war, against people's reaction to the war, even against the outcome of the war. I wanted to say, 'Sorry, no, this is all wrong, this isn't in the script at all, can we just have some completely different news please.' Dejected Argentine troops were shown on the television, their heads drooping and their tatty clothes hanging loose around them. They reminded me of Michael Foot. The news informed us that Argentine prisoners of war were assisting the British army in locating land mines. Which I presume meant that some sergeant-major shouted at them, 'Right, you dago bastards – you go, play football, that field over there.' Their defeat led to the overthrow of Galtieri and a prompt return to democracy in Argentina. Presumably Argentine socialists were delighted with the war's outcome – unfortunately I was unable to have a wide enough perspective to share their joy.

Worse was yet to come. Every day for weeks, it seemed, the news would open with the 'Emotional Return of Troops' slot in which thousands of people gathered at the quayside in Portsmouth or Plymouth to wave Union Jacks and cry while the band played 'Don't Cry for Me, Argentina' for the hundredth bloody time. The ships couldn't all come back at once, of course – it had to be one ticker-tape-covered ship a day to stretch it out for as long as possible and really rub our unpatriotic noses in it. On one occasion the news showed two topless girls standing on a rock waving their bikini tops at some squaddies who had a big banner on their ship saying, 'Call Off the Rail Strike or We'll Call in an Air Strike'. I had died and gone to hell. And hell was a Rupert Murdoch Theme Park.

What galled me so much was how lucky Margaret Thatcher had been. Before the war she had been trailing in third place in the opinion polls, her government had been at fault for allowing the crisis to develop and then suddenly here she was with a five-year extension on the lease of 10 Downing Street. One of the commanders of the task force (I can't recall his triple-barrelled name) said that Britain had been very fortunate that so many of the Exocet missiles that struck British ships had failed to go off. If they had detonated, he said, we would have suffered too many casualties to allow him to risk keeping the task force in the area, and we would have

81

failed to recapture the Falklands. So that's what kept Mrs Thatcher in power. A few faulty detonators on some French-made missiles.

In the middle of the war Labour faced another drubbing in a Parliamentary by-election, in the safe Tory seat of Beaconsfield. A young Labour candidate lost his deposit. As I watched the result come in I still hoped that Michael Foot could lead us to victory at the general election. But of course the next victorious Labour leader would not be Michael Foot, nor even the man who followed him, nor even the Labour leader after that. It would be this twenty-nine-year-old novice who had just lost his deposit in Beaconsfield – Anthony Charles Lynton Blair (3886 votes). I think if I had known that we would have that long to wait, I might have given up all thought of joining the Labour Party there and then. But I had decided that going on occasional demos and boycotting Outspan oranges was not enough – it was time for me to become actively involved. Maybe it was the disappointment I had felt when I actually voted that made me want to sign up and do more. Maybe it was just the obvious fact that Labour needed all the help it could get. But I resolved to get involved. I had a form to join the Labour Party which I had cut out of the newspaper. I was going to commit myself because they needed someone dynamic like me, someone who got things done, who didn't sit around talking but actually got in there and made a difference. About twelve months later I finally got round to sending the form off.

Labour hold Jarrow

General Election – 9 June 1983

In 1983 the United States of America went to war against the tiny Caribbean island of Grenada. This, however, was a far more equal battle than the British general election of the same year. It was said that the Labour campaign started badly and then fell away, but this is being generous. It was the worst campaign in electoral history, and it hurt to watch it. There are various things that can lose a party votes in elections. You might have a leader who does not look like prime ministerial material, you might have a manifesto that alienates many of the electorate, you might have a hostile media, you might appear hopelessly divided as a political party, or your campaign might be poorly organised and unfocused. Or, like Labour in 1983, you might manage all of the above.

Mrs Thatcher called the election for 9 June – two days after my finals ended, cleverly keeping me out of the campaign until the last possible moment. Labour had a great deal of work to do in those four weeks if it was to get any sort of result, although not quite as much work as me. It was not that I had been a lazy student, it was just that I hadn't realised that doing a degree in English and Drama would involve reading lots of books and plays.

There had been a lot of discussion about whether the prime minister would go to the country a year before she needed to. She teased the country, saying that it reminded her of the old song 'Maggie May', which rather surprised me as I had never had her down as a Rod Stewart fan. She whipped up election fever until she reluctantly announced that she was now forced to dissolve Parliament because all this speculation was not good for the country. I was outraged by the dishonesty of this process. She had deliberately engineered speculation and then used it as her excuse to take advantage of her opinion-poll lead. What sort of politician was she to engage in this blatant ... er ... politics.

I had really hoped that the election would be on one of the later dates that were being talked about, to give Labour's poll position a chance to improve and to allow me to get involved, but when I walked into the front room where Rochdale Randle was watching the news he said grimly, 'It's June the ninth,' in a way that confirmed that we both knew that this was really bad news.

'Right!' I said with a steely resolve. 'We're really going to show them.' And I sort of looked around for a way in which we could really show them, and then just slumped down depressed in front of the television.

At the beginning of the campaign Labour were a million miles behind the Tories. Then, from out of the blue, a poll was published that put us only three-quarters of a million miles behind. One shadow cabinet member said on the news with a completely straight face, 'If Labour continues to improve its standing at this rate, we will win the election.' I clung to this straw and waited for every poll with the anxiety of a relative waiting for news after a major operation.

My support was limited to pathetically small contributions. I had a *Vote Labour* sticker which I wore everywhere. During my finals I stuck it on my pencil case and put this face-up on my desk. My reasoning was that the invigilator who walked up and down the aisles during the exam might notice the sticker and be persuaded to vote Labour by the force of its argument. I think I was more concerned about whether he had noticed my sticker than I was about my essay on Dickens. Every time he came towards me I would look at him and then look at the sticker meaningfully. Eventually he looked long and hard at it just to make sure it didn't have the entire text of *Bleak House* scrawled on it in tiny writing. Ah, he's looked at it, I thought. That's one conversion done, only about another four million to go.

I stuck a big red 'Evans for Exeter' poster in the front window and also one in the back window, which I hoped might get noticed by the parents taking their kids into the Scout hut that backed on to our garden. I put one in the back of my car and was forced to drive with extreme care and courtesy for the entire month.

But strangely my efforts did not seem to be shifting Labour's poll position. About a week before polling day my radio alarm came on just as the *Today* programme was leading with the latest poll findings. A bigger Tory lead than ever. Any tiny chink of light at the end of the tunnel was snuffed out in an instant – the Conservatives were going to win, they were going to win by a mile, and the whole country was completely mad if it couldn't see how wrong they all were.

But in the four weeks available, the Labour Party had not exactly deported itself with the dignity of a statesman-like team ready to take the reins of office. An early party political broadcast featured Michael Foot wandering into an old people's home to talk to some of the residents. He chatted a bit with the old people, wandered around a bit more and at any minute you expected one of the nurses to say, 'Time for your medication now, Mr Foot.' Michael Foot was a great politician, the person I had ultimately wanted to become leader of the Labour Party, but somehow you sensed that in 1983 Margaret Thatcher was not lying awake thinking, He's making a fool of me. I'm going to lose. Photographers from the *Sun* would follow him around hospitals and wait till he was standing next to the sign saying 'Psychiatric Ward' or whatever. 'Could you move to your left please, Mr Foot, we want to get you under the sign saying "Terminal Cases Only".' Then he would head off to the next photo-inopportunity on our secret weapon – the Labour Party Battle Bus.

This was an open-topped double-decker bus which toured marginal constituencies helping to make them into Conservative strongholds. Its route was carefully planned to take in as many tree-lined avenues as possible so that overhanging branches could whiplash across the top of the bus knocking members of the shadow cabinet to the deck. The evening news would feature Margaret Thatcher being presented with flowers by rosy-cheeked schoolchildren, all waving Union Jacks and cheering. Then it would cut to Labour's campaign and we'd see Jill Foot getting back to her feet and picking a bird's nest out of her hair with the tannoy booming, 'Vote Labour – for an end to the NHS queues', as the injured headed down to the nearest casualty department to make them even longer.

Throughout all this I would defend Labour's campaign against charges of incompetence and amateurism because the same charges were being made by the Tory press so they must be malicious lies designed to undermine Labour's chances. But deep down I had to admit to myself that if it wasn't even inspiring me then the floating voters would have floated away long ago. If it was possible to do something wrong, Labour managed it. The election leaflets were printed on a kind of paper normally reserved for prison toilets. One of them showed a rather unconvincing black-and-white photo-montage of hundreds of people being swept down a drain. These were supposed either to represent all the unemployed people that the Tories didn't care about or all the voters that Labour was losing as a result of this campaign – I was never quite sure which. It did less damage than I feared, however, because the paper was so flimsy that the thing ripped in seven places every time you tried to push it through a letter box, thus avoiding any danger of it being read.

In the final few days the polls looked worse than ever with the Alliance gaining ground on Labour and momentarily overtaking us – which prompted David Owen to pronounce that Labour was finished. I knew we must really be in trouble when Margaret Thatcher started campaigning for Labour. 'The Labour Party would never die,' she said. 'The only good opposition would be a reformed Labour Party.' Cheers, Margaret, thanks for the support. Much appreciated.

On election day I turned up at the committee rooms in the north side of Exeter eager to do my bit, knowing nothing of how elections are organised. They sent me out to knock on doors and although I knew I was on a council estate and that this should be natural Labour territory, I was actually pleasantly surprised by just how many Labour supporters I found on my way round. At the first door they were Labour. At the second door they used to be Labour but were voting Conservative this time. The next couple were voting SDP, but might vote for us 'if we got our act together'. Then another Labour voter, another Labour and then one Conservative. On these figures we were ahead. I happily reported this news back to the committee rooms and they explained to me that the list of voters that I had been calling on was the Labour *promise*: the people who had been canvassed earlier in the campaign and had said they would definitely vote Labour. That's why I had only been knocking on every fourth door. If support was haemorrhaging like that across the country we were doomed. And my little snapshot was exactly what was happening across the country. My first day of knocking on doors for the Labour Party was the day it recorded its lowest share of the vote since 1918.

When the polls closed at ten o'clock, there was a sense of relief that nothing else could now be done. Like the moment before an execution, all the appeals and petitions had failed and the inevitable was now upon us. During my years as a student I had resolved the impossible equation of high alcohol consumption and low income with a craze for home brewing. Every new barrel of beer had had a topical name. There had been 'Task Force Tipple' and 'Malvinas Mild' and on the announcement of the election I brewed a 'Labour Landslide Bitter'. I timed it so it would be ready on election night. It was undrinkable.

Why I stayed up to watch the results is a mystery to me. I suppose it was for the same reason that I cannot help slowing down and glancing across at horrific motorway accidents. As the first couple of results came in that night I remember Peter Snow actually bursting out laughing and saying, 'Look what's happening to the Labour vote!' We had lost one in four of our voters since 1979 – itself a heavy defeat. As election parties go, the evening of 9 June was not a swinger. On the positive side it did not produce that awful anxiety of some election nights – the nail-biting finish, the vital recounts and the eventual disappointment of narrow defeat. But in the circumstances I would have settled for that. Grim foreboding gave way to depressing confirmation. A couple of the people in the room burst into tears when Tony Benn lost his seat. But it was not the loss of individual MPs that was so depressing, just the unrelenting barrage of little blue bars flashing up across the bottom of the screen, places that sounded like they really, really ought to be Labour: Con Gain Newcastle Central, Con Gain Newport West, Con Gain Barrow-in-Furness, Con Gain Slough, Con Gain Clywd South West, Con Gain Glanford and Scunthorpe, Con Gain Leicester East, Con Gain Bradford North, Con Gain Lewisham East, Con Gain Manchester Withington, Con Gain Darlington, and then finally one little red bar across the bottom of the screen – Labour Hold Jarrow.

Labour Hold Jarrow; oh rejoice, rejoice! Well done, Labour, another great triumph for socialism. I don't wish to take the Labour votes of Jarrow residents for granted, but it strikes me that Jarrow is the sort of place that Labour really ought to hold. This was a caption that the BBC always saved for the most depressing moment on election nights – usually when Mrs Thatcher was waving out of a Tory central office window to the Young Conservatives who were pouring champagne over each other's heads. The editor of *Election Special* would say, 'OK, let's try to cheer up the Labour voters a little bit – put up *Labour Hold Jarrow*.' The implication is that we should try to look on the bright side because in the midst of another catastrophic election at least the Tories haven't taken bloody Jarrow. It's a bit like saying to Jackie Kennedy, 'Don't worry, that blood will wash out of your coat, no problem.'

On the morning of 10 June, I woke up and for a brief second did not remember the enormity of the disaster that had hit Labour. And then it struck me. That another five years of Margaret Thatcher started today. And that Labour's defeat was so enormous that she would probably win the next election as well and that politically speaking everything but everything was lost. With the sort of depression that pulls down the pit of your stomach, I closed my eyes again and tried to take in the scale of it. The news on the radio confirmed my worst fears. Labour had not just lost an election, they had effectively been destroyed as a political force. Even before universal suffrage, candidates for the Labour Representation Committee had averaged a greater share of the vote. With a majority of 144, Thatcher could do exactly as she pleased and not even the saner members of her own party could hold her back.

Why could the country not see the rightness of our cause? How could it be that the simple basic precepts of left-wing politics were not in themselves enough to make everyone want to vote Labour? A philosophy that did not leave anybody out of the equation. A way of looking at the world that saw an injustice to one person as an injustice to us all. A belief that we were all impoverished if we lived alongside 3 million unemployed people. A knowledge that envy and hatred and crime and violence would flourish unless we gave people dignity, security and justice. Couldn't everyone see how their world had improved? That in the past 100 years they had gained decent wages and working conditions, and homes with sanitation that they could not be easily evicted from? That it was the left that had won them all these basic human rights, but that it had always done so in the face of fierce opposition from the establishment? Was it not obvious that this process was far from complete, that too many people still lived in poverty or suffered from avoidable ill health or that their children did not have the opportunity to achieve their greatest potential? What did people think the Conservatives wanted to do for them? These arrogant, remote and vicious people who knew the price of everything and the value of nothing. Did they have a history of helping people worse off than themselves? Did they have a record of granting more freedom, improving living standards and fighting inequality? Had they wanted the abolition of child labour? Had they wanted the abolition of the slave trade? Had they wanted to grant the right to form trades unions? Had they wanted shorter working hours or the establishment of a decent basic wage? Had they wanted universal suffrage? Had they wanted votes for women? Had they wanted the National Health Service, the Welfare State, universal state education, or anything else that improved the rights, power and prosperity of the majority of ordinary people in Britain? Of course they hadn't. Why did people think that the Conservatives might suddenly have their interests at heart now? The anger and frustration spun around my head as various radio journalists delivered their obituaries of the Labour Party. It wasn't just the Conservatives' record that convinced me they were the worst possible people to be in charge of the country, it was their whole philosophy and outlook. They were not the answer in 1983 and they never could be. I surmised that the Conservatives' answer to every social problem must be automatically wrong because their analysis of society was so totally misconstrued. If you believed the world to be flat then you could not successfully navigate a ship around it. And if you believed that people were only motivated by greed, selfishness and fear then you would not be able to build a happier, safer, more prosperous society.

I remembered a political argument I had had during the election campaign with a Conservative friend of my parents. He had said to me: 'The reason I am voting Conservative is because I do not believe in interfering in the marketplace. You have to allow the market to decide everything.'

To which I said: 'Sorry, who is this "Market" bloke? Who elected him then? Listen, the market is something we have created for our own purposes, not some law of physics as unchangeable as the ebbing of the tides or the waning of the moon. When you Conservatives say that you cannot interfere in the market what you really mean is you cannot interfere with *me* – with my desire to make as much money as I can, at the expense of everyone else. The market is our servant, something we have created – if it is causing poverty and destitution then we must interfere to stop it doing those things.'

Or was this the reply that I came up with that night in bed, reconstructing the argument in my head? Yes, that's right ... my actual reply to his point had been, 'Oh, that's just Tory rubbish.'

He had said that the same rules applied in nature and that you could not defy the survival of the fittest. 'Oh, *heil Hitler*!' I had replied, searching hard for an example of unacceptable right-wing politics. So I worked out what I should have said to this point as well. That the survival of the fittest is a means by which creatures may evolve from one species into a superior species. It explains how we got from being lungfish to *Homo sapiens* who could understand and analyse the world around us. The challenge before us now was not how we could evolve further. No one was saying, 'Vote SDP for a larger cranium and the abolition of the appendix'. The challenge was to live together in society and achieve the greatest amount of happiness for the greatest proportion of the world's population and this could never be achieved by imitating the survival of the fittest. Things are not morally right because they happen in nature. I'm young and strong enough to go round to the old man who lives next door to me and steal all of his food for myself. That's what a young lion would do to an old lion. 'Well, it happens in nature – that's just the way of the world; your child failed her eleven-plus so natural selection has taken place and we're feeding her to a pack of hyenas ...' We are human beings, with a soul and a conscience and a unique ability to see things from other people's point of view. The survival of the fittest created species. But what makes a decent society is the responsibility of the fittest.

That was what I should have said. But I think saying 'Oh, *heil Hitler*!' got my point across almost as well.

* * *

I lay there thinking in my studenty, sci-fi, Kurt Vonnegut way about how far mankind had come. About how it wasn't economic competition that had got us out of the caves, it was *co-operation*. One caveman cannot dig a huge pit and chase a mammoth into it, skin it and cook it. *Homo sapiens* advanced by doing things together, with a plan. They spent millions of years evolving a brain, learning to fashion tools together, communicating this information, inventing languages, building civilisations together, originating philosophies, founding the arts and culture and developing technology till they could walk on the ocean floor and explore the void of space. And then after all that miraculous achievement, after having come so far, at the final hurdle they blew it and went and re-elected Margaret bloody Thatcher.

I lay there all morning, not wanting to venture out into the world that had just chosen her. I could not face passing people in the street and thinking, 'They voted for her ... he voted for her ... she voted for her.' I felt like crawling under the duvet and staying there until the next general election.

It seemed that there was no point in carrying on caring about anybody else, that there was no chance of making a difference to anything. Of course I had no choice.

Around this time W. H. Smith were selling A4 writing pads with famous quotations on the cover page under a line drawing of the relevant figure from history. Some of the lines seemed a bit pointless and random, such as Winston Churchill saying, 'We are waiting for the invasion. So are the fishes.' But one of the quotations really inspired me. There was a sketchy drawing of Martin Luther King and underneath it said, 'All that is necessary for evil to triumph is that good people do nothing.'

That was the key to why it was impossible just to walk away from what had happened. That good in the world had only ever come about because good people had actively fought for it. That to do nothing was to surrender all the precious things that still made our society basically decent and civilised. That the forces of greed, intolerance, selfishness and bigotry had triumphed and now bore all before them because too many people had stood back and done nothing. And because I knew and understood this, it was impossible for me to do nothing.

So that was my inspiration. A quotation on the cover of a W. H. Smith jotter pad wrongly attributed to Martin Luther King. Underneath it said '200 sheets, lined, narrow feint'. I re-read this bit a couple of times, but it failed to stir the same emotions. I dug out the newspaper advertisement from the Labour Party, which like the party itself was now in a rather sad state. I ticked the box that said I would like to join Labour's campaign to stop Mrs Thatcher being re-elected. I addressed an envelope. Once I had accomplished the Herculean task of organising a stamp I would be almost there. Perhaps because I did not know what to expect, or perhaps because I was nervous that I would have to obey lots of rules, for me to join a political party felt like a very big step at the time. And yet within a year of getting my Labour Party card, I would have also joined the World Development Movement, the National Council for Civil Liberties, Amnesty International and the Nicaragua Solidarity Campaign. The only one I never got round to joining was the Anti-Apartheid Movement. I tell myself that it is pure coincidence that this was the only campaign of the left which was to achieve all its aims.

Before I sent off the form there was one more hurdle to cross. After foolishly revealing my intention of becoming a political activist, I was persuaded to go along to a meeting of the Communist Party by the captain of my pub quiz team. He was an English lecturer turned British Rail guard whom I rather admired because he did not own a television or radio and he spent every waking hour of the day reading books. I might have tried a pose like this but I never would have been able to keep it up for more than a week. The walls of his house were covered from top to bottom with books. The hallway, the stairs, the toilet – nothing but shelves of books right up to the ceiling. 'How many of these have you read?' I asked him. 'All of them,' he replied, as if it was a ridiculous question. When I told him I was joining the Labour Party I was disappointed that he did not think this a political route worth pursuing. He said that he was holding a meeting of the Exeter Communist Party in his house and he suggested I came along before making any firm decision. So that's how it happened, Senator McCarthy.

A week or so later seven of us sat around in his front room and the South West regional organiser came all the way from Plymouth and addressed us as if we were the grand meeting of all the Soviets. In the middle of this woman's oration about the great success of that year's National Conference an old man sitting in the chair in the corner piped up, 'Never mind all that, I want to know what the young people think. That's what we need to know, what the young people think. What do *you* think?' and he looked to me to speak and I froze with panic about the breadth of subject matter before me.

What do I think? About what? I wondered. I think that beer and chocolate don't taste very nice together, I think that David Bowie's version of 'China Girl' is not as good as Iggy Pop's, I think that I should have revised more for my French A Level ... what does he mean what do I think?

I mumbled something about not actually being a CP member, just being there to observe, er, probably not allowed to speak ... and the regional organiser jumped in and continued reading out the list of the fraternal greetings that had been announced at conference from comrades in Eastern Europe.

Finally came a discussion about the future of communism. The man who had enticed me to the meeting and in whose house we then were spoke: 'The most important job for the CP must be the rehabilitation of the reputation of Comrade Stalin. It is scandalous that Kruschev was allowed to blacken the name of the supreme defender of the Soviet revolution.'

And there was a pause and a few embarrassed coughs around the room which suggested that this was not the first time they had heard this speech. It was then that I noticed that our host had a big picture of Stalin on the wall – the only picture which did not have stacks of books piled up in front of it. He continued in this vein for some time, about how Stalin's 'pranks' had been misunderstood and how Uncle Joe's interpretation of communism was the only way forward. Nobody argued or contradicted him, or pointed out that he was trying to defend one of the greatest mass murderers in history, they just let him finish and then carried on with what they were saying. They were either too embarrassed, too worn out by him or simply worried that to cross him might necessitate moving to Mexico before getting an ice pick in the head.

The following Sunday night, at the end of our next pub quiz match, he asked me whether I had reached a decision about joining the Communist Party, and he was rather surprised and hurt when I said I had decided not to. He obviously felt that I had witnessed one of their better meetings. But I was not going to join a party where a few sad people with no concept of reality sat around and made long-winded speeches that bore little relationship to the real world. Well I thought I wasn't – but then of course I hadn't been to any Labour Party meetings yet.

Eventually the form was posted, and I awaited the Labour Party's grateful reply. You would have thought that a party in the state that Labour was in by the summer of 1983 would have welcomed new members with open arms. But to join the Labour Party in those days you had to go through several stages of endurance to test that you were really committed.

First the long silence. No reply, no visit, no welcome pack. Just silence for weeks. Maybe they've got a lot of membership applications to sort through, I thought naively. Then, instead of an apology about how long they took to get back to me, came a query about my suitability to join. 'What union are you in?' 'Oh, you're a student? Shouldn't you be joining the University Labour Club? Oh, you're about to graduate? Well, if you're about to leave you're wasting your time joining here.' Finally grudging submission – a letter telling me that my application had been passed by the General Management Committee and that I was now 'accepted'. No glossy brochures, no booklet on the thoughts of Keir

Hardie, no car stickers, no list of forthcoming events and certainly no 'thank you and welcome'. Just one rather frosty letter. It had been more exciting when I joined Lloyds Bank.

In politics everyone starts at the bottom. And you don't get any more rock bottom than the Labour Party in 1983. As a student I had a tendency to arrive at a party just as everyone else was leaving. My arrival in the Labour Party was no exception.

Gissa job

Exeter Guild of Students Elections
– 7 March 1984

To get heavily involved in the intricate internal battles of student politics when you are at university is self-indulgent at the best of times. To do it after you are supposed to have left the university is just sad.

The problem was that I did not have the faintest idea what else I could do with my time. So I successfully applied for the popular post-graduate course in Milling About For a Bit. I don't know whether the seven stages of man includes a period in your early twenties when you just drift along aimlessly, becoming increasingly bitter and frustrated, but this occupation seemed to keep all of us not-very-busy at the time. It was the usual problem of being unable to get a job because you had no experience and not being able to get experience because you could not get a job. What made this situation worse was having to nod in agreement while sympathetic relatives said, 'Well it's so hard to get a job without experience and you can't get experience without getting a job.' In one moment of heroic over-reaching optimism I applied to be the editor of *New Socialist* magazine. For some reason they decided that a twenty-one-year-old with no professional experience of journalism was not even worth an interview.

Eventually I resolved that the best use of my degree was to get occasional driving jobs with an employment agency. As a quick lesson on how capitalism worked, this organisation confirmed all my suspicions. They were paid around £4.50 for every hour that they supplied me to work for somebody, of which I received just £2. I was exploited, poorly paid and had no rights. It felt great.

I was given the job of delivering the polystyrene cups that are fitted into automatic drinks machines. For a young idealist it felt good to be able to do something really worthwhile for society. But when I looked down the list of places I had to go I suddenly spotted a problem.

'Ah, sorry, no. I'd rather not do this one.'

'What you talking about?'

'Hinckley Point Nuclear Power Station. I'm against nuclear power, you see.'

The foreman looked somewhere between bemused and murderous. 'I'm asking you to deliver some paper cups, not the bloody atom bomb.'

I tried to explain that by delivering the cups I would be contributing to Britain's nuclear power programme – because the provision of coffee and tea to the power workers was an essential part of the maintenance of the nuclear industry.

'Would you like me to hire another driver just to do that address then?'

'Oh, that would be great, thanks,' I said, failing to

spot that he was being dangerously ironic.

'And while he's at it, he could do all the other fucking deliveries as well.'

I realised that I was being threatened with the sack.

'All right, I was just saying that I didn't believe in nuclear power.'

'Well don't use electricity then, you stupid twat.'

And he threw me the keys to the van and went back into his office. I made the delivery and told myself as I drove up the M5 that given that the nuclear power station was already in place, wasn't a workforce that had been refreshed by plentiful supplies of hot drinks less likely to make a mistake and therefore cause a major nuclear accident? Giving them polystyrene cups was actually a very socialist thing to do.

I think word of this exchange must have got back to the office, because the offers of driving jobs rather suddenly stopped. And so although I got one or two temporary jobs after that, for the best part of two years after graduation I was unemployed. Not genuine 'they've closed down t'pit' unemployed, but deliberate 'I don't want to train to be an accountant' unemployed. All the same having nothing to do for weeks and weeks on end is a challenge to anyone's morale. Things that would now take me less than half an hour were subconsciously allowed to take the entire day just so that my time was kept occupied. Right, a letter to the bank, that's my task for Monday ... and I'd sit down with a cup of tea at ten o'clock and maybe type out the final draft at around half past four in the afternoon. And as I signed the letter with a confident flourish I felt the satisfaction of having done a good day's work. I wouldn't post it straight away because going into town to get a stamp could be my task for Tuesday. After a while I took to going up to the university library to self-consciously read books on Difficult Subjects that I felt I should know more about. I didn't just wander up there every now and then, I got up at eight o'clock every day, put on my smartest clothes and strode up the road with all the other people setting off to work. Then I hid there until half past five in the evening when it was time to come home again. I think for a while I convinced myself that I was gainfully employed doing something worthwhile, until the landlady of my local pub unwittingly rumbled me. She had seen me walk past several days in a row and eventually came out and said excitedly, 'Ooh, John – did you manage to get a job then?'

She looked so pleased for me, almost proud to see me setting off in the morning with a briefcase and a sense of purpose. Half swallowing my words I mumbled, 'Er, no – I'm just going up to the library, actually.'

I felt about six inches high.

Fortunately for me, many of my contemporaries had also failed to find an acceptable route into the world of work and so we all ran back to the comforting bosom of our former university campus. We hit upon the idea of setting up an alternative left-wing publication which we called *New Times*. The plan was to produce a readable radical journal which would follow in the long line of successful left-wing publications like the *Daily Herald*, the *News on Sunday* and *New Society*. There's a first time for everything.

While I had been a student I had written the occasional article for the official student publication of which one of my housemates was the editor. Thrilling features, like my account of a day spent on the non-stop picket of South Africa House, or articles on the arms race packed with factual inaccuracies. But in a surprise

103

coup a bloke who claimed to be 'apolitical' packed out a student meeting with a number of friends and got himself elected editor of the magazine by promising to make it less left-wing. Then, as now, 'apolitical' was a euphemism for 'right-wing but doesn't realise or admit it'. So we hit back by launching our own independent and, we thought, superior student magazine – which we published more regularly and sold for half the price. We did of course have the slight advantage that we were working on it full-time, but all those extra hours just meant that the articles were even more verbose and numerous than they had been before. We sugared the pill with a bit of comedy – I wrote a humorous diary of an imaginary first-year student – and we tried to make the design of the magazine as radical as the content. Before long *New Times* was actually quite successful, making enough surplus money for us to put on the odd exhibition and give away a free flexi-disc. But for some reason we never would have dreamed of paying ourselves any wages out of it. We had unwittingly created a successful small business but we would have been horrified if anyone had told us we were entrepreneurs. I think we believed that making a living out of *anything* would have been right-wing.

Running a student magazine meant that I started following student politics more closely, caring whether this or that motion got through the Guild of Students General Meeting and worrying which shade of politics were represented by which guild officers. (Only a snobby university like Exeter would have a Guild rather than a Students' Union.) I got to know some people from the University Labour Club to whom I casually boasted that 'I was a member of the Labour Party in the town actually' and before long I was roped into some of their campaigns.

For several years the excuse of Rag Week had been used to organise a beauty contest on campus. Girls (and some boys, as a means of deflecting charges of sexism) paraded around in swimming costumes and if they were drunk enough and sufficient money was promised to charity they ended up revealing even more. But it was all OK because it was for Rag Week. If the university rugby team wanted to wave their genitals at passing motorists it was OK if it was for Rag Week.

So I went along to join Labour's picket of the beauty contest and gave out leaflets to a lot of rather excited students who for some reason were not persuaded by our arguments that they really ought not go in and pay money in the hope that one or two over-enthusiastic first-years might take their bras off. Having failed to persuade a single student we then went in and watched the proceedings. We offered the occasional heckle, but in the bear pit of drunken students cheering semi-naked women our muted objections were drowned out. One particularly game lass got up and started to thrust about the stage in a rather over-stretched bathing costume and, as she toyed with the lace of her bikini top, a chant grew from the mob: 'Off! Off! Off! Off!'

At that point we made a spontaneous decision to occupy the stage. The Labour Party was never particularly good at choosing battles that would make it more popular and this was no exception. We were booed and jeered and Labour's poll rating in that room must have plummeted off the bottom of the graph. The compère of this event was a prominent Conservative who had prepared for the possibility of our invasion by having half the rowing team on stand-by to act as improvised vigilante-type security guards.

'Right – get rid of them!' she said, like a Translyvanian princess releasing the hounds. Suddenly we were being dragged off by burly third-years who looked like muscle-bound super-heroes except that they all wore rather naff university sweatshirts.

'Violence against Women!' shouted the protester next to me.

'Oh, is it?' said her assailant rather apologetically, and he let go of her again.

As I was being dragged off I had the embarrassing experience of realising that I knew the bloke who had hold of my legs. He had shared a student house with a former girlfriend of mine.

'Oh, hello!' I said.

'Oh, it's you, hi! Sorry about this.'

'Oh, that's quite all right.'

The boos were growing as the audience realised that the moment had gone when Miss Rag Week might have bared all in the name of local good causes. So in that sense we had achieved our goal. Obviously the breasts of a twenty-one-year-old blonde held no interest for me. Ahem.

'It was so outrageously sexist,' said the girl from the Labour Club afterwards. And I agreed with everything she said because I was hoping to get off with her at some point later in the evening.

That was the most militant thing I did in the whole year. And yet 1984 will be scorched on the soul of every socialist as the year when the greatest strike in the history of the Labour movement took on the might of the Conservative government and lost. The year when police were pitched against pickets, courts against unions and sequestrators against support groups. And I was in a little office gluing down adverts promising 10 per cent discount for students at the record and tape exchange.

The trouble was that the Miners' Strike just felt so far away. All I could do was transfer my little yellow *Coal Not Dole* sticker from one T-shirt to the next and put my loose change in the buckets that were being shaken in the town centre. I wanted to do so much more but I did not have the initiative or confidence to volunteer myself to anyone. This was a strike about unemployment and I was unemployed but I felt it had nothing at all to do with me. My membership of the Labour Party at least meant that someone occasionally came round to collect food donations. So I apologise now to whichever miner's family received that tin of anchovy paste I had had since Christmas 1982. But for the rest of the year, the Miners' Strike was just something that happened on the television and in the newspapers. Something that happened far away in places I had never been to the sort of people I had never met. I listened to every bulletin and pored over every report, article and editorial, like a teenage boy reading dispatches from the front line. But in terms of actively doing anything, my contribution to the battle for socialism went no further than selling student magazines or organising film festivals and poetry readings. However torn my donkey jacket was, this still felt like a poncey middle-class pursuit.

Although alternative poetry evenings are clearly less likely to result in pitched battles with the police than major industrial disputes are, we did come fairly close one evening. We had as our guest Michael Smith, a radical Jamaican performance poet. After a very successful and well-attended event we took him and his companion down to one of the nightclubs on Exeter's quayside. These clubs normally catered for lager-swilling university rugby teams and their petite posh girlfriends and so the sight of a Rastafarian and a very tall Jamaican poet was not quite what the bouncers were expecting. Exeter did have a black population but he had recently completed his law degree and left.

'Sorry, we're full.'

'What?'

'We're full – you can't come in.'

'What do you mean, you're full – you're never full. This is Devon.'

'Well, we are tonight – and *he's* pissed,' he said, pointing to the Rastafarian.

Then the penny dropped. This was nothing more than petty vindictive racism. And apart from anything else he wasn't pissed, he was stoned. A fierce argument developed, during which, just to rub our noses in it, other people were admitted to the 'full' nightclub. Eventually the police were called and when they were confronted with two shouting black men they excitedly radioed back to the station to tell them to get the beds in the cells made up.

An hour earlier, Michael Smith had been on a stage in front of hundreds of students who were applauding his brilliant poems about oppression and racism. And now he had some spotty policeman telling him, 'One more word out of you, sunshine, and you'll be spending the night behind bars.' I hazarded a guess that this particular officer did not have any of Michael Smith's albums. As it was generally our policy to try not to get our guests locked up in police cells overnight, we were trying very hard to defuse the situation. Eventually we managed to drag them away and back to our house, with them still seething with anger and lambasting us for effectively caving in to the racism of the bouncers and the police. 'Police international behave the same way!' Michael Smith kept saying over and over again.

We should have fought the police, they told us, we should not have co-operated and kept the peace and done what the forces of authority wanted. But for the same reason that we weren't on the picket lines throwing stones at riot police we had shied away from any trouble outside a Devon nightclub. We were soft middle-class kids, destined to join the establishment not fight it. One of the women in the house was getting some more drinks when she was approached by Michael Smith.

'I want justice!' he implored desperately.

She turned to him with words that will stay with me for ever.

'I can't give you justice, but I can give you a hug.'

You would be hard pressed to a find a more succinct definition of liberal middle-class politics than 'I can't give you justice but I can give you a hug'. They should have had that inscribed in Latin under the SDP's logo.

The argument raged long into the night, with us nervously proposing that there was nothing to gain from being locked up in a cell and them countering, 'But you have to fight them – because police international behave the same way!' They were angry with us and we were apologetic and terrified of the idea that we might be tarred with the brush of racism for accepting the decision of the bouncers.

There are only a few people that you meet in life who are genuinely charismatic and inspiring and for me Michael Smith was one of them. On stage he was fearsome and compelling, with an infectious anger about the injustice of the world that shone out of his fiery eyes. He did not care if his deeply held beliefs caused offence or made him enemies. A few months later, in the middle of the Jamaican general election campaign, he was set upon by a mob in the street and stoned to death. It was an impossible, incomprehensible piece of news.

I tried to picture the scene – a dusty shanty town or some run-down suburb. The moment when he realised he was in real danger. Then the rocks raining down upon him, the anger in his eyes turning to fear. For some reason I couldn't hate the people who had done it – all I could feel was a sense of enormous waste. What a pointless, stupid waste of a death it was. What a waste of all that talent and energy. That awe-inspiring man now a bruised and chilly corpse in some far-away morgue. It made me feel physically sick.

Perhaps in his memory we should have gone to the front line of the Miners' Strike and charged the police shields and been arrested and beaten up and then bailed so that we could return to the fray again the next day. But we just carried on fighting our own little battles in our own protected pretend society, too preoccupied to stand back and consider the insignificance of what we were doing.

In the summer a note from my local Labour Party came round informing us of a scheme to give holidays in Devon to the children of striking miners which asked if any party members would be prepared to put a few kids up. Our lefty student household thought this was a great idea – modern-day evacuees coming to our house to escape the violence and deprivation of the pit villages – so we eagerly put our names down and waited for the grubby children in flat caps to be delivered to the front door. A few days later the local party sent someone round to check that our home was suitable. The ring on the doorbell woke me up at around half past ten on Saturday morning. They had a quick look around the house. They looked at the various groggy couples wrapped in duvets emerging from smelly bedrooms to see who was at the door. At the barrels of home brew dripping in the kitchen. At the chickens leaning through the open window and pecking at the dried-on crust of last night's washing-up. At the ashtrays spilling over with torn-up packets of Rizla. For some reason they decided that our house was not quite right. Maybe they wanted somewhere with a bigger garden.

The only other contribution that I felt I could make was to do my bit towards the 'six o'clock surge'. This was an underground plan that was relayed to me by some bearded lefty I had listened to at a party as he sat on a bean bag taking far too long to roll a joint. He told me that the media were suppressing news of an effective campaign by socialists everywhere, a scam which was rapidly exhausting the government's huge reserves of coal. The idea was to suddenly increase the demand for electricity at a given point in the day because a huge surge apparently made far greater demands on the power stations than generally increased consumption.

Every day thereafter I ran around the house at six o'clock in the evening turning on kettles, immersion heaters, steam irons, electric fires, hair dryers and the yoghurt-maker in the hope that the resultant draining of electricity would bring power cuts and the collapse of the Thatcher government within a couple of weeks. The campaign lasted right up until the arrival of the next electricity bill when I realised I had almost bankrupted us. Perhaps I might have been wiser to give all that money to the miners rather than to the electricity company who then went off to spend it on importing more South African coal.

But that was one of the great things to come out of the Miners' Strike – just how much so many people wanted to help them. If we had thought swimming the English Channel would help their cause we would have given it a go. The Labour Party rank and file provided a network of support of which we should all still be proud, a structure that provided food, money, clothing and an education to both sides. It was perhaps the only time that Labour was more than just a political party.

Set against the generosity of the miners' supporters, the inspiring acts of self-sacrifice, the social education, the new friendships and the incredible courage, there was heart-wrenching suffering. I was moved and angered by every story I read. A miner crushed to death by a lorry crossing the picket line. Families torn apart by debt and the fear of losing their homes. Miners weeping and apologising as they crossed the picket line because they had no financial choice. Miners sent to prison for assault who had simply been plucked out of the crowd. And all this suffering was precipitated by a prime minister hell bent on avenging the miners' defeat of the Conservatives in 1972 and 1974. A government whose policies were not based on economics or the national interest but on their own party political and class interest, to bring the British trade union movement to heel by crushing the most militant and symbolic union of all – the National Union of Mineworkers. I hated Mrs Thatcher more and more with the passing of each day. I hated her more than was healthy. I hated her so much I wanted her to die.

112

I would invent all sorts of elaborate scenarios whereby she would cease to be prime minister of Britain. Some involved a sombre deputation from the 1922 Committee and others involved me popping up with a machine-gun during her standing ovation at the Conservative Party conference. And so in October 1984 when the Brighton bomb went off I felt a surge of excitement at the nearness of her demise and yet disappointment that such a chance had been missed. This was me – the pacifist, anti-capital-punishment, anti-IRA liberal – wishing that they had got her. Why did she have to leave the bathroom two minutes earlier? I asked myself over and over again. I just hated her so very, very much.

But with some justification, it has to be said. And though some might argue that I should not have been prepared to countenance undemocratic means to get rid of her, she was not being particularly democratic in the way she exercised and extended her power. Apart from the outrages of the Miners' Strike, all sorts of sinister and draconian things were happening. CND leaders were picking up their phones and hearing their last conversations being played back, trade unionists were receiving their post in resealed envelopes, Clive Ponting, a civil servant at the Ministry of Defence, was arrested under the Official Secrets Act for leaking the truth about the sinking of the *Belgrano,* and elections for the GLC were to be cancelled and an unelected Conservative body to be put in the authority's place until abolition. The miners had to win or nothing would stop her.

But the strike was already effectively lost, though its actual end was painful and slow. The drift back to work by impoverished and indebted miners eventually

113

passed 50 per cent of the workforce and a special meeting was held to vote whether or not the strike should be ended. You might have thought that for such a massive political event there would have been live news coverage from outside the meeting, but instead I was forced to watch the usual Sunday morning television in the hope of a newsflash.

The BBC were showing *Dad's Army*. I remembered this episode from my childhood. *Dad's Army* had been my favourite programme, one that we had watched together as a family after tea in another, more innocent time. And now I watched it dispassionately and without laughter waiting for the grim news from the TUC headquarters. Eventually the caption was flashed up over the antics of Captain Mainwaring and Corporal Jones. 'Miners' delegates have voted 98 to 91 to end the strike and return to work.'

My heart sank. This is where it all ended. A caption along the bottom of *Dad's Army*. The words hung there for a couple of seconds before they faded away and allowed the comedy to continue as if nothing had happened. How could the audience keep laughing? How could the characters keep trotting out their catch-phrases? After a whole year, the Miners' Strike was over. Thatcher had beaten everything the British labour movement could throw at her and now her power was the greatest it had ever been. On the Tuesday morning proudly defiant miners marched slowly back to work behind noble banners and evocative brass bands. Ten years later only a fraction of them would have a job in the industry to march back to at all.

And I felt ashamed as I realised that the only campaigning I had done during that long and painful year was for the election of the president of the Exeter

University Guild of Students; an organisation of which my friends and I were no longer even members. The irrelevant posturing of student politics was our only outlet – like the pretend soldiers in *Dad's Army* we imagined we were part of the wider struggle, but in reality our efforts were more for the benefit of our own morale than for any difference we made. And despite what was happening in the rest of the country, the students elected the son of a former SDP Member of Parliament who promised to be 'apolitical'. Above party politics. Well it had clearly worked for the Civil Service and the judiciary and the television news and the police so the students obviously thought it worth giving a try. Apolitical! I think I prefer active Conservatives to people who think they are apolitical. How could anyone be alive during the Miners' Strike and think they were apolitical?

But that's the way student politics seemed to be going at the time. They were reacting against people like us. When I had arrived at Exeter it had had a Labour president. We had a left-wing student newspaper which we sold in the Nelson Mandela room. We lost control of the paper and Labour lost the presidency – it was time I stopped pretending to be a student and moved on. A few years later it wasn't even called the Nelson Mandela room any more. I heard that a group of students moved a motion that it be renamed after Frankie Howerd. How fucking hilarious.

Working for London

North Battersea, GLC By-Election – 27 June 1985

'Hello, I'm calling on behalf of the Labour Party about the forthcoming GLC by-election. I wondered whether we might be able to count on your vote?'

'Me no money,' said the scared Vietnamese woman cowering behind the chain over her door.

'No, I'm not selling anything – it's about the election. I wondered if you were going to vote Labour.'

'Me no money.' And the door closed in my face. 'Hmmm – better put that one down as a 'Don't Know'.

I moved to London in the spring of 1985 just as the bill to abolish the Greater London Council was passing its final stages in the House of Commons. Yet again I was arriving to join a fight after it had already been lost. My party membership was transferred via the super-highway that was Labour's membership system, finally arriving at some point in the late 1980s. Effectively I had to rejoin in Battersea. There was no special reason for choosing this part of south London to be my home –

that's just where the flat I found happened to be – and yet a random decision like this can end up affecting the rest of your life. There happened to be a local GLC by-election campaign already underway and I volunteered myself to help ...

'Hello. I'm canvassing on behalf of the Labour Party and I wondered whether we could count on your vote.'

'What election's this then?'

'It's a GLC by-election on June the twenty-seventh and your Labour candidate is Norman Lucas—'

'GLC? I thought they'd abolished it.'

'No, they haven't yet. They've just confirmed that they are going to abolish it.'

'So what's the point in voting for it then?'

'Er, well, to show the government how strongly people feel, er, so that they'll decide not to abolish it.'

'I thought you said they had already decided.'

'WELL MAYBE THEY'LL CHANGE THEIR MIND!'

Normally you can entice Labour supporters out with the argument that Labour must retain control of the authority to protect local jobs and services et cetera, but in this election it was far too late to protect anything. Or you might say that the Tories are working really hard and are poised to win the seat. But the Tories weren't even bothering to stand. What was the loudspeaker supposed to say on election day? 'Vote Labour! Vote Labour *for the sake of it*!'

I was fighting my first campaign in a 'special intro-ductory election'. No Tories, no significance attached to the result and no one interested in the campaign. But as I wandered the windswept estates of North Battersea, calling at the tatty doors whose musical doorbells could

117

hardly muster the energy to play 'There's No Place Like Home', I started to meet people who had really suffered under the ideological steamroller of Thatcherism. Unemployment here was well above the national average and the local council had complete contempt for its tenants. The mongrels whose pitiful howling echoed across from the Dogs' Home had a better chance of a housing transfer than Wandsworth Council's tenants. I started to see genuine poverty for the first time in my life. Working for Labour started to be less like supporting a football team and more a way of trying to change the lives of people whose circumstances shocked me. I would be invited inside people's homes to be shown the mould growing up the walls of their kids' bedrooms or be given a demonstration of how the plaster crumbled in their hands as they touched it. In one flat I expected Roy Castle to pop up and announce, 'And this is the world record for the greatest number of small children living in a tenth-floor two-bedroom council flat! And that makes Wandsworth Council a record breaker!'

Obviously they weren't all poor and demoralised. Some people had incredible displays of flowers in their front gardens, but then these would be offset by next door's interesting modern sculpture created from a broken-down fridge and an old mattress. One woman had about thirty cats although it only smelt like twenty. Some people (like the Vietnamese lady) spoke no English and were too scared ever to go out, leaving their teenage children to translate, shop and generally liaise with the outside world. You could see the House of Commons from the walkways on the Patmore Estate but the people who lived there could not have been further from the government's mind. And tucked away on the edge of the Borough of Wandsworth I'm not sure if the ruling Conservative councillors knew it existed either, unless it was them who kept coming along to urinate in the lifts. The people of the Patmore Estate were the kind of people who needed Labour most. But by the laws of politics they were the people who were the least interested. People would stand there listening to me ask them about their voting intentions and then just say, 'No thanks, mate' before closing the door. Was that *Politics – No thanks* or *Labour Party – No thanks?* Better put them down as 'Against'. One first-time voter said to me, 'I've been unemployed for over a year so I'm going to have to vote Conservative.' Sometimes I just wanted to pick voters up and shake them by the lapels.

While the poorer parts of the ward generally expressed indifference, the richer areas responded with naked hostility. Despite this I was still surprised and pleased at how much political canvassing was an accepted part of our culture and at how people never questioned my right to call on them to ask their voting intentions. I thought this was fantastic. 'Labour Party? You must be joking. You're a dangerous shambles and I'll vote for whichever party has the best chance of keeping you out!' As I walked away part of me was thinking, Isn't it marvellous that we live in a country where we can openly say these things to one another?

The only certainty when you knock on someone's door is that you will have chosen the least convenient time possible, that the voters will be in the middle of a blazing row, in the middle of a crucial moment in the snooker or in the middle of burying their partners under the patio. One woman came to the door in her nightie at about three o'clock one Saturday afternoon and was

119

hardly able to answer any of my questions for so much wine-induced giggling.

'Ah, hello, yes, um, sorry to have got you out of, er, bed – I was wondering if you had decided what you might be voting in the forthcoming election.'

'Election – ooh, I dunno, love, I don't live here.'

'Right, um,' (*glance at canvass card*) '... yes, I've only got James Morgan registered at this address – is, um, is he up?'

'He was, dear, till you rang on the doorbell!' More hysterical laughter. James has heard the important nature of my visit and calls out to express his feeling on the forthcoming election.

'Tell them to piss off.'

'Jim – it's the Labour – what you voting?'

'What?'

'In the election – this bloke wants to know what you're voting.'

'Come back to bed.'

'He is Labour, don't worry,' and she closed the door.

So I leave it at that and put a tentative red mark on my canvass card next to his name. In an important election you value every Labour vote. You knock on the door where your records show that 'Agnes' and 'Herbert' have always voted Labour and you cannot let any of these votes go, even if it is a council by-election you probably can't win. There was a by-election in Southfields ward in Wandsworth in which a victory would have brought us control of the council. Under such circumstances it is very easy to lose hold of one's perspective. I knock on the door and a very anxious Agnes takes a long time to answer. I'm ready to confirm the two votes when she pulls the rug from under me.

'My husband – he's dying.'

'Right – so what you're saying is you want to arrange a postal vote for him.'

'They've sent him home from hospital, there's nothing more they can do for him.'

'Yes, that's under-funding in the Health Service for you, and by voting Labour at this council by-election you will be sending a message to the government about the need for more beds in the NHS.'

'He's dying . . .'

'Yes, um, I've just seen on my sheet here that it's too late to register for a postal vote – now if we organised a car do you think he'd be all right to go and vote on Thursday?'

'Oh no, dear, going all the way down there and back would finish him off.'

I just manage to stop myself saying he only has to make it *there*.

One trick always played by election organisers is to present new canvassers with 'The Address That Doesn't Exist'. Every ward has one house that has always been on the electoral register but that no one has ever found. If you sent out a canvasser and they never came back, it probably meant that they did eventually find it but were sucked into the fourth dimension in the process. I'm sure these addresses are made up by council employees who wait until election time and then sit in cars giggling at the party workers walking back and forth scratching their heads and looking at maps.

Eventually you decide that you have had enough of canvassing for a while and you ask whether it would be possible just to do a bit of delivering. Back in 1985 this was fairly straightforward. You just had to put the leaflet through the various spring-loaded guillotine letter boxes without scrunching it up so that the rabid dog on the other side could scrunch it up for you. It is important to put the leaflet all the way through the door. On one occasion we got a letter from a very irate voter who said that Labour leaflets had been left sticking out of his letter box as a clear sign to potential burglars that he was not home. He then went on to be very rude about the Labour Party. We looked him up on our canvass cards, checked that he had consistently voted Conservative and then wrote him a very polite and sincere letter of apology which we left sticking out of his letter box.

Computer-addressed mailshots had not yet been developed, so personalised letters were sent in envelopes that had been painstakingly addressed by house-bound elderly party members who were delighted they could still contribute in some way. The handwriting was always ornate and elaborate with little curly bits on all the capital letters, as if the envelope contained a secret love letter from Lady Hamilton to Lord Nelson instead of some dreary pamphlet about deadlines for postal votes. It's rather sad that the advent of the computer has made these volunteers redundant.

Targeted mail on various issues had not yet evolved, although canvassers could use their own discretion. If you had four or five different leaflets in your canvass pack, you could give the one on crime to the old lady with four locks on her front door, the one on nursery education to the woman with five toddlers around her legs, and two copies of all five leaflets just to annoy the bloke with the Ecology Party poster in his window.

That is, of course, if you managed to get into the block in the first place. The greatest bane in any party footsoldier's life is the entry-phone. For years Labour councillors had fought for council blocks to have entry-phones, only to discover that the buildings are now impossible to get into in order to ask to be re-elected. Canvassing via an entry-phone intercom is like trying to chat to a Dalek on a cheap mobile phone.

'Hello, it's the Labour Party.'

Pause. 'Sorry, that was last night, mate.'

I buzz again. 'What was last night?'

'The neighbour's party. They've all gone home.'

'No, can you let me in to deliver leaflets for the Labour Party?'

Another pause. 'Whose party is it?'

After five conversations like this you give up and push the leaflets one by one through the tiny crack under the security door, knowing that they will be trodden on and ruined by the first person to come in out of the rain.

But in my first campaign I was too young and keen to let any such obstacle stand in my way. I turned up most days to canvass or deliver or address envelopes in a burst of enthusiasm that got me so deeply involved in the Labour Party that soon it would be impossible to escape. After all, this was a GLC election, the famous GLC, the largest local authority in the world; with 'Red Ken' and 'Fares Fair' and 'Working For London'. I had read with excitement about the innovative brand of municipal socialism pioneered by Labour's young Turks in London and felt that by taking part in the last ever GLC election campaign I might just become a little part of it. If Margaret Thatcher wanted to abolish them, then they must be worth fighting for.

My mother had said that the only reason Maggie was abolishing the GLC was to get rid of that big poster on County Hall telling Parliament how many unemployed there were in London. I have to say that I think this simple analysis probably hit the nail right on the head. I was only there at the fag end of the GLC's existence, but nothing became that authority like the leaving of it. There were free concerts and festivals all summer long. The 'Jobs For A Change' festival took place in my very ward, in Battersea Park, and local party members worked as stewards. Me! A steward for a GLC festival! I nearly framed the T-shirt.

There were further concerts at Jubilee Gardens on the South Bank and elsewhere. Sometimes it was Billy Bragg supported by Hank Wangford and sometimes it was Hank Wangford supported by Billy Bragg. On the one occasion when they tried someone new, a concert by The Smiths was ruined by a group of skinheads climbing on the stage and *Sieg Heil*-ing to the crowds of lefties down below. That was about as constructive as the arguments against a London-wide authority got. On the night that the GLC was officially abolished thousands of pounds worth of fireworks lit up the sky. It was fantastic – if only all those Conservative voters in Bromley and Finchley could have seen how much of their money was being wasted! Then, on the stroke of midnight, workers from the London Residuary Body moved in and started ripping everything down, signs, placards, banners – anything with a GLC logo on it – while the crowd looked on and booed.

Unsurprisingly we won our by-election and the old constituency of North Battersea had a new GLC councillor who would serve for less than a year before his seat was abolished. Election day itself had been a bizarre phoney war, with no other political parties visible on the ground. At the count there were a handful of Social Democrats and some people from the Ecology

124

Party who looked like extras from *The Addams Family*. But even if no one else was particularly excited about this Labour victory, I was. It was the only election I had to care about. A bloke called Gorbachev got elected head of the Soviet Communist Party during our campaign, but that was obviously far less significant. I had taken part in a real election and we had won! I had got my Boy Scouts' canvassing badge.

It struck me that politics would be so much more simple if it was always like this – if the Conservatives just decided not to take part any more. If the Labour Party could just get on with planning its policies and choosing its candidates as if the Tories did not exist. The trouble was that this was exactly how the Labour Party behaved anyway. Despite the rout we had suffered two years earlier, the party rank and file were not interested in how we were perceived by the voters we still needed to win over. Most of the stories about councils banning black dustbin bags and making children sing 'Baa Baa Green Sheep' were actually made up by the tabloids, but I witnessed people taking their cue from these fictitious examples and starting to condemn people for asking for black or white coffee.

A friend of mine was writing an article for the *Greater London Arts* magazine and suggested that perhaps the inclusion of a cartoon strip might lighten it up a bit. They said they couldn't possibly have a cartoon without black people in it. OK, he said, have a cartoon strip with black people in it. They were horrified. Print caricature drawings of black people? *That would be racist!* You could almost hear the *Daily Mail* journalist sharpening her pencil.

Most Labour Party activists I knew worked in the public sector and were surrounded by like-minded people, only ever read the *Guardian* and were simply not aware that the rest of the country thought we were stark staring bonkers. Which made the shock all the greater for me when I did enter the real world and find myself surrounded by Tories. And not just Tories but working-class-should-be-voting-Labour-but-very-very-right-wing Tories. My brother had got to know the builders working on his house, and I asked them if they wanted a labourer. They offered me £15 a day, which even then was a ludicrously small amount of money, but I took it because I couldn't think what else to do with myself. The political gulf could not have been wider had I been working with a group of Canadian baby seal clubbers. When on my first day I made the mistake of revealing my allegiance the plasterer said, 'The Labour Party – what are you in that for? You're not a lesbian are you?'

Declaring that I was a socialist was like saying, 'I am completely misguided and vaguely deviant – please be as hostile as you like.' The lies and prejudice they were fed by the tabloids were thrown at me as proof of my ignorance. I used to keep the drill on for longer periods than I needed to, just to postpone the next round of liberal-baiting. It was not as if the arguments I got into were ones I could ever win.

'I suppose you agree with social workers, do you?'

'What do you mean, do I agree with social workers? Do I agree with them when I'm talking to them or do I agree with the fact that they exist or what?'

In the end the mental energy required to argue my corner was more than I could muster so I would avoid the issue. I certainly couldn't face explaining the convoluted arguments that had made me decide to become a vegetarian – although once or twice I was

126

nearly exposed for the weirdo I was. 'Four bacon sandwiches, please,' said the foreman on my first morning in
the café, as if there was nothing else that any of us might
possibly want to order.

'Er, actually I don't fancy bacon, er ...'

'Sausage sandwich?' suggested the lady behind the
counter helpfully.

'Er, no ...'

And they all looked at each other and tutted, unable
to believe how fussy I was.

'How about egg?'

I just stopped the words 'Are the eggs free-range?'
coming out and agreed to that.

Something had gone very wrong somewhere. I was the
one with the posh voice pathetically arguing liberal
social policies, while all the working-class people were
arguing for the abolition of trade unions and unemployment benefit. They should have had a two-way
mirror in that café and charged Norman Tebbit forty
quid a time to watch from the other side.

This was not a great time to be a leftie. When his-
torians come to write their dissertations on Thatcher at
the height of her power, then the year 1985 must be
favourite: a majority of over 140, the 'wets' expelled
from the cabinet, the Argies and the miners beaten, the
Metropolitan Councils on their way out, and before
the Westland crisis, which was to cause a series of resignations over her style of government that began with
Heseltine's and ended in Howe's and her own. Any
opposition to her was completely ineffective. Just as we
had had the pleasure of fighting a by-election without
an opposition, she was running an entire country
without an opposition. Neil Kinnock was a better leader

than Michael Foot but he had too many battles to fight inside the Labour Party to be able to focus his fire on the all-powerful Mrs Thatcher. Every now and then she might get a letter from a senior churchman tentatively suggesting that perhaps she consider the social cost of her policies. But since she had recently destroyed the Labour Party and the NUM, I don't suppose that she worried too much about the odd Church of England vicar threatening her grip on power.

It was this strength which appealed to the builders I worked with. They didn't say they voted Conservative, they said they voted for Maggie. These were men who did not let their wives drive their cars but were more than happy to have a woman run their country. Yet the level of sexism on the building site was one of the hardest things to cope with. They would shout really unpleasant things out of the windows of their van and I would wince embarrassedly in the middle seat. Later in the day girls walking down the road would look up and see me shovelling cement and brace themselves for a barrage of catcalls and whistles. I wanted to tell them I wasn't like that. What could I shout as they crossed the road to avoid me? 'Wha-hey – look at the brain on that!' 'Here, darling, what about you and me going to a gender studies evening class together?'

I remember one of the workmen showing me a picture of Samantha Fox and saying, 'Look at those tits – I'd be satisfied if my missus had one tit that size,' which did not conjure up a particularly attractive image. As well as being one of the stupidest and most bigoted right-wing men on the site, Terry was also one of the poorest people I had ever met. Like me he was an unskilled labourer, only with a wife and children to support. Unlike me he did not have a return ticket –

that was his future. There were millions like him – no car, no holidays, behind on the rent with no prospect of life improving. But Terry voted Conservative and tore into my beliefs like I was threatening the very existence of his country. A voice at the back of my brain wanted to shout, 'Look, I don't go to all these Labour Party meetings for *my* benefit, you know. I do it for the likes of you – so that your kids can have a proper education and not end up banged up in jail like you were, you stupid fat bigot.' But obviously I didn't say that because it would have been patronising and unconstructive and because he would have punched me in the face.

I spent months working with Terry and by the end optimistically hoped that maybe I might have made him a tiny bit less prejudiced and a tiny bit more sensitive. On my last day the builders dropped me off and came in and had a cup of tea in my flat. Looking at my posters, the foreman said, 'These paintings are by Degas, aren't they?'

And then Terry said, 'Yeah, well, they're all by bloody dagos aren't they?'

At some point in the mid-1980s an MP started a 'working-class section' of Labour MPs. I can only conclude that having voted Labour would have automatically disqualified you from membership, because not one person I encountered on the building site admitted to voting Labour. One carpenter told me in private that he thought Neil's speech at conference had 'done us proud'. But he made sure the others were out of hearing, as if he was happy to confide in me but not ready to come out of the closet in front of everyone else just yet.

But this was the year that Neil Kinnock was determined to change Labour's image and outlook. To make the Labour Party realise that there *were* Tories out there and that we could not exist in a political vacuum and still expect the votes to come our way. And I would be there when he did it. My enthusiasm for the Labour Party led me to attend all of the 1985 Labour Party conference. Not as a delegate with the right to vote or anything worthwhile like that, but with an observer's ticket – just to be there and soak it all in and buy Labour Party biros from the souvenir shop. But it felt great to show the security guard the special pass pinned to my chest and be ushered towards the doors as crowds of activists behind the crash barriers thrust leaflets into my hand and shouted 'Support Composite 17!', even if I hadn't the faintest idea what they were talking about.

The highlight of any party conference is the leader's speech. And the speech at Bournemouth in 1985 was a turning-point in the party's history. It was the speech in which Neil Kinnock finally 'lanced the boil of Militant', as the papers objectively put it, precipitating the expulsions and signalling Labour's long haul back to the political mainstream. The *Guardian* called Kinnock's speech 'The bravest and most important speech by a Labour leader in over a generation' – and I was there! The speech that changed the complexion of the Labour Party and I was in the room when he made it! Except I wasn't; I was somewhere else. I was physically there, sitting in the room. But by the time he reached the famous bit that they showed on the news criticising Liverpool City Council, it felt like he had been speaking for an eternity and I had been lulled into the same semi-conscious state that I used to fall into when I was listening to my geography teacher describing drumlins.

And as Kinnock roused and pleaded and impassioned, my focus slowly drifted from the argument that he was developing to the appalling dandruff of the man sitting in front of me, and finally to deciding that when I got home I would throw out that packet of desiccated coconut that had been at the back of my food cupboard for years.

I tried to concentrate on what he was saying again and then I remembered that I had to ring my dad who was going to come and have lunch with me on Friday, and I thought maybe we could go to that pub near the sea-front that I had passed that morning, and then I thought about the nice pub on the seafront at Exmouth where I'd had a lovely Scotch egg, and I thought, Ooh, I haven't had a Scotch egg in ages – oh, of course that's because I'm a vegetarian. Suddenly a commotion brought me back to the conference. Delegates in the hall had leapt to their feet and some were booing while many others were cheering and applauding. Eric Heffer was walking off the platform, Derek Hatton was shouting 'Rubbish!' I didn't have the faintest idea what was going on. What could Neil Kinnock have said to precipitate such a reaction? Should I boo like the people behind me? Should I clap and cheer like the people in front of me? I settled for glancing around the hall with a confused look on my face.

I had to watch the news in my hotel that evening to find out what had happened in the very hall I'd been sitting in. And when I got back to Battersea, party members asked their 'observer' what I had thought when Kinnock said that bit about 'the grotesque chaos of a Labour council scuttling round in taxis to deliver redundancy notices to its own workers'.

I had to lie. How could I tell them what I had really

thought? Oh that bloke doing the sign language has got a nice shirt – I wonder where he got it from. And 'Kiki', yes, that was it. That was the name of the frog in *Hector's House*.

Despite my inability to concentrate on anything for more than ten minutes, I spent the entire week at conference. I had got a lift down to Bournemouth with Alf Dubs MP – which itself was exciting enough for me. He kept saying, 'A whole week? Are you sure you won't get a bit bored?' But I really didn't get bored, even though I was on my own all week. I went to meetings and exhibitions and read pamphlets and left-wing journals and I enjoyed every minute of it.

The only company I had was that of a man who worked as a research assistant to a Labour MP. He started chatting to me at some fringe meeting or other and I said that I really envied him – working for Labour in the House of Commons and being paid for it! He was obviously flattered by my enthusiasm and suggested I come to the Commons and allow him to show me round. This was music to my ears.

After conference he gave me a ring and invited me to Westminster, where he showed me his office and told me about what he did. We walked around the Houses of Parliament before going out for a meal. What was most gratifying was that, although he was about twenty-five years older than me, he was interested in my opinions on the state of the Labour Party and the way to defeat Margaret Thatcher and so on. Maybe he could get me a job as a Labour researcher, I thought. Before we went out to eat he quickly rang home to say he would be late. He explained why to the people he lived with. 'I'm just taking a young gentleman out for dinner.'

The person at the other end of the phone fell about

laughing. The voice repeated this to other people in the house – 'He's just taking a young gentleman out to dinner' – and more distant laughter could be heard.

Then it suddenly struck me. I was on a date. This fifty-year-old man wasn't interested in my politics at all. It was an elaborate seduction ploy. My mind went back to the way we had met at conference: he had kept looking at me across the room and smiling and I had smiled back. The way he had insisted on paying for the meal we had in Bournemouth, and his offer to take me out to dinner this evening. He wanted me to be his boyfriend. Oh my God – all the things I had said about the Labour Party dragging their feet on gay rights! I had been leading him on. I felt embarrassed and guilty for accepting dinner under false pretences. I made no comment about his strange phone call, we went out for dinner as planned, and references to my girlfriend were sprinkled liberally throughout the rest of the evening. I felt so mean. He'd paid for two meals and I didn't even give him a peck on the cheek. He didn't ring me again after that.

My hopes of getting off the building site and working for the Labour Party had evaporated. But the tour round the corridors of power had kindled some sort of ambition. I really wanted to work in politics. To be part of Labour's attempt at opposition. The Labour Party were always going on about creating jobs – why couldn't they bloody give me one? Doing anything in the Commons would be enough. I answered an advertisement in the *Guardian* for a trainee transcriber for *Hansard* – the official record of Parliamentary debates. This sounded like a great job, just being paid for listening to *Today in Parliament* all week. Unfortunately it required basic typing skills of 30 words a minute. My preferred method of typing at the time was to hit the first letter very hard with my index finger before the same finger began a 30-second search for the next letter. This was until *Hansard* wrote back and said I had been short-listed for the job. I was horrified – I was to have an audio-typing test. I had just one week to get my typing up to the required standard or face abject humiliation. So I bought a 'teach yourself to type' book and sat down with a typewriter and practised and practised and practised.

The night before my interview I timed myself. It was a major achievement! I really could type at 30 words a minute! The only catch was that they had to be the right words. I would be fine as long as the only sentence the MPs used in their debates was 'the quick brown fox jumped over the lazy dog'. I tried to imagine a debate in which this sentence might possibly come up a hundred times or so. Maybe some hunt saboteurs had drugged a dog, making it appear lazy, with the result that the quick brown fox had jumped over it.

'Would the Minister confirm the unusual events witnessed at the North Devon Hunt on Sunday?'

'Mister Speaker, Honourable Members, I have to report that ... the quick brown fox jumped over the lazy dog.'

'Is the member for Devon North suggesting that the quick brown fox jumped over the lazy dog?'

'Yes indeed, as I said to the House only seconds ago, the quick brown fox jumped over the lazy dog.'

It looked like a long-shot. When I eventually sat down to do the test, the debate coming through my earpiece was a committee discussion on immigration and political asylum which I could not get down because I kept emitting horrified shrieks at the outrageous opinions being expressed. None of the other applicants seemed to bat an eyelid. When I settled down I did manage to type at the required rate but the words were from a strange Indo-Gaelic language that had not yet evolved.

Though inevitable, the rejection letter still depressed me. Everywhere around the Commons there had been Young Conservatives my age, bustling around in stripy suits escorting rich-looking businessmen to meetings with Conservative MPs. Posh-looking Tory girls fetching order papers and collecting MPs' mail. I bet I could have got a job if I'd been a Tory. But there were not enough Labour MPs to provide the work. And of six by-elections in Tory seats since the general election, Labour had failed to make a single gain. Labour Party members simply could not get into the Commons as MPs. And I couldn't even get in as a bloody typist. Never dreaming that within a year my ambition of working in the House of Commons would be realised, I dragged myself back to the freezing-cold building site. As I listened to the bigoted invective, the non-stop anti-gay and xenophobic diatribes, I thought, Oh, well – at least in this job I don't have to type it all out.

Labour of love

Election of Queenstown Ward Secretary
– 13 January 1986

There are some elections that change history. 1832, 1906 and 1945 all spring to mind. All those elections spelt disaster for the Conservatives and an end to the established order. Somehow my election as secretary of Queenstown ward Labour Party did not send the same political shockwaves through the British political system. The *Evening Standard*'s headline did not read 'Is This the End for Thatcher?' but for me it was a big day. Labour Gain O'Farrell South. It was the day I really committed myself to the religious cult known as the Church of the Labour Party Activists.

By early 1986 I had been out of university for two and a half years and was still doing nothing more impressive with my life than mixing cement. I was going out with a girl I had met in my final year at Exeter and we would occasionally attempt to make life more interesting by splitting up and then getting back together again. But when people asked me what I was up to I could only mumble 'This and that', which they knew and I knew meant that I was too embarrassed to say, 'I'm not doing anything of the slightest interest or merit, and so I'd rather not talk about it thank you very much'. Into this vacuum went the Labour Party. After my enthusiastic arrival at Queenstown ward during our historic by-election victory over all the other parties that could be bothered to stand, I was asked to be (*fanfare*) … 'Vice-Chair of the Ward'. I was genuinely very flattered. Flattered to be asked to be vice-chair of my ward Labour Party! Looking back, I didn't realise my self-confidence had been that low. The reality was of course that there were fewer active members than there were posts to be filled, but to say that I was vice-chair of my local Labour Party still felt better than saying 'this and that'. The vice-chair attended the informal officers' meetings that planned the full ward meetings. As far as I could make out the same six people attended both.

Religious cults are well known for preying upon people who are low or lacking in self-esteem. They praise them, shower them with love, tell them that more people ought to appreciate them. They say things like, 'You'd be a really good vice-chair of Queenstown ward', and thus you are subtly drawn deeper and deeper into the cult. You have new friends who convince you that your inability to find a job is not your fault – no, 'tis the work of Satan (a.k.a. Mrs Thatcher). Only you and your friends have the answer to save the world, for the end of the world is nigh, especially since Reagan got in. Yours is the only truth, but the truth must be spread – so it's a membership drive on the Savona Estate on Sunday morning.

As part of the process of assimilation I started to wear the same clothes as my new fellow believers. In the

137

1980s Leftie chic was dungarees and a T-shirt for the women, and jeans, T-shirt and a donkey jacket for the men (brightened up with a few badges proclaiming support for that season's lost cause). The T-shirt need not be directly political. For example, if it featured Black Uhuru it showed you were into reggae and therefore had an affinity with the black community. If it featured a football team, it suggested you had an interest in working-class culture. If your T-shirt did feature a political slogan it was far better to have one from a good few years back just to show you weren't some nouveau arriviste to left-wing causes. For example: 'Support the Grunwick Picket', 'NUPE Says £60 Now' or, if you were really cool, 'Reject the Partition of India'. There were dozens of different ways to display your politics on a T-shirt without being so obvious as having Che Guevara on your chest. As long as you did not wear one from Millets featuring a heavily armed mouse with the caption 'I'm on a Pussy Hunt' you were generally OK.

The one thing I found a little uncomfortable when I first joined the religious cult was being addressed as 'comrade'. There are still some people who use this form of address in the Labour Party, though I can't imagine that Peter Mandelson and Alistair Campbell called each other 'comrade' when they were discussing the latest feedback from the focus groups. I suppose being called 'comrade' reminded me what a fraud I was. It would have been fine if I'd been one of those dynamic workers featured on 1920s Russian posters hammering a sickle into shape. But I was from Berkshire. The only time I had had to share a cramped bedroom with my brother was in our family's holiday cottage in Brittany. The word 'comrade' did not come easily to my lips. Oc-

138

casionally, I would try to grapple with less embarrassing replacements: 'Well, I'd like to thank all the *party members* who helped at the stall on Saturday. And if any more, er, *people* would like to come next week, then all, erm, *boys and girls* are welcome.'

What finally convinced me that I must have been captured by the Moonies was the weird selection of hot drinks consumed by party members whenever they came round to my house. Was it just in Queenstown ward or was it everywhere in the Labour Party that nobody wanted anything as simple as 'tea, white, no sugar'? I would find myself coming back from the kitchen saying, 'Hang on, let me just make sure I've got this right: one earl grey, nearly all milk, one lapsang souchong, milk in second, one plain hot water with just a drop of milk, and one camomile tea with half a spoon of honey.'

Nobody had coffee when they came to my house after the first time.

'John, I don't mean to be rude but this coffee is really disgusting.'

'Yes, it's Nicaraguan.'

'Oh, sorry, that's all right then.'

Before long came the defining test of any activist's commitment – the Annual General Meeting. It is not possible to go to a Labour Party Annual General Meeting and not agree to take on a job for the rest of the year. Like Ulysses listening to the sirens I have tried it. You go along thinking, It's fine – I've held every post there is – it's time for someone else to take something on, and then silence falls after each vacancy is announced and eventually the out-going chair says: 'Well, if we don't have anyone to be membership secretary, we won't have any members to fight the election, then this seat will fall to the Tories, and the government will get back in with a majority of one and sell off the NHS, abolish state education and destroy the entire Labour movement so that they can remain in power for ever. But if that's what everybody wants we won't have a membership secretary.'

Not many people can withstand this sort of psychological pressure. So you say, 'Well, look, I'll do membership on a temporary basis – until we can get someone who'll agree to do it for the rest of the year.' And then you say that the following year as well. This was the month of the Westland crisis, and as Margaret Thatcher carried out her enforced reshuffle I wondered if the same long silences happened in cabinet. 'Come on – who's going to be secretary of state for Northern Ireland? Someone has to do it ...'

But in 1986 I was that rare person – a party member who wanted to take on more than they were doing already. And so when the election of a new ward secretary came up, my name was proposed as if out of the blue and as if this had not all been cleared before the meeting. I acted half surprised, a little cautious and yet flattered, before saying, 'All right then, I'll do it – but you will have to show me the ropes and give me a bit of support', while inside I was going 'Yes!' as if I'd just seized control of the Soviet Communist Party. The other party officers were elected unopposed in the usual game of political musical chairs. Last year's treasurer became this year's membership secretary; last year's secretary became this year's chair and so on. Democratic structures are fine, but they do rather lose something when there are no candidates and no voters.

As ward secretary my main job was to get out a ward

notice once a month to all the members. This reminded them of the forthcoming meeting, informed them of the agenda, included the minutes of the last meeting and ended with a rather desperate plea for more people to come to the meeting. In 1986 the state-of-the-art way to duplicate a ward notice eighty times was to type it onto an inky stencil and then try to attach the peeled-off stencil sheet to a hand-powered Gestetner duplicator. This then had to be filled up with thick black ink and on the first turn of the handle the stencil would rip because you hadn't fixed it on properly. So you had to re-type the ward notice, while cursing the amount of black ink that had sprayed onto your *Coal Not Dole* T-shirt. Eventually you would reset your new stencil a little more carefully and watch the sweet-smelling ward notices roll off the machine with each turn of the handle. Perhaps the letter 'o' isn't normally represented by a filled-in circle, and perhaps the ink had smudged rather where I had typed a row of 'x's over a mis-spelling, but the finished ward notice was an object of great beauty and pride. Then the same operation had to be repeated again for the minutes of the last meeting. Staple 80 copies together, fold them all three ways and then they just had to be delivered to 80 doors around the ward.

And after all that six people come to the meeting. And what's more, they were the six people you knew would come to the meeting, because they were the same six people who always came to meetings. Six phone calls to the same people would have had exactly the same end result. But you have to give everyone else the *opportunity* to come. Much of the evening would then be taken up with discussing ways of getting more people to come, but short of hiring some supporting artists from a film and TV agency, we couldn't think of any way of padding out our meetings.

We tried moving our ward meetings to the Patmore tenants hall to encourage more people from the estates to come. The same six people came. I hired videos from the Labour Party and carried my telly and video player into the hall. The same six people came. I organised guest speakers: refugees who had fled Pinochet's Chile, NUJ delegates to talk about the dispute at Wapping and on one occasion a fairly senior Labour MP who was expecting a mass meeting and walked in to find the six of us sitting round a little table. Sometimes I could not be bothered to organise anything, and it didn't make any difference – the same six people came. Every few months there would be a surprise and a new member would suddenly turn up, but we were probably so over-attentive and enthusiastic towards them that they were too terrified ever to return.

There were of course other times when fewer than six people came. I remember welcoming a Labour councillor who came to address us on the need for Labour Party members to become school governors. He projected his over-rehearsed speech like he was Nye Bevan rousing the pit villages of South Wales. But there were only three of us listening to him, all seated around a little trestle table in a dusty tenants' hall in south London. I felt like saying, 'Richard – hello? There's only us here. It's OK – we're all school governors already.'

On one occasion, however, nobody came. I produced the ward notice the week before, travelled round my patch of north Battersea giving it to the deliverers, got to the hall early, set out the chairs and sat there waiting for everyone to turn up. A couple of the usual loyalists had telephoned to say they wouldn't be able to make it, but I had sort of hoped the numbers might be made up with some of the new members we'd signed up during the recent election. I waited. And waited. I felt that same sinking feeling that I had had in my teens standing against the railings outside the cinema in Maidenhead, slowly realising that the girl who had said she would meet me there was not going to come. After fifteen minutes I went from hoping that someone would arrive soon to hoping that *no one* would arrive soon. If a new member had turned up to find just me and ten wildly over-optimistic chairs set out in an empty semicircle, then no amount of excuses could have covered up the pitiful state of Queenstown Labour Party. As I walked home on my own after waiting thirty minutes, it was hard not to ask oneself what was the point of it all. Maybe I'm wasting my time, I said to myself. Maybe I should chuck it all in. But when something you've given so much time to is on a life-support machine, it's hard to be the one to turn off the switch deliberately.

Then I had the inspired idea of moving our meetings to a pub. There was a pub opposite Battersea Dogs' Home that had a big empty room above it. The landlord said we could use the room for free after I had described the scene of dozens of Labour Party activists queuing to get to the bar on the second Monday of every month. The reality was the usual six members, most of them ordering mineral water or asking if the pub did camomile tea with half a spoon of honey.

Strangely, I found that the ward meetings were made much more enjoyable by drinking pints of bitter throughout. The problem was that by the end of the evening I had turned from earnest ward secretary into a half-drunk pub bore: 'You see the trouble is ... we won the war, but we *lost the peace*. I mean look at Germany and Japan now – see? We lost the peace – can I fill that glass up for you?' Fairly soon the landlord stopped unlocking the upstairs room and told us that he was putting us at the table in the corner of the bar, that is, the table between the telly and the fruit machine. The councillor's report back on the threat to our local city farm would then have to compete with *Brookside* at full volume.

'Wandsworth want to evict Elm Farm so that they can sell off the site, despite the fact that the farm is so well supported by all the kids off the estates, most of whom have no garden.'

'No way, Sinbad, the bizzies are gonna find I fixed the leccy. I'm not doing time for no one.'

And she'd try to continue and then someone would win the jackpot on the fruit machine.

But disruptions need not be limited to external factors. Just as every village has its idiot, every ward has its nutty Labour Party member. These come in a variety of guises. A common variety is the 'agenda-dyslexic'. This is someone who can read, write, converse, listen and understand, but does not know the meaning of the word 'agenda'. For example, the members of Queenstown ward are discussing item three on that month's agenda – organisation of the jumble sale on the Patmore Estate.

'So, Libby, if you can bring a couple of trestle tables as well, that should be enough ... Yes, Michael, you had your hand up.'

'What are they doing about Battersea Power Station?'

'Sorry?'

'Battersea Power Station – it's just sitting there rotting

away. It seems to me that someone ought to be doing something about it.'

'Er, well, the Battersea Power Station Community Group have actually been doing quite a lot about it, but we are discussing the jumble sale at the moment.'

'There ought to be a petition or something.'

'There's been quite a lot of petitions, but if you like we can discuss it under Item Eight – Any Other Business. Now getting back to the jumble sale. Any suggestions for what to do with the stuff that we don't sell?'

'I've got an idea.'

'Yes.'

'Turn it into an industrial heritage museum. And you could arrive by steam train from Victoria.'

At which point you explain to him that we have to deal with what is on the agenda, because if we didn't we would never progress or decide anything, so it is really important to talk about one issue at a time. He nods and says he understands and then you start discussing Item Four on the agenda, the treasurer's report, and his comment on this is: 'I think the Labour Party should start telling the truth about Thatcher taking orders from Murdoch.'

This theme is then taken up by the next sort of ward idiot – the paranoid conspiracy theorist. As secretary of a ward Labour Party you represent Authority and the Establishment as surely as if you are Norman Tebbit or Alexander Haig. So if you tell them, 'I'm afraid we can't affiliate Battersea Labour Party to the Friends of the Malvinas Campaign – that would have to be done by the General Management Committee – you'd have to propose the motion to them', they will nod and look at you in a way that says, 'I understand what you're trying to do. You're trying to obstruct my motion because it threatens the Labour Party's silent conspiracy with the Conservatives over the British occupation of the Malvinas Islands.'

Another common infiltrator is the single-issue fanatic. I had one member from Dublin who was only in Battersea Labour Party as a means of ending 800 years of British oppression of Ireland. On election night he came along to knock up, but only wanted to call at the addresses where people had Irish surnames. I thought Ireland might be a good place to start, but I didn't suggest it.

Most constituencies also have an honorary martyr, moaning about how they end up doing everything themselves but never delegating or accepting offers of help. Perhaps that's how the Tolpuddle Martyrs got their name. 'I think we should organise the first union here in Tolpuddle.'

'All right, I suppose *I'll* have to do it, since I do everything else.'

Then there is the mute, who comes to meetings but has never been heard to say anything. We had a mute turn up a few times at the tenants' hall and I don't think I ever established whether he spoke or understood a single word of English. For all I know he might have thought he was at a meeting of Alcoholics Anonymous.

But the most common of all the varieties is the common or garden pedant. In the Labour Party they blossom like flowers in spring. Is it that the process of devising policy, passing motions and following standing orders is what attracts pedants to join the Labour Party or is it that we all just naturally metamorphose into nit-picking droning bores after a few years as political activists? When a new member comes along to their first meeting you want to make it interesting for them, but you sit there powerless as some old bore who was on the council in the 1950s takes half the evening to point out that if a comrade wants to put something new on the agenda then they must vote to suspend standing orders which they can only do if you have a two-thirds majority of a quorate meeting blah blah blah blah blah. He is then utterly perplexed during the next item for discussion, 'Why don't more people come to Labour Party meetings?'

Thankfully none of Queenstown's core members was anything like this. Most of the people I describe were occasional attenders or people I encountered in other wards. Apart from my friend Phil who chewed vanilla roots through every meeting and insisted on calling his personal stereo a 'walkperson', Queenstown were a very normal and sane, not to say hard-working and prin-cipled, group of people who quite frankly deserved better voters. If the British Labour Party is the army, the local ward members are your platoon. You are thrown together, you fight battles, win some, lose a few more, and experience all your highs and lows together. Some will inevitably go off to fight elsewhere, some will get promoted (one former Queenstown secretary is now an MP) and some might desert to more left-wing parties like the SWP or the Liberal Democrats. But the active members of your ward become friends and you share a pride in your local patch. When Battersea Labour Party had a new banner made, I remember feeling faintly smug that the skyline depicted landmarks that were all in my little ward: the Power Station, the Peace Pagoda, the Dogs' Home; I even thought the trees must be from Battersea Park! When people are divided into groups they end up feeling an inward solidarity and even a rivalry with neighbouring wards. My parents are members of Cookham ward in Berkshire. It was proposed that the ward party should stop organising separately and merge with Maidenhead. They fought it with all the anger and energy of the miners fighting the pit closures.

I never used to be able to understand what motivated Labour activists in the true blue shires. That was what had been so great about moving to London – for the first time in my life I was surrounded by Labour voters, and here was I, running their local Labour Party! Had I been living in a constituency where Labour had no chance of winning anything, I doubt whether I would have become so immersed in local politics. But when I became secretary of Queenstown we were the proud owners of two Labour councillors, a Labour MP, a Labour GLC councillor and a Labour ILEA councillor. By the time I resigned four years later the Tories had either won all these seats or simply abolished them. I didn't have to imagine what it must be like to be a Labour activist in a solid Tory seat, it was just a question of staying put for a few years and finding out. Religious cults had mass suicides. We had elections.

Westminster, please

Fulham By-Election – 10 April 1986

As part of the process of my being sucked into the Labour Party a couple of early victories were arranged so as not to disillusion me before I was really hooked. First had been the easy GLC victory. Now came a fully fledged by-election in a Tory-held seat to really whet my appetite: a seat next door to our own constituency that Labour might gain from the Conservatives. 'Labour Gain From Conservatives' – the words had an unfamiliar and unreal sound to them. Victory for Labour in Fulham would bring the Tories' majority right down to the psychologically important figure of 138 seats over all the other parties, so obviously there was everything to fight for.

Fulham is what they call 'socially crunchy', which means that it has very rich people with very poor people living nearby to clean their houses in the daytime and burgle them at night. Every door had to be canvassed. In the GLC by-election we had concentrated just on getting out the Labour vote on the estates and not disturbing the

149

Conservatives lest they went out and voted SDP, so I was not used to ringing the doorbells of very, very wealthy households while wearing a Labour rosette. But during the Fulham by-election I canvassed some of the poshest people I had ever met.

When they are electing a new pope they don't make the cardinals canvass the Protestant heartlands of Belfast's Shankill Road. So I never quite understood what was the point of knocking on all these huge blue doors and saying, 'Ah, hello, yes, I'm from the Labour Party, are you Camilla Forbes-Patterson?' to a rather confused Filipino maid. Residents of Fulham's tree-lined avenues would glance out from behind their puffy curtains and give me a dismissive whisk of their hand which was their way of saying, 'No, we will not vote Labour, now get off my path, you horrible little oik.'

There is something vaguely heroic about canvassing an entire street knowing that behind every single door is a staunch Conservative supporter and yet ploughing on regardless. It would have been so much easier for me to get out of the rain, sit in a pub and sip a pint while methodically putting a blue mark next to every name on the canvass card. The end result would have been exactly the same but, unfortunately, you just have to do it the hard way.

You can generally tell how someone votes before they come to the front door. Immaculately swept front steps, well-trimmed hedges and a mud-splattered Range Rover parked in the drive with a sticker saying *I Slow Down for Fox Hunters* do not augur well for a Labour canvasser. But if next door the hedge is a bit more overgrown and the door is painted red and through the window you can see stacks of paperbacks untidily piled up on the bookshelves, you can knock on the door with a little more optimism.

Much as it pains me to admit it, Conservatives just take a lot more trouble with the appearance of their homes than socialists do. Their cars are cleaner, their window sills are not all cracked and flaky and they don't have broken-down old mopeds rusting away in their front gardens. And if Labour Party voters neglect the appearance of their homes, imagine how the combined efforts of activists leave the appearance of Labour Party premises. Perhaps it's our way of empathising with the slums.

Conservative clubs, like their members' homes, are always immaculate. I remember at the count at one election overhearing a Conservative lady saying, 'I've been so busy with this election I haven't washed my net curtains for a whole month!'

I hadn't realised you were supposed to wash net curtains at all. When I got home and looked at mine I realised that they were disgusting. So I washed them on too hot a wash, attempted to iron them with too hot an iron and ended up putting back a pair of very crinkled nets with holes melted in the middle. No canvasser would have bothered calling at my house – it was too obvious I was Labour.

If you are at all unsure about which way people vote before they open the front door, you are generally in no doubt the moment that you see them. Girls with up-turned stripy collars, little skirts, blue tights and gold buckles on their shoes have generally not just arrived home from Greenham Common. Chaps with brown leather brogues, dark green thick corduroys, stripy shirts and floppy fringes have probably not been outside Woolworth's selling *Socialist Worker*. As a simple guide, stripy shirt equals Conservative, grubby white shirt equals Labour and stripy shirt with white collar means you're David Steel and have no taste in clothes. There are all sorts of other codes which I learnt over the years: middle-class people with Dr Marten shoes equalled Labour, new front door on council house equalled Tory, and so on. But the other difference between Labour voters and Conservative voters, and I don't just mean when I was knocking on their doors with a red rosette on, is that Labour voters were just nicer people. Less snotty, less fussy, less prejudiced, less pompous and simply more polite and friendly. And the higher you went up the social ladder the more discernible this distinction became. You would think that with all their education and refinement and social advantages the British upper classes would be charming, considerate people, but they are not; they are rude. Loud, insensitive, arrogant, patronising and rude. As I walked the streets of Fulham it struck me as being one of the worst areas of London for these types – it was full of young braying ex-public school boys who hadn't yet made enough money to move to Chelsea and stood outside pubs blocking pavements while old ladies had to step into the road to get round them.

How can it be that they are taught the polite way to hold a fork and the correct way to tilt their soup bowls but no one told them how rude it was to perch their bottoms on the edge of the pub table that my friends and I are sitting around? And in the same way that Conservatives are unaware of how their behaviour affects other people on a day-to-day basis, their lack of consideration affects the way they behave in government. 'Sorry – I didn't notice you queuing there' is basically the same syndrome as 'Oh, sorry, north of England, I didn't notice you there'.

As they get older they improve slightly, in as much as they no longer find it as amusing to throw bread rolls around in restaurants, but the tendency to make you feel inferior increases. My accent has always been too middle-class to allow me to have any street cred, but as soon as I start talking to older golf-club-type Conservatives I feel like a cockney chimney sweep come to thank his lordship for the ha'penny tip what he give us, gawd bless him! Apparently this is how Margaret Thatcher felt in her first cabinet. So eventually she sacked all the Old Etonians and surrounded herself with the Tebbits and the Majors.

It struck me that the classes in Britain were still basically divided along the lines of the Normans and the Saxons. The Normans of Fulham still drank wine and owned land in France and the Saxons of Fulham still drank ale, used 'Anglo-Saxon' vocabulary and tended small strips of land behind the playing fields. And while Robin Hood robbed the Normans and gave to the poor Saxons, we went round Fulham promising to take a little bit from the rich and give a little bit to the poor, although not too much, obviously . . .

When I finally saw Conservative activists, especially the dreadful people who ran Wandsworth Council, I needed no further convincing about the rightness of my cause. Complex political debate is all very well, but generally most issues can be sorted out simply by deciding who are the nicest people. Nelson Mandela versus the Afrikaners – no contest, there has to be majority rule in South Africa. The Dalai Lama was always smiling whereas Deng Xiao Ping was always miserable. So independence for Tibet it is. Michael Foot versus

Margaret Thatcher – what clearer argument could you want for voting Labour? Ayatollah Khomeini versus Saddam Hussein? Hmmm – that was a more tricky one.

So that's all that socialists needed to say: Vote Labour because we're *nicer*. Don't vote Conservative because they are just not very *nice*. This criterion also determined my political shading inside the Labour Party. The handful of people on the far left of Battersea Labour Party had no sense of humour and glared at me, and the bearded councillors on the right of the party were pompous and patronising, so I just blended into somewhere on the soft left, with all the people who liked a laugh and a pint after the meetings. And during crucial policy votes I looked around to see what all the people that I liked were voting, and just stuck my hand up with them. If I had been interviewed about my reasons for voting for a certain policy during a meeting I would have had to have said: 'Well, let's just look at the facts. Pat and Barbara Roche are nice, and they voted in favour of it. Sarah Newens is nice and she voted for it. Martin Linton is not only nice but supports the same football team as me. How many more reasons do you need?'

As it happened the football team that Martin and I supported was Fulham FC. This was another reason to want a Labour victory in the by-election. Nick Raynsford the Labour candidate lived in Fulham and was well armed with reasons why the club should be saved. I had visited nearly every London ground on moving to the capital but had decided to adopt Fulham as they were fairly local and seemed like they needed my support more than most. 'You're a great one for lost causes, aren't you, John?' said my Conservative-voting uncle when he heard I started supporting Fulham.

Although the Battersea activists had vital council

elections to fight in a month's time, we sent quite a few helpers over Wandsworth Bridge. I remember the man from Fulham Labour Party coming to address us. 'Greetings,' he said, 'from *Minder* country to the *Lavender Hill Mob*', and we laughed and appreciated that he'd taken the trouble to think of a joke just for us. We were given a choice of several addresses from which we could canvass, and it always seemed that I turned up at the same one that Alf Dubs had said he would be going to. For during the high-profile campaign to get Nick Raynsford into the House of Commons as the Labour MP for Fulham, a subtler, more covert campaign was also taking place: the campaign to get myself into the House of Commons as an assistant to Alf Dubs. I did not know whether Battersea's MP already had any help or indeed whether he even wanted any, but I thought it would certainly not do any harm to chat to him at social events, happen to sit next to him in the pub after meetings and generally crawl and creep myself into his favour. My qualifications for the job were minimal. But if he ever wanted someone who could flick a cheese biscuit from under his nose into his mouth, and could recite the lyrics to 'Up the Junction' all the way through, then I was his man.

I had offered to help him when he was setting up the Nicaraguan Health Fund – a scheme to send medical assistance to Nicaragua, which had involved me ferrying boxes of leaflets around London. After that I said more than once that if there was anything else I could do, he only had to ask. Then, miraculously, one day there was a message on my answerphone.

'Hello, John, it's Alf here. I wondered if you could give me a ring at the Commons – I wanted to talk to you about a job I was hoping you might be able to help me with.'

He *wondered if I could* ring him at the Commons! A job *he was hoping I might be able to help him with*! I listened to the message again, but he hadn't changed his mind. I listened to it a third time just to make sure it wasn't a friend with a gift for impressions playing a cruel trick on me. Then I braced myself and rang him back.

'Ah, hello, John — do you know anything about computers?'

'Oh — a bit.' I was lying. I knew nothing about computers.

'And are you working at the moment?'

'Er, not really.' I was lying — I was still working for Goering & Sons the builders.

'Well, would you be interested in coming to have a chat about something that I'm trying to set up in here?'

'Sure,' I said, trying to sound cool, and we arranged a time.

I put down the phone and thought about what this chance meant. As it was six o'clock I went into the kitchen and began opening a tin for my dog. She spun round in excited circles and barked. And that was just how I felt.

The night before I was due to go in to see Alf I went to a Labour Party disco where I thought there would be food but there was none and the music was so loud that it was impossible to chat so I just kept taking involuntary swigs from can after can of lager. Perhaps my excitement or nerves got the better of me, because the next morning I had a headache so powerful I don't know how it fitted inside my head. I glanced at my radio alarm. I was supposed to be at the House of Commons in half an hour. If I had had the energy to

156

panic I would have done so. I thought I had better shave although stubble would have looked better than the collage of scabs that I hurriedly left on my face. I was still slightly drunk and dizzy and was feeling increasingly nauseous.

I was only about ten minutes late at the House of Commons for which I apologised probably too profusely, but Alf hadn't even noticed. He proudly showed me his new Amstrad 8256 computer, the Model-T of computers, and explained to me a way it could be used to keep constituents informed of issues about which they had written to him. I was forced to pretend again that I had a passing acquaintance with computers although he looked a bit surprised when I genuinely asked, 'What's a cursor?'

As he explained the basics of the software to me, I could feel myself swaying back and forth as my body began to punish me for not allowing it time to recover from the excesses of the previous night. What I really wanted to do was lie down right there on the carpet and go to sleep in his office but this job was so important to me that I was forced to plough on, attempting the occasional over-earnest nod that made it look as if I was really concentrating.

'You see, John, by recording the name and address of every constituent that writes to me and indexing them according to what their letters are about, we can then send them copies of any subsequent questions or speeches that I raise in the House on that subject.'

He glanced at me to see if I was impressed but all I could do was burp ominously. It was impossible for me to take in his instructions because I was focusing so hard on presenting a facial expression that I thought would say, I am listening to what you are saying, I understand

157

it, and I am in no way about to puke up all over your new computer.

I dutifully looked at the computer screen as he demonstrated, but the glare and the rhythmical flashing of the cursor made me even more nauseous. I attempted to ask a pertinent question about how it printed, but as he went through the procedure my mouth was flushed with the cool saliva that informs you that you are about to vomit.

'Ah, well, to print you enter the code for a certain subject – say the NHS – and the code for that is "NHS" and then it's "print" followed by "enter" and it prints out the address labels. Do you want to try it?'

Involuntary muscular contractions were building in my stomach.

'Excuse me, Alf – I just have to go to the toilet,' and I rushed out and found one of the toilets in the Mother of Parliaments just in time to throw up in it. As I stared into the bottom of the toilet bowl I tried to memorise the computer instructions that Alf had given me. Code, then 'print' followed by 'enter'. I think that's what he said. Code, then 'print' then 'enter'. Then I was sick again. And then I was sick a couple more times before I wiped my mouth and blew my nose. The toilet paper dispenser had a little Palace of Westminster portcullis logo on it. That's classy, I thought.

I can only imagine there were no other candidates for this task because I started work the following week. He had made it clear from the outset that he did not have any money to pay me with and that the work was purely voluntary and part-time, but I didn't care. To have gone straight to this from the freezing-cold building site was the most rapid promotion this directionless twenty-three-year-old could have imagined possible. I had a special House of Commons pass with my photo on it. It said, 'Research Assistant to Mr Alf Dubs MP.' And on the back it said the pass was to be shown whenever entering the Houses of Parliament. It didn't say anything about whether you had to show it to your friends at every opportunity but I thought I better had, just to be sure.

Close inspection of the dates on the pass would reveal that I was a new boy to the Palace of Westminster, but that was already blatantly obvious from the way I walked around looking up in wonderment at the stained-glass windows, the huge paintings, the grand columns and panelled walls. I learnt one or two routes through the building off by heart, but if I ever deviated from those I would find myself dangerously lost and in fear of opening a door into Margaret Thatcher's private office. But over the following weeks I began to feel this strange sensation, which can only have been that precious, elusive quality – self-confidence. Alf Dubs gave me an injection of confidence which stayed with me ever after and for which I will be eternally grateful. In all the work he did for all his constituents, I felt like he could never help anyone as much as he'd helped me. I would get on the 77 bus and say, 'Westminster please' in the vague hope that the conductor would ask me why I wanted to go to Westminster. Alf would mention to people at Battersea Labour Party that I was working for him at the Commons and I would try not to beam too obviously. At night I would go to bed and listen to *Today in Parliament* and the chimes of Big Ben and think, That's where I was today. One night as I lay there listening to the midnight news I heard that Labour had just ambushed the government with a successful amendment. And not just some minor revision of offshore fishing quotas but a clause that drastically increased the amount that MPs would receive to pay their research assistants. That's me! I thought, sitting up in bed. That's money for what I do! The next morning I walked in the door and Alf immediately announced that he could give me a wage, employ me for more days a week and back-pay me for all the days that I had come in and worked for free. Oh happy day.

For two or three days every week I sat in the corner of his office in front of a primitive green-screen Amstrad computer. Every time I made a mistake the computer went 'beep' and he would leap up from far more important business to see what the problem was. We both thought this computer was amazing. It was supposed to save time, but it didn't because we just stood watching it and commenting how clever it was to be able to print out all these addresses just from me entering a little code. It impressed a few voters as well. During the 1987 election campaign someone said to me, 'He's a very good MP, that Alf Dubs. I wrote to him ages ago about the education cuts, and he never forgot, he sent me something the other day about an education question he had asked in the House of Commons.' Part of me wanted to say, 'I did that! That was me! I photocopied the bit from *Hansard* and got your name off the computer and stuffed your envelope,' but obviously that is not part of the deal.

There were three of us in his office: Alf, a front-bench spokesman on Home Affairs, Frank Dobson, Labour's shadow health secretary, and me. Two shadow ministers and twenty-three-year-old me. Alf apologised that he couldn't provide me with an office of my own. 'Oh, er, no problem,' I said nonchalantly.

It seems ridiculous that British MPs have to share offices; that we elect someone to represent about 80,000 people and we can't even give them an office of their own to do it in. When Tony Blair was first elected, he shared an office with Dave Nellist, the Militant MP for Coventry South East. That must have been fun for them both.

Alf liked to get on with his work. Frank Dobson liked to chat.

'Did you see *Local Hero* on the telly last night, Alf?'

'Er, no, no, I didn't.'

Alf continues with his paperwork.

'Did you see it?' he asks me.

'Yes. What a good film.'

'Oh, it's a great film! Have you never seen it, Alf?'

Alf looks up from his bulging in-tray. 'Er, no, no, I haven't.'

'There's this bit where they run over a rabbit, and the bloke in the hotel says he'll see what he can do for it, and he serves it up for their dinner and he says, "I had to kill it – the leg was completely broken – look at the bone,"' and we both laugh and Alf who is only half listening as he works attempts a smile although he didn't hear the joke.

'No, I had to go to the Balham ward barbecue,' he says by way of an apology for not joining in this conversation.

'The Balham ward barbecue?' says Frank in horror. 'What do you want to go to that for? I never go to those bloody things if I can avoid it.'

And the Member for Battersea humbly defends his dutiful attendance at every ward meeting, social event

161

and street stall, and the Member for Holborn and St Pancras insists that there are better things to do with one's time, and I am Mister Speaker, seeing both points of view and offering the occasional comment.

I was providing a service to two MPs. For Alf I would fetch mail, collect early day motions and continue to log and inform constituents of Alf's work on their behalf in the House. And for Frank Dobson I would listen as he read out his favourite bits from his speeches to me and just generally chat while Alf tried to concentrate on what they were both supposed to be doing. When Frank Dobson was struggling with a speech on the Health Service I told him a convoluted Health Service joke I had once written in my university magazine. And he laughed his hearty Yorkshireman's laugh and asked if he could put my gag in his speech. I just oozed pride.

It was down to Frank Dobson to decide Labour's response to the AIDS crisis. Some people wanted to use the onset of AIDS to try to impose some sort of old-fashioned sexual morality that had of course never existed in the first place. Frank Dobson thought about what Labour's position should be, then came in one morning and announced, 'You won't stop people shagging!' And of course he was quite right. So Labour's approach was that people should not be told not to have sex, they should be provided with better education about safer sex. I sat in the public gallery and watched him make his speech, which was basically a long-hand way of saying 'You won't stop people shagging!', and I told him it was a good speech and he liked me even more after that. Eleven years later, Frank Dobson saw me at the Royal Festival Hall on election night 1997. His face said, I know you from somewhere but I can't quite

162

place you. I smiled and he smiled cautiously back and he was whisked away by a TV crew.

I got to know quite a few Labour MPs, which was like a ten-year-old being introduced to the England football team. Alf and I would have lunch together with Kate, his over-qualified secretary, and often we would be joined by Chris Smith or Clive Soley or some other MP and Alf would introduce me and they would chat to me about things and treat me as their equal and find it completely normal that I should have chosen to become a vegetarian. Then I would go up to the counter again to get us all some coffees and get stuck between Ian Paisley and Peter Robinson in the queue as they discussed the situation in Northern Ireland. Once Paisley boomed at me, 'Does this apple pie come with custard?', and I nervously replied that I thought it did, and hoped that I hadn't helped the Unionist cause at all.

On one occasion Alf organised a group of London MPs to join the picket of a factory in Roehampton, where staff had been sacked for being members of a union. I was to drive the minibus. As I nervously drove along Millbank with about ten Labour MPs in the back I thought, If I crash into the Thames now, Labour will be virtually without representation in London. We went along Chelsea Embankment and Alf pointed out landmarks from his constituency to his colleagues. 'And that's the new Peace Pagoda. It's rather effective, don't you think, the way it reflects in the Thames ...' And they looked at his constituency in the way that dinner-party guests look round someone's house when it's been redecorated.

'Yes, that's lovely, Alf – very nice with those trees either side as well.'

'And over there, look, is St Mary's church, where

163

William Blake was married – that's one of the oldest churches in London.' It was very endearing. Alf was proud of Battersea.

We marched once around the factory in the pouring rain and I found myself walking back to the minibus sharing an umbrella with Ian Mikardo. I was suddenly plunged into the situation where I felt that I should make small talk with a Labour legend who had just announced he was retiring from the Commons after 42 years. What do you say to someone who was elected in the Labour land-slide of 1945? There was so much I would have liked to ask him, to chat about. Attlee and Churchill, Suez, Labour's years in opposition in the 1950s, the Profumo scandal, the Wilson government … And all I could think of to say as sheets of rain lashed down on the other MPs and the picketers was, 'Well, they can't accuse us of only being fair-weather friends.' And Ian Mikado said, 'No.' And then we walked in silence back to the minibus.

When I'd been working there a year or so Alf gave me the job of drafting some amendments for a Fire Safety Bill which he was discussing on a Home Affairs committee. This was being introduced mainly in response to the fire at Bradford football ground in 1985. The Fire Brigades unions had contacted Alf with some provisions that they wanted inserting into the bill, as had the Shopworkers Union, and so I tried to amalga-mate these overlapping amendments while adding a couple of other shortcomings to the legislation that Alf had pointed out. All I had to do was phrase all these points in the appropriate way for him to present them to the Conservative majority on the committee.

However, the laws of the United Kingdom are not written in the sort of English that most of us understand. If you want to say 'you can't just have a fire escape that leads onto the roof above where the fire is', you have to say: *In this Act 'escape' in relation to premises, means escape from them to some place of safety beyond the building which constitutes or compromises the premises and any area enclosed by it or enclosed with it; and accordingly, for the purposes of any provision of this Act relating to means of escape, consideration may be given to, and conditions or requirements imposed as respects, any place or thing by means of which a person escapes from premises to a place of safety.* That was section 4, subsection 2. And just in case anyone was left in any doubt, subsection 3 said *'escape' has the meaning assigned to it by section 5(5) of this Act and 'means of escape' is to be construed in accordance with that subsection.* When I first sat down to try to understand all this stuff, I had to concentrate so hard that my head hurt. I thought that by reading the bill out loud to myself, putting the emphasis in different places, it might start to make sense.

I went up to the library and got down some law books which I hoped might provide me with appropriately long and cumbersome phrases that I could adapt. I then wrote out the required amendments in my best impression of this strange archaic language – adding an extra clause or unnecessary line whenever possible. When I had finished my amendments sounded suitably incomprehensible, and to my shock and delight Alf got nearly all of them accepted by the committee. And so somewhere in British law are a few paragraphs written out by a twenty-three-year-old English and drama graduate who was making it up as he went along. Nobody on the committee seemed to notice because they were probably pretending to know what it all meant just as much as I was.

On 10 April, after the most intensive house-to-house campaign since Stalingrad, we won the Fulham by-election and London had another Labour MP. In the sweepstake I had randomly guessed that the Labour majority would be 3,500. It was 3,503 and even though I got the cash I rather regretted successfully knocking up those three voters in that one house at five to ten. The same swing in a general election would have left Labour just one seat short of an absolute majority. 'Yes, but don't forget Plaid Cymru's basically a socialist party,' I said to Alf with my customary optimism, as if that would be good enough to govern with for five years. We were watching the result come in at an activist's house in Fulham. I remember that the side of their fridge featured stickers from every battle that the left had fought over the last ten or so years – Coal Not Dole, GLC Working for London, Refuse Cruise, Union Rights at GCHQ – and I was struck by the fact that every one of them represented a defeat. The fridge was a memorial to lost left-wing causes. But tonight we had won and won well.

Neil Kinnock organised a boat to bring the victorious Nick Raynsford from Fulham to Westminster. I wanted it to stop off at Battersea Wharf and pick me up along the way. When Peter Snow did his graphics demonstrating how many little red men would fill up the government benches there should have been another graphic: 'And there's all the little red research assistants filling up the library.' I had the best job I could imagine, and after a well-run and successful by-election campaign Labour looked like they might be capable of ousting Thatcher. Maybe Labour really could be the next government. Alf would be a minister and I would work in his private office. At last there was everything to hope for.

But of course Labour did not win power. And one year after this triumph, the Conservatives regained Fulham in the '87 general election. I was too devastated that night to mourn the fact that Nick Raynsford had lost his job. Because the same night, Alf Dubs lost his seat too.

The jewel in the crown

Wandsworth Council Elections
– Queenstown Ward, 8 May 1986

For some reason not even well-educated people seem
to understand who represents them on the council or
the differences between wards, constituencies and
boroughs. At school I was taught that a nunatak is a peak
protruding through the ice sheet which is affected by
frost but not by glacial erosion. However, at no point
was I taught the difference between the area that my MP
represents and the area that a councillor represents.
While there are many people who can have informed
conversations about Shakespeare's tragic heroes, or the
difference between a coal tit and a marsh tit, only political activists seem to understand the very basics of local
democracy. Very briefly it works like this. A borough
is the area governed by your local council. A borough is
made up of wards, the divisions which the councillors
represent. A constituency is an area usually smaller
than a borough, made up of a number of wards, which
is represented by an MP. And a nunatak is a peak

168

protruding through the ice sheet which is affected by frost but not by glacial erosion.

If this was even slightly interesting, it would be basic general knowledge. But although it is clearly important, only strange sad people like political activists find it interesting. While there have been plenty of exciting TV dramas about other people working in the public sector such as *The Bill, London's Burning* and *Casualty*, no soap has yet hit our screens portraying the thrilling day-to-day running of a local authority.

> 'Listen, Mike, either we renew this estates manage-ment contract or those bastards on the Housing Committee will be down on us like a ton of bricks!'
>
> 'I know your game, Steve – you don't even want an internal bid for that contract! What's the problem, scared you can't cut it with the big boys?'
>
> 'We just can't handle it, Mike (*breaks down and sobs*). I've not seen my kids for a week – and it's the Leisure and Amenities Sub-Committee meeting tonight.'

Local government is not what the guys in the marketing department would call 'sexy'. It has an image of grey-haired old men who like the sound of their own voices sitting round in meetings talking about rather mundane things. One famous newspaper clipping somehow said it all: 'The Old Town Hall Renaming Committee which was established to come up with a name for the old Town Hall has settled on the name "The Old Town Hall".'

Disinterest and ignorance about local politics suited Wandsworth Conservatives down to the ground. It meant that their outrageous behaviour was never

169

front-page news and the complexity of their scams was impossible to explain on the doorstep. Although it received more publicity elsewhere, the idea of selling off council houses to all comers, which could build up the Conservative vote, was pioneered in Wandsworth. The chair of the housing committee would openly boast which wards would soon be going Tory. Whole blocks were emptied of council tenants and turned into luxury private apartments. Council properties were sold off below the market price to speed up the whole process. The traditionally Labour-voting council tenants were not only rehoused away from marginal wards but often placed outside the borough altogether. If local residents could have seen what Wandsworth Council were up to, or even witnessed the arrogance with which they behaved in council meetings, then no one would have voted Conservative. But as far as many of the residents were concerned their bins seemed to get emptied and the rates bills were low so Wandsworth must be doing a good job.

Living in Margaret Thatcher's flagship borough made us all the more determined to win back the council that would have been Labour last time round but for the Falklands War. Just a few weeks after our triumph in Fulham Labour was expected to make significant gains in the May local elections. And the sweetest prize of all we thought would be her favourite council, Wandsworth. I counted myself lucky to be involved in the campaign that was to be centre of the political stage. That spring I had attended a weekend course in Sussex organised by the Greater London Labour Party to train election organisers. When people heard I was from Wandsworth it gave me a special status. 'Wandsworth?

Oh, make sure you get those bastards out in May.'

'Don't worry, we will.'

Becoming an election organiser was the only way to avoid going out in all weathers to knock on voters' doors. It is the political equivalent of First World War general. 'I don't care if there isn't a single Labour vote in Primrose Mansions – I'm sending you to canvass it anyway.'

'No, sir, please not Primrose Mansions ...'

In the peculiar way that boys do, I drew up charts and coloured in maps and generally gave the impression of being very busy, constantly updating my records of all the work that still had to be done. When I was doing my O Levels I think I spent more time re-drawing my revision timetable than I did actually revising, and the same law applied now.

There were 4,183 front doors in Queenstown ward behind which lived 6,468 voters. Among them were three Labour MPs (who shared a house and always needed nagging to put up their poster), a couple of lords, two dozen nuns, one first-division football manager and the guy from *Yes Minister* who used to be Basil Brush's straight man. There was an old man who would sing 'The Red Flag' at you before assuring you he was Labour, there was a woman who wanted me to get her Harold Wilson's phone number, and there was a man called James Brown who rather unsurprisingly wasn't *the* James Brown.

My job was to get our six canvassers to make contact with as many of them as possible. If to start with I didn't realise what a serious responsibility being an election organiser was, I was soon to find out. Before the campaign proper got underway I organised a 'voter registration drive'. This was a plan to call at all the addresses that did not appear on the electoral register, check whether the residents were Labour voters, and if they were to register them in time for the council elections. Half a dozen activists gave up their Sunday mornings to traipse around the estates in the snow and it was a very successful operation, with about twenty or thirty new Labour votes to add to the lists. All I had to do was get the forms down to the town hall by the deadline and the votes were in the bag. And the deadline was ages away so I had plenty of time.

Those are the worst sort of deadlines. The envelope sat on my desk for weeks and every time I noticed it I thought, I must send off those forms. Eventually it became something I was so worried about forgetting to do that I put it out of my mind altogether. The deadline came and went. Perhaps deep down I always knew I was going to miss it, even though I had put myself and those people through all that effort. It was as if some pathological subconscious force was willing me to be that useless. And for months afterwards the envelope stayed on my desk staring at me like a body I hadn't disposed of. One unregistered voter had been so delighted that we cared so much about his vote that he actually joined the party. And on election day he went down to the polling station and argued furiously with the woman from the council, insisting that he *did* have a vote because the man from the Labour Party had come round specially, and he had filled out the form and everything. When he bitterly recounted this scene to me and railed against the Conservative conspiracy to deny him his democratic right I did not have the moral courage nor the heart to tell him whose fault it really was. 'Hmm ...' I nodded. 'Well, that's what we're up against.'

After this scare about my ability to blow the election single-handedly, I became methodical and obsessive with the way the campaign was run. Every canvass and delivery was recorded and I took great care that Labour activists looked the part. One new volunteer walked in my front door wearing a filthy Clash T-shirt and was sent out canvassing ten minutes later squeezed into my one and only suit. One of the candidates thought I was a bit too autocratic at times, but I don't think it was unreasonable to suggest that he might shave his beard off. To be honest, I was rather enjoying bossing everybody about. 'Look, nothing can stand in the way of the task of getting rid of this despotic, undemocratic council. We want local politics to be about tolerance and caring and listening to people. So if I say you're wearing a tie and canvassing Riverside Court, that's what you're bloody well doing.'

Every night for weeks I would have people out knocking on doors and delivering leaflets, and when they came back ready for a well-earned cup of tea I'd have another quick street for them to do. And at the end of the evening when we added up how many Labour votes we had been promised I could colour in a few more little boxes on my giant red bar chart.

Although Phil and Eileen, our two Labour candidates, were very involved with the local community, nothing could compare with the commitment of one of the Tories they were up against. His election leaflet informed us that he was 'monitoring the improvements to Queenstown Road Railway Station'. Greater devotion to duty hath no man than this. British Rail were improving Queenstown Road station and he was

173

monitoring it. So while Phil and Eileen were addressing the tenants associations about how the flats could get central heating, or were attending meetings at local primary schools of which they were both governors, the Conservative candidate was busy walking past the railway station saying to himself, Yup, they've repainted that entrance – I thought they were going to do that when they put up that scaffolding.

In the battle to win control of the borough we were only aware of how we were getting on in our little corner and we all felt that things were going rather well. In the Battersea constituency we reckoned that we would win probably seven of the eight wards and we hoped that the other constituencies felt the same way. The night before the election we finished our final canvass early and over a bottle or two of wine set about the task of copying out our 'Reading pads' (the lists of voters in each street who had promised to vote Labour, named I think after a Reading by-election in which they were first used). I proudly put up the Labour Committee Rooms poster in my window, and displayed the statutory sheet of Local Government Act regulations in a prominent position, which gave my front room a rather pleasing official look about it. Morale was high.

Just to entertain ourselves we decided to watch the Conservative Party political broadcast scheduled for that evening. We laughed as it began but by the time it was finished the mood was rather more sombre. The whole broadcast had been about Wandsworth. Millions of voters going to the polls the following day in every part of the country and the only authority they had talked about was Wandsworth, the Brighter Borough. Its enduring image was that of Conservative councillors giving out bundles of banknotes to passers-by in the street. That was the message about voting Conservative: Vote for us and we'll give you free money. We knew that this might sway a lot of voters. Apparently a number of local residents did vote Conservative because they'd rather liked the look of this idea. There were rumours that one or two of them were spotted wandering around the Arndale Centre the next day looking for those nice people with bags of cash that they'd seen on the telly. We were even worried enough to think that this broadcast might affect the size of Labour's majority on the council.

Running the committee rooms on election day is an exciting and satisfying experience. You get to write out big notices on bits of paper with marker pens and stick them up all over your front room. You need biros and rulers to cross out voters who have voted, jotter pads to keep a tally of the figures and coloured felt-tipped pens to mark which streets should be done together. The amount of stationery that is called for is one of the best things about it. The excitement does not really get going until the evening. At ten in the morning you have lots of adrenaline but nothing to do with it. Endless cups of tea are busily made and trestle tables moved slightly forward and then back again. But from the time that the children are picked up from school onwards the trickle of voters becomes a steady stream until eventually the closing bars of the *EastEnders* theme signals such a rush to the polls that no system has yet been devised to keep up with who has and has not voted.

All sorts of people arrive to help that you are not particularly familiar with and you have to trust that they are not Conservative double agents who have come to sabotage your campaign. On this particular night a man with a moustache appeared at my flat to offer his help and immediately had a bundle of sheets thrust into his hand with instructions to knock up Ingelow Road and then come back for more. As he was leaving I thought, I recognise him – that's Larry Whitty. What's the general secretary of the Labour Party doing turning up at my flat to help?

Finally the polls close and there's nothing more you can do. As we surveyed the chaos of my flat we estimated that enough of the voters who had promised to vote Labour had done so to give us victory in Queenstown, and we headed down to the count to have this confirmed. Our ward was the first count to be completed. I stood eagle-eyed behind the tellers watching the votes being divided into piles and keeping my own mental tally of how many votes each party had polled. Despite the terrifyingly high number of people who voted only once, or who voted for one candidate from each party or who voted for every single candidate just to be sure, we were clearly edging ahead. As the bundles of votes were wrapped up in red or blue paper and stacked into little piles, the red column was inching ahead. Finally it was announced. We had won, we had increased the Labour majority and I had succeeded in my task. I gave a huge sigh of relief. Eileen gave me an excited hug and a kiss and much to my embarrassment so did Phil. Labour activists cheered and clapped their speeches. It was going to be a great night.

But within seconds there was cause for concern. Martin Linton, who worked for the *Guardian* as a journalist and psephologist (an expert on elections), quickly calculated that the swing in Queenstown was not enough to win the borough. When he told me this I didn't really take in the enormity of what he was saying. We were not going to win Wandsworth. I carried on enjoying the moment of victory and assured myself that the Labour swing would be greater in the target wards that we had worked harder to gain, and that my little 'South Chelsea' corner of the borough had been more prone to gentrification. But as the evening went on, Martin's extrapolation looked like proving correct. Seats whose names I recognised from our lists of target wards were being won by a whisker by the Conservatives. For a couple of hours we hoped we might still do it, that one or two wards might buck the trend, but although we were making a few gains the Tories always looked to have a very slight edge. The last of our target wards was announced. If we won this ward, then the council would be Labour. The first two figures were read out – the first Labour total just beat the first Conservative total and we cheered. But in the cruellest of electoral tricks, the other two votes went the other way. The ward would be represented by one Labour councillor and two Conservatives. It is quite possible that if the Labour names had been higher up the ballot paper alphabetically we would have won the council. But the agent confirmed to me that it was no longer possible for us to win it. This possibility had never occurred to me and I walked out of the town hall in shell-shocked disgust. On my way I walked past the throng of Tory activists; mostly old ladies with blue rosettes and hair to match. They were all too busy congratulating each other to notice me glare at them. The thing that annoyed me most was that they didn't even seem particularly surprised that they had won.

I dragged myself back to the 'victory party' at my flat and joined in the bewildered wake. An hour or so later the agent came and confirmed the last few results, lay on my sofa and drank an entire bottle of vodka. Finally he rolled off onto some wine glasses and we ended the night picking pieces of broken glass out of his bottom. And the evening had started so well.

Of sixty-one seats on the council, the Conservatives had won thirty-one and Labour had won thirty. One seat – that's all we lost by. A handful of votes in any number of wards would have robbed Mrs Thatcher of the jewel in her crown. We got *more* votes than the Conservatives across the borough but just not in the places that mattered. And what we did not realise then was that 3 May 1986 had been our last chance to win Wandsworth back from the Tories and that we would not get another one. If we had won in '86, we would have increased our majorities in '90 and '94, like every other Labour council in the country. 'We won six out of the eight wards in Battersea so at least our constituency is safe,' I said brightly, precipitating our next disaster.

With the bitterness of unexpected defeat came recriminations and the search for blame. There were rumours that in one ward in which we lost by only fifty votes Labour activists had been so confident of victory that they had stopped knocking up voters a couple of hours before the polls closed. In another marginal ward, one Labour councillor was elected while the other Labour candidate, who was black, was not. The same split happened where one of the Labour candidates was openly gay. Why were black and gay candidates not put up in safe Labour wards? Why were there not fewer target wards so that resources could be better focused? Why had we lost when every other Labour Party in the country was celebrating victory, dammit? In the London Borough of Newham they had won sixty seats out of

178

sixty! That's just greedy. Every other council in the country seemed to have gone Labour. Why did I have to live in Wandsworth, the Brighter Bloody Bastard Borough?

Whether one council was Labour or Tory all those years ago may seem fairly unimportant now. But there are people walking around today whose lives would have been very different if Labour had got those few extra votes and won control of the town hall that day. Of course it's an impossible thing to measure. For most people the difference would have been invisible. A larger library fine here, or a different parking scheme there. But for others the difference would have been enough to change their lives completely.

A year or so after the election there was an explosion in Balham which destroyed several properties. A girl who lived in one of these had just popped out to the launderette and came back to find her road blocked off by the police and her bedroom half demolished. The accident had left her with nowhere to live. Had the council been Labour her statutory right to be rehoused would have been taken seriously. She would eagerly have accepted a council flat and would not have got chatting to me about the accident a few days afterwards. I was going on holiday the next morning and, although I'd never met her before, she was a friend of a friend so I was more than happy for her to stay in my flat while I was away. Three years later we were married. I've still got the thank-you note pinned to my noticeboard. 'Thanks for letting me stay. It's a lovely flat. I don't suppose you want a permanent lodger? No, only joking.' (What did she mean 'only joking'?)

So it is conceivable that if Labour had won that election I would never have married Jackie and my two children would not exist. That is just one possible consequence of 3 May 1986. But a council's failure to rehouse the homeless does not usually have such a happy outcome. Who knows the knock-on effects that Labour's failure in Wandsworth had on less fortunate people's lives. I wish it was possible to pick out other individuals from the quarter of a million people who live in the borough and be shown the paths their lives would have taken if that election result had gone the other way. Children who grew up in the one room of a bed-and-breakfast hostel. Families that split up from the stress of overcrowding. People who ended up sleeping on the streets. Kids that were taken into care. Former council workers who lost their jobs or had their wages slashed by the private contractors. Tenants who got into debt because Wandsworth charged the second highest council rents in the country. What would they be doing today if they had been allowed to live normal comfortable lives? What sort of childhood might their kids have had? I wonder. And even though I am aware of all that, I can't help looking at my own two children playing with Jackie in the garden and thinking, Well, thank God the Labour Party blew it.

Three cheers for Alf Dubs

General Election – 11 June 1987

Two things struck me simultaneously on the evening of 26 February 1987. One was that there was no way that Labour was going to win the forthcoming general election, and the other was that Rosie Barnes had remarkably sweaty armpits. As she held her arms aloft to celebrate her victory in the Greenwich by-election she exposed the huge dark circles of sweat that had soaked through her dress as evidence of just how hard she had worked for this victory. She turned this way and that, waving to supporters and clasping her hands together in the air again, just in case there were one or two TV crews or photographers who had not yet recorded that she had forgotten her Sure Extra-dry under-arm spray that morning.

But the dampness of Rosie Barnes's armpits should never have been exposed to the nation in this way. Greenwich had been a Labour seat for 50 years, and here we were losing it to the SDP only months before a general election. A party that is going to overturn a majority of 100 at a general election does not lose one of its safest seats in the run-up to the campaign. I climbed dejectedly into the bath and lay there listening to the analysis of the result on a Radio 4 by-election special which described the SDP's victory as 'spectacular' and 'historic'. I could foresee these superlatives being wheeled out again in a few months' time to describe Margaret Thatcher's third successive general election victory.

Greenwich is a lovely place when the tide is in. But the tide was most definitely going out. Labour's victory a few miles upstream in Fulham was a distant memory. In the autumn of 1986 Nigel Lawson had performed a dramatic U-turn and injected £5 billion into the economy, successfully creating a 'feel-good factor' in the run-up to the general election. When Wandsworth Council had faced re-election, they had given thousands of households free window boxes that were carefully timed to come into bloom just before election day. On polling day every window sill in my road was a riot of blue and violet flowers (not red, obviously). The government's dramatic abandonment of monetarism in 1986 put money in people's pockets and increased spending on schools, hospitals and public services. It was the £5 billion equivalent of free window boxes. Labour's poll rating gradually slipped back and was now frighteningly low.

The mood among Labour MPs in the House of Commons was one of grim foreboding. As Frank Dobson got his papers together and put them into a box file before leaving for the duration of the campaign, I said to him in my annoying, optimistic way, 'That'll be a red box in a month's time.' He attempted an upbeat 'Aye, we'll show them' sort of reply, but he did not sound very

182

convinced. The swing that we required to evict Mrs Thatcher was enormous. There was a poster in Alf's office that the party had produced after the débâcle of 1983 in order to depress ourselves even further. It was entitled 'The Size of Our Task' and featured a map of Britain with all the Labour constituencies coloured red. Suffice to say that the bill for red ink at the printers did not set the party back very much. South of a line from the Wash to the Bristol Channel, there were only three Labour seats outside London: Bristol South, Thurrock and, rather surprisingly, Ipswich. Or 'Ipsweetch' as it was dubbed because its MP was Ken Weetch, and Ipswich Labour Party were very proud that they alone had survived the wipe-out. This pride seemed rather misplaced to me – like one of the crew of the *Titanic* swimming ashore and saying, 'Didn't I do well?' They published a pamphlet about Fortress Ipswich, 'the town the Tories couldn't take', boasting of their unique achievement and how it was an example to constituency parties everywhere. Needless to say when Labour was gaining seats in the general election of 1987, Ipswich Labour Party bucked the trend again, and lost the seat to the Tories.

Ipswich was one of six gains that the Tories were about to make from Labour. I did not appreciate that even when a party's share of the vote increases across the country it is still possible to lose individual seats in certain constituencies. If I had done, I might have been more prepared for what was to happen in Battersea. The Sloane Rangers that had been spilling into Fulham were by now getting their passports stamped and coming south of the river as well. As I drove back from the Commons with Alf past the forest of 'For Sale' signs that dominated the roads of my ward, I commented on how

183

many properties were being done up by the influx of yuppies. 'Every skip contains a couple of Labour votes,' he said ominously.

It was true. My road contained old working-class couples who voted Labour and young upper-middle-class couples who voted Conservative. If we could just stop enough of the old ones dying this side of the general election we would be all right. We kept putting leaflets through their letter boxes. We should have been giving them vitamin supplements.

The day after the election was declared I organised a canvass of Queenstown Road, the main thoroughfare of the ward, with the sole intention of getting people to put Labour posters in their windows. Canvassers were just to call on previously identified Labour supporters and new voters, armed with bundles of window bills that already had a little bit of Blu-tack stuck in each corner. It worked like a dream. Before the Tories had even knocked on their first door, one of the major roads in the constituency was a sea of Labour posters. And every morning the hundreds of people who looked out of the 137 bus could see nothing but day-glo yellow and red squares that proclaimed 'Dubs, Labour'. I overheard one Labour activist from another part of Battersea say excitedly, 'Have you seen Queenstown Road? It's fantastic!' I was so proud.

Because I liked Alf so much and I hated Margaret Thatcher and the local Tories, there was no way that I was going to be a half-hearted election organiser. I put in every spare minute I had, shamelessly roping in friends and family to help achieve the only thing that mattered. At the end of the campaign the agent Ann Creighton and I looked out over the estates from one of the walkways and she said, 'You've done a marvellous

job on the Patmore, John. You should be really proud.'
I realised that it was partly because of people like her
and Alf and Phil and Eileen that I had become a Labour
Party activist. They made me feel that I was good at it.
And for someone who had been a mediocre pupil at
school, who was useless at sport and who had been one
of the tutors' least favourite students at university, it felt
rather nice to be good at something.

Unexpected praise was also coming the way of Neil
Kinnock. The campaign was adjudged to have been by
far the best with the leader featured in a much-
acclaimed party political broadcast. He was shown
walking along the cliffs with Glenys. I was just relieved
that this time he didn't fall into the sea. The leaflets were
better, the organisation was better and the discipline
was better. Best of all, the campaign seemed to have
some imagination.

Somebody gave my name to Labour Party headquarters as the sort of person who might be able to take
part in a scam that they were organising. My task was
explained to me down the phone. I was to phone up
Election Call, which was being broadcast on Radio 4 and
BBC1, and ask the party representatives a question.
When I had heard their answers I was to say, 'Well, up
till now I've always voted Conservative, but after
hearing the minister's reply I think I'm going to vote
Labour.' I practised this line a couple of times and felt
pretty comfortable with it.

I rang *Election Call* and the telephonist took my
question and said they might ring me back. So I sat
and listened to the programme. A fairly ordinary-
sounding housewife was asking the panel about the
economy. She sounds like a Tory, I thought. The
Conservative gave a very convincing reply, packed with

impressive-sounding statistics, and finally he boasted that Britain had the fastest-growing economy in Europe.

'Caller,' said Robin Day. 'Does that answer your question?'

'Well,' she replied. 'I've always voted Conservative, but after hearing the minister's reply I think I'm going to vote Labour.'

'What?' said Robin Day incredulously. 'Another one? How can you change a lifetime's voting habits because of what the minister's just said to you?'

But she was not there to explain. She'd panicked and hung up. Hmm – maybe this plan needed more subtlety.

But the same sort of thing was happening on a local scale. The Battersea Churches organised a public meeting at which all the main candidates were to speak and answer questions. We asked our planted questions and the Tories asked theirs. John Bowis, the Tory candidate, performed well and had clearly rehearsed his answers. But then a woman near the front hurled an accusation at Alf that sent a ripple of tension across the hall.

'Mr Dubs, I wrote to you about a very serious matter three times and you never did anything about it.'

Alf was thrown on the defensive. 'Well, what was the issue that you wrote to me about?'

'Black magic is being taught in a school in Battersea. Children are being encouraged to dabble in the occult, to learn voodoo and witchcraft.'

To an audience of church-goers this was a shocking claim. That children were being exposed to some sort of ritual satanic mass and that Alf had turned a blind eye. This could be a major scandal. They anxiously awaited some sort of explanation.

'Ah yes, I remember your letters, madam. I did contact

186

the headmaster at the school concerned and wrote back to you to explain that it is perfectly normal, as part of their Religious Education, that children learn about the different religions of the world.'

The audience heaved a collective sigh of relief. Oh, I see – she's a nutter, they all thought.

I was proud of the way that Alf charmed the audience, tackled the questions head on and displayed such a thorough knowledge of local and national issues. By the end of the meeting I was fairly sure he'd be getting my vote. And if everyone else couldn't see how much better he was than John Bowis then they must be mad. But those more experienced than me could sense a shift. An article in the *Daily Telegraph* during the campaign said that the Conservatives were poised to snatch Battersea, and I dismissed this out of hand as right-wing propaganda.

But when Fiona Mactaggart said to me a few days before polling day, 'Do you know, I think we might lose?' I was shocked. Here was one of the people with the best political antennae that I knew, a leading councillor whose political analysis and opinions often guided my own, and she thought that Battersea, inner-city Battersea with its council estates and its power station and its railway lines, might become a Tory seat. Despite the evidence piling up against me, I still refused even to consider this was a possibility. 'But we had a three thousand majority in eighty-three,' I said. 'Labour has to be stronger now than we were then.'

On election day my dad took the first shift sitting on the local polling station. 'There were an awful lot of BMWs pulling up, John,' he said afterwards, with the air of a parent worried that their child might be about to suffer a disappointment. Dad always enjoyed sitting on polling stations and was always more than happy to chat to the opposition. 'Yes, I was sitting next to this young Conservative girl, she was absolutely charming,' he said, which I knew translated as 'she was a beautiful posh young girl who laughed at my anecdotes'.

Mum brought over lots of food for all the helpers and kept making cups of tea in that 'everybody mucks in and helps' sort of way. I was proud to introduce Alf to them when he turned up at my flat. During the day the candidate tours the constituency, geeing up all the activists in each committee room and urging people to vote Labour through the loud-hailer bolted to the top of his poster-covered car.

I had had the job of driving Alf about a few days earlier. We had driven past the market stalls of Northcote Road, passing a group of jeering Conservative activists who were giving out leaflets. Alf just carried on talking through the loud-hailer: 'This is Alf Dubs, your Labour Candidate, Vote Labour on June the eleventh.' He only turned the loud-hailer off to say, 'It's probably best *not* to do V-signs at the Tories, John.'

On the lunchtime news on polling day voting was described as 'brisk', but then voting is always described as 'brisk'. The agent rang me up and asked me what the voting was like in Queenstown and I told her it was 'brisk'. Members who were not seen from one year to the next turned up offering their help, stirred by the excitement of election day. Part of me wanted to say, 'There's more to it than just one day's work you know,' but somebody had said something like that to me in 1983 so I restrained myself. By the evening more and more voters were crossed off our lists and the table tops of carbon-copied Reading pads changed from blue to pink to yellow to white as sheet after sheet was torn off for all

188

the foot-soldiers out knocking up. Finally, as ten o'clock approached, the cardboard backing cards of the Reading pads were ripped off the table and people were sent out with those to bully the last few reluctant voters out of their houses.

One newcomer came in from knocking up at a quarter to ten and was rather surprised I wanted her to go out again.

'Is it worth it?' she whinged.

'Is it worth it? We lost Leicester South by seven votes last time round! Seven poxy votes! You could easily get seven votes out between now and polls closing. Is there anything more important that you can think of doing during the next fifteen minutes?'

So she dutifully went out again. I felt like a football coach who had given the crucial team talk that would win the game. When the polls finally closed she came back and rather pointedly told me that she hadn't managed to get out a single extra vote.

I went straight to the lower hall at Battersea Arts Centre for the count. As I crossed Lavender Hill, somebody chased after me and shouted, 'John, the BBC exit poll is predicting a hung Parliament.' I felt a surge of excitement. Could we possibly do it after all? Could this be the night that Thatcherism was done away with? Alf came in with his wife and his daughter Sarah, whom I had got to know quite well over the previous couple of years. I patted him on the back and told him the rumour about the exit poll. He didn't seem very impressed. The Tories were there in large numbers, looking younger and even cockier than they had in the past. They had loud voices and laughed too much for my liking.

Soon the ballot boxes were unlocked and tipped out onto the trestle tables where council workers who needed the overtime would sort them into piles. Our job was to stand too close to them, watching their every move over their shoulders, and make them so nervous that they would eventually put a Labour vote on the wrong pile. We could then point this out and say to each other, 'It's a good job we're here.'

Different ballot boxes have different ratios of Labour votes to Tory. Where I stood the votes were splitting evenly, but I had no idea which polling district this ballot box was from. Alf had done a lot of work trying to help the leaseholders in the mansion blocks around Battersea Park. He had held public meetings and even proposed a private member's bill that would prevent leaseholders being stung for extortionate service charges. I went and stood behind the people counting the votes from that polling district. Conservative, Conservative, Conservative, Conservative, Conservative ... I counted forty Conservative votes in a row before there was a Labour vote. Ungrateful bastards, I thought.

Eventually all the votes were counted and there was much brisk walking back and forth by the returning officer who was enjoying being the centre of attention for a few hours. Ann Creighton and Alf were called over by him to have a word by the side of the stage. Although it was too far away to hear what was being said I watched their faces for any trace of news. It did not look good. Alf was nodding and listening and Ann looked very displeased. A recount I thought. We're going to have to have a bloody recount. How could we have gone from having a majority of 3,276 to needing a recount? Ann came over to a group of us who were waiting to hear what had been said to her. As she approached she just blurted out, 'We've lost. I'm very sorry. I'm *very* sorry but we've lost. I'm very sorry.'

This just did not compute with me at all.

'How many by?' somebody asked.

'Eight hundred and fifty-seven.'

'Is that too many to have a recount?' I asked, desperately clutching at a possible straw.

'Yes,' said Ann. It was a stupid question. It was possible to miscount ten votes, maybe even fifty votes. But not 857 votes.

'I'm very sorry,' Ann kept saying.

'Don't say sorry, Ann,' I said. 'It's not your fault – nobody did more than you.'

I just could not believe it. This was Alf Dubs. Battersea's Alf Dubs. How could anyone not vote for him? I turned to his wife and said, 'We'll want him to stand again.'

'Thank you,' she said.

Alf was shuffling up to the stage for the official announcement. What an ordeal to have to go through. The other agents had not shared their news with their activists and most of the room did not know the result. The returning officer said all the boring bits about the number of votes cast and the number of spoilt ballot papers and then a hush fell over the room. '*John Crocket Bowis*' (and then a pause in which I wondered why Tories always had such stupid middle names) '*twenty thousand nine hundred and forty-five votes.*

'*Alf Dubs, twenty thousand and eighty-eight votes.*'

A roar went up from the other side of the hall and podgy rugger buggers punched the air and waved blue flags. The noise went on while the other votes were read out. Alf and the other candidates graciously shook the winner's hand as the Tory MP for Battersea went to the microphone to speak. John Bowis's speech revealed that they had not expected to win the seat. 'We had thought we would need two bites at this cherry, but we've done it in one,' and he finished and they all cheered some more and chanted, 'Five more years!'

Only five more? I thought. That's if we're lucky.

And then it was Alf's turn. I put my arm around his daughter who was biting back the tears and she put her arm around me. Alf thanked all the people who had worked so hard and then he added: 'If it's anyone's fault it's mine.'

'Rubbish!' I shouted at the top of my voice. I could have hit him for saying that.

'Well you might think it's rubbish ...' he said, and then couldn't think of anything to say about it. His speech trailed off and there was polite applause. This wouldn't do at all, I thought, and in a voice that was cracking with emotion I shouted, 'Three cheers for Alf Dubs!' and even the council workers cheered. Bowis came down off the stage and Ann Creighton said, 'Keep the seat warm for us.'

I commiserated with Alf who was professional enough to realise that he had some very distraught supporters to comfort. Eventually I left the count and looked across the road at the tatty headquarters of Battersea Labour Party. On the steps of our building was a small group of Young Conservatives cheering and waving their blue flags, like soldiers who had captured the enemy's capital. It was so provocative and I hated them so much for what they had done that I wanted to go and punch them in the face. But there were three of them and they were all bigger than me so I didn't. As I walked through the Shaftesbury Estate at two in the morning I looked at all the houses with people asleep in their beds, blissfully ignorant of what a terrible thing they had done.

In my flat were the supporters I had left so full of optimism earlier in the evening. They had been watching the results come in when the bombshell had suddenly hit them. A little blue bar came across the screen, *Con Gain Battersea*. No warning from the BBC; no 'We would like to warn viewers in the south London region that they may find one of the following results disturbing'. Just there suddenly and then gone, commented on maybe by David Dimbleby before the analysts carried on discussing the likely size of the Conservative majority. Total and utter shock had hit them, just as it had hit me at the count. We watched the disappointment unfold but the scale of Labour's failure had been eclipsed by the loss of our seat. It was not until the cameras showed us the Conservatives celebrating that we realised that we had to face disaster on two fronts. At Conservative Party headquarters Margaret Thatcher was leaning out of an upstairs window waving to supporters and holding up three fingers to denote that she had won three elections in a row. And in the fore-ground the blue posters that were being waved said 'Bowis for Battersea'.

Alf rang me the following morning to ask if I could come in and help him clear out his office. He sounded remarkably cheerful. Before I went in I went to Pizza Express at Clapham Junction where a few party members had said they would meet. About thirty people turned up. When someone dies there is a need for all the friends and relatives to come together. So it was with the loss of our MP and our constituency. More and more activists arrived and we sat around in silence and disbelief. Battersea had always been Labour. John Burns (the first working-class cabinet minister) had won the seat in 1892, Saklatvala (the first black MP) had

193

represented the seat in the 1920s and Douglas Jay after the war – all Labour MPs for Battersea. And now our Member of Parliament was some flabby-faced Tory who did comic turns for the 'Blue Revue' at the Conservative Party conference.

I set off from Clapham Junction for the House of Commons. A few Alf Dubs posters still peppered the constituency in futile defiance. Alf was in the middle of his office filling large black bin liners with piles of now moribund paperwork. Eight years of work as an MP were crammed into a couple of bin liners. As we sorted through files and cupboards the only interruption were the occasional phone calls from former colleagues who rang to offer their sympathy. All my favourites rang that afternoon: Frank Dobson, Clive Soley, Chris Smith ... people that Alf had been friends with. Even Neil Kinnock found the time to give Alf a call.

When it was all done we had a drink outside the Red Lion in Whitehall and the sky looked dangerously overcast as thunder rumbled in the distance. Alf told me that when his mother had died he was kept so busy sorting out everything it took his mind off the loss, and I suppose he was saying that was a bit like how he felt today. He told me how his mother had been the source of much of his socialism and how she had got him out of Czechoslovakia after Hitler had invaded. As a little Jewish boy he had been forced to give the Nazi salute in school. I imagined how hard it must have been for him coming to England as a refugee with nothing. But he had learnt a new language, become involved in the Labour movement, been elected to Parliament and finally risen to become a Labour front-bencher. Until Wandsworth's housing policy and an influx of yuppies conspired to

194

turf him out of the job he did so well and into apparent oblivion.

He talked about the need for active Labour peers in the House of Lords and I understood his meaning. I pleaded with him not to go to the Lords, feeling he had too much to give the Labour movement to sit between the old duffers who fell asleep on the red benches of the Upper House. 'How can you represent something you believe should be abolished?' I said. Actually I still couldn't accept that he was no longer in the House of Commons and I certainly didn't want him to tear up his return ticket, least of all in a way that would be so vilified by the left. Twice during this discussion I called him 'Dad' by mistake. I don't think a psychologist would take too long working out the significance of that. Some years later when he finally did join the Lords I thought, Good luck to him, and dropped him a line to say so.

We went our separate ways and resolved not to lose touch. The skies went so dark that the streetlamps came on, the heavens opened and I was soaked to the skin in a torrential downpour. Even God was disgusted with what had happened.

On the Saturday night I drowned my sorrows at a friend's party in Bethnal Green and ended up staying the night. The next morning the whole house was woken up by a woman screaming in the middle of the Bethnal Green Road. We ran to the window to see what the commotion was.

'You stupid idiots!' she was shouting. 'You stupid fucking idiots! You voted her back in! Can't you see what you've done! You stupid idiots!' Between the ranting she was crying. She did not look like the sort of

195

woman who normally walked in front of oncoming traffic screaming and swearing, but the election result had clearly precipitated some sort of breakdown. One of the girls in the house was shocked. 'I know that woman,' she said. 'She goes to my evening class. She's really quiet and shy.'

But she was only saying what I wanted to say. Because of the dreadful outcome in Battersea I had not really taken in the scale of the disaster across Britain. But it was, as Neil Kinnock put it, 'a devastatingly disappointing result'. For all our red roses, slick broadcasts, glossy leaflets and Red Wedge Billy Bragg concerts, Labour had increased its share of the vote by around 3 measly per cent. The Tories had a majority of 102 – a landslide win, if you can have a landslide on top of a previous landslide. It was our second worst election result since the war.

The consolation in 1983 was that it had been so obvious why we had lost. 1987 felt even worse because we'd got it right and they still hated us almost as much. There were very few crumbs of comfort. The handful of gains that Labour made from the Tories were at the expense of Conservative back-benchers that no one had ever heard of. Not one Conservative minister lost their seat. The only front-bencher to go was Alf Dubs.

And so on the Monday morning Alf went to sign on. The form asked what his previous job had been. Alf put 'Member of Parliament'. Then it asked the reason he had lost his job. There was just enough room in the box to write 'Not enough votes'. He handed this to the girl behind the counter who read the form and seemed slightly confused.

'So you were an MP?'

'That's right, yes.'

196

'And when did you lose your job?'

'Erm – on Thursday,' said Alf. 'The general election was on Thursday.'

She seemed a bit irritated.

'Well why didn't you come in on Friday?'

Welcome to the world of the unemployed.

I know thee not, old man

Labour Party Leadership Election – 1 October
1988

During the 1987 campaign the *Sun* ran a full-page article
entitled 'Why I'm Backing Kinnock, by Stalin'. They
had helpfully arranged for a psychic medium to canvass
the spirits of major figures from history in order to estab-
lish who they were supporting in the forthcoming
general election. Winston Churchill was right behind
Maggie, as were Henry VIII, Nelson and Boudicca. Keir
Hardie had switched to the SDP. The only person who
said he was backing Labour was Joseph Stalin. Terrific.
Great to have you on board, Joe.

The journalist responsible would no doubt argue that
this article was clearly a bit of fun and that no one was
expected to take it all seriously. And anyway Stalin
would have probably got into the polling booth, worried
about Labour's tax plans and voted Conservative at
the last minute. But the general impression given to the
reader by this and hundreds of other articles was that
the Conservatives were the patriots and that Labour was

the party of extremists. There were outrageously big lies, like the alleged plot by left-wing MPs to make Ken Livingstone prime minister if Labour were elected, and then there were the subtle distortions that you needed a left-winger's paranoid eye to spot. I remember one piece in the *Telegraph* reporting that a Labour council was flying the red flag outside the town hall 'on the extreme left of its three flagpoles'. Hang on, I thought, if you have three flagpoles, there's one on the left, there's one on the right and there's one in the middle. How can you have an extreme left of three flagpoles? Especially when the same flagpole would be on the right if you looked at it from the other side. But the words 'extreme' and 'left' had been smuggled into the story and thus the journalist had done his or her job.

Although the television news was supposed to be impartial, it quite often took its cue from the predominantly Tory newspapers. I shouted at the television in frustration when at the end of *Newsnight* Jeremy Paxman said, 'And there's just time to see the headlines in tomorrow's papers.' The *Sun* have gone with 'Labour are Bonkers', the *Mail* have 'Bonkers Tag Damages Labour' and the *Daily Telegraph* leads with 'Minister Questions Labour Sanity', so there we have it, all pretty well agreed on that one ...'

During the right-wing heyday of the *Sun*, the left simply could not deal intellectually with the fact that lots of working-class people might prefer tits and bingo to savage indictments of government policies. Any way that you looked at the figures, the *Sun* was outselling *Tribune* and *Labour Weekly*. This paradox was discussed at a Weekend of Marxism that I attended at City University. (Obviously I had to book early to avoid disappointment.) One of the main speakers said that many ordinary people were not informed about what was happening in Nicaragua because this issue 'is only covered in the sort of newspapers that working people do not have the time to read'. I grasped this explanation with both hands. Yes! Working-class people are forced to read the tabloids because they work so hard that they *don't have time* to read the *Guardian*! That's it! And the impossible political equation in my head had at last been solved. It was simple and it was unpatronising. Unfortunately it was also complete bollocks.

I abhorred the *Sun*, not just because it was so dishonest and debasing, but also because it was so infuriatingly effective. When Rupert Murdoch sacked 5,000 News International workers I found it hard to shed too many tears for those journalists who had known they were supping with the devil, especially after all the damage their work had done to the Labour movement. I felt they should have resigned on principle years ago. However, I was persuaded that they'd never be able to resign on principle unless Murdoch gave them their jobs back, so on this basis I supported the call for their reinstatement. In any case Murdoch hadn't just sacked the journalists; the secretaries, messengers and even the cleaners had been locked out simply for belonging to a union.

On the day that Prince Andrew married Fergie, a handful of Battersea members decided to go down and join the print-workers' picket at Wapping as a symbolic gesture. It was a surreal scene, like a ragged siege outside an impenetrable hi-tech castle. Under the cold and eerie glare of the arc lights we watched helplessly as huge juggernauts carrying the first edition of the *Sun* trundled out into the night, and we booed from behind the lines of police officers and razor wire. The driver was so far away and the noise of his lorry so great that I'm sure he couldn't hear the insults any more than Rupert Murdoch could. By the mid-1980s, booing was all the unions could do. They couldn't stop Murdoch printing the papers, they couldn't stop people buying the papers. They couldn't even stop *me* breaking the boycott when I saw the *News of the World*'s headline TORY BOSS ARCHER PAYS VICE GIRL.

In a bid to counter the global domination of Rupert Murdoch, four of Wandsworth's Labour councillors pooled their expenses to employ me for one day a week writing press releases to the local newspapers. This project was the idea of Fiona Mactaggart, who before long was to become the leader of the opposition on the council and eventually the Labour MP for Slough. Every Friday I would sit on my own in her office, chatting to the cat and trying to decipher her handwriting. Sometimes I just stared and stared at her instructions because I simply did not understand them. 'Get breakdown of capital and revenue expenditure on this project from Establishment Committee.' What's capital and revenue expenditure? I just didn't know. Capital? I wonder if that's anything to do with the fact that London is the capital – as in *Capital Radio*? I rang my dad.

'Dad. What's capital and revenue expenditure?'

In these situations parents are always far too helpful to be of any help.

'Ah, I tell you what, John, there's a whole section on economics up at the London Library. I'm going there tomorrow, I can get you some books out if you want.'

'Er, no, it's all right, Dad. Not to worry.'

At the end of the day I would send off a few press releases written in my very best journalese: *Council in Double Rubble Trouble, Public Toilets: Tories Pull the*

Chain, and the lazy local journalists usually reproduced them almost verbatim. And so thanks to Fiona's plan and the income provided by her and the other three councillors, Labour were at least mentioned in the local papers from time to time, even if my story on page seven of the *South London Press* did not quite counterbalance all the articles attacking the Labour Party in the *Evening Standard*, the *Sun*, the *Star*, the *Express*, the *Mail*, *The Times*, the *Daily Telegraph* and the *National Trust News*.

Somebody suggested I try to pursue a career in journalism, but I felt that I did not know enough about the issues and had never been very good at working long hours. I suppose that's why they thought I was perfect for journalism. In careers sessions at school we were regularly asked to fill out questionnaires that were a roundabout way of saying, 'What do you want to be when you grow up?' I used to put 'journalist' for want of any idea at all. If I had pursued that line, then it is quite possible that I could have ended up writing articles saying 'Why I'm backing Kinnock by Stalin' (I certainly would have been proud of a joke as good as 'Genghis Khan's a Don't Know'). But what I really wanted to be was a comedy writer. I just did not have the nerve to put this down on the form. I didn't want to put the careers master in a position where he would have to say, 'Ah yes, Comedy Writer; you'll need a "B" in biology, at least a "C" in technical drawing . . .' So I put 'journalist' and thanked him for the inspired suggestion that I ought to think about doing A Level English.

But with the new-found confidence that my two jobs as MP's researcher and councillors' press officer had given me, I plucked up the courage to pursue my long-held ambition and I started going to uncommissioned writers' meetings for Radio 4's *Week Ending*. In January '87 I got my first sketch broadcast, and I continued to get the occasional quickie in the script. Then I teamed up with a bloke I met there called Mark Burton and as a writing partnership we were very suddenly given a three-minute commission in the week that the general election was called. For a moment I panicked. The script was always written on a Thursday. I said, 'Er, I'm afraid I won't be able to make Thursday June the eleventh – is that all right?'

Mark's background was almost identical to mine. He had grown up in Berkshire in a middle-class home with left-wing parents. He had gone to a comprehensive school, and a redbrick university where he had got a first-class honours degree in being late all the time. Apart from sharing the same politics and sense of humour, we agreed on most other things – except his tragically misguided belief that there was some point to the game of cricket. With Mark I could see myself becoming a full-time comedy writer.

Alf Dubs had said that after the election I could work for him five days a week. The producer of *Week Ending* said he had another show that he wanted Mark and me to write for. The voters of Battersea made the career choice for me. Writing left-wing satirical sketches seemed to fit in very well with the ideologically pure image I had of myself. The little Labour Party badge that I always wore featured a shovel crossed with a quill. I had done my fair share of shovelling and had failed to make any inroads for socialism on the building sites. So now, armed with my quill (or rather, broken Silver Reed manual typewriter), I would tell the masses the truth about Thatcher's Britain. Who knows, I thought, perhaps people would be influenced by the things Mark and I wrote and be persuaded by the rightness of the left's cause. As if the C2s in the West Midlands marginals were all sitting around waiting to hear what Radio 4's *Week Ending* had to say before they voted.

'Ere, Brian, coming down the polling station to vote for Maggie?'
'No, hang on there, Kev. 'Cos whilst I was polishing my Sierra, I was listening to this satirical sketch about the budget done like an episode of *Star Trek*. And although it made me laugh, it made me think as well. It's Labour for me this time, and no mistake.'

I very quickly learnt that the stuff that gets on was the stuff the producer wanted to hear. Our first producer was far from being a natural Labour supporter. Just before I got my commission, an election story broke in which Labour claimed it had an old tape-recording of Norman Tebbit saying it would be very difficult for the Tories to get re-elected with 3 million unemployed. It then transpired that Labour had paraphrased Tebbit's words and that the tape did not say exactly what Labour had been claiming. I casually joked to our producer that all that the recording actually said was, 'Hello, this is Norman Tebbit, I'm sorry I'm not in at the moment, please leave a message after the beep.' The producer laughed and said, 'Oh, that's great — write that up as a sketch,' and suddenly I found myself, in the middle of an election campaign, writing a sketch that was ridiculing the Labour Party and taking the *Daily Mail* line on what had occurred. I was so keen to get sketches on that I went along with whatever angle pleased the boss. In my own little way I was doing what all those *Sun* journalists had always done.

Up till then living a life of political correctness had not been that challenging. Boycotting South African tinned peaches in syrup had not been a huge inconvenience. In fact, joining the odd boycott was a rather therapeutic way of thinking that we made any difference after our consistent failure to win any sort of political power. If there was an official boycott of anything I joined it: News International, Nestlé, Barclays, Chile and South Africa ... My friend and local councillor Phil Green went a bit further and pursued a one-man boycott of the Jubilee Line. As a staunch republican he had been outraged when it had been named the Jubilee Line instead of the originally intended Fleet Line, and swore that he would never travel on it again. The first time I journeyed on the underground with him was the last.

> 'Charing Cross to Bond Street – it's just two stops.'
> 'No, no – it's the Bakerloo Line, two stops to Oxford Circus and then change for the westbound Central Line. I don't use the Jubilee Line.'
> 'What do you mean, you don't use the Jubilee Line?'
> 'I'm boycotting it. As a protest.'
> 'Phil? No one cares! London Transport are not going to rename it now because one solitary and impossible bloody leftie inconveniences himself *and* his friends by using two other lines instead. The Queen is not thinking, Oh dear, I'd better abdicate because Phil Green is not using the sodding Jubilee Line!'

'No – but it's a matter of principle, isn't it?'
he said, as we headed off towards a politically
acceptable combination of underground lines.

If you tried to live an entirely politically correct life, you would go mad having every little moral trespass pointed out to you. (I know this because I have been on holiday with Phil.) I was coming to the conclusion that it is impossible to live a totally pure socialist existence in the middle of a capitalist society. Every time we switch on a light we consume nuclear energy, every time we buy washing-up liquid we line the pockets of the multi-nationals. But just because it is impossible doesn't mean that people don't expect you to try it. 'Oh you're a vegetarian, are you? I see that you don't mind buying books held together with cow gum ...'

We had to live in society as it was, with all its in-justices, biased newspapers and petty prejudices, even if sometimes we tried to pretend that we were living in the society we wished existed in its place. This was also the harsh reality that faced the Labour Party after its third successive election defeat. The manifestos of 1983 and 1987 had been excellent documents in all respects except one – that people did not want to vote for the policies in them. The Labour leadership now faced a harsh decision. They could either have policies that appealed to the party membership or they could have policies that appealed to the voters. In a break with recent Labour tradition, Neil Kinnock decided to go for the latter. And so was born the Policy Review. By 1988 Labour's left-wing policies were being reviewed in the same way that the government was 'reviewing' the economic viability of the remaining coal mines.

Queenstown Ward Labour Party loyally took part in

the policy review, even though deep down we must have known that our participation was part of a PR exercise. It was a huge feedback operation, with every ward and constituency Labour Party discussing our policies: which principles were sacrosanct and which tenets of our programme might be modified. Labour Party HQ collected all these opinions together in one great thick document for Neil Kinnock, which he could then place under his desk to stop it wobbling.

It was the widely held view on the left that the policy review was a right-wing foregone conclusion which finally prompted Tony Benn to challenge for the party leadership. I thought his challenge was more of a gesture; a way of saying, 'Let's have a proper debate about our policies. Let's have a vote about how many people want our party to move that far to the right.' But not at all. I went to see him speak in Battersea. He opened his speech by talking with apparent total sincerity about how he was going to win this election for the Labour Party leadership, and how he would lead us to victory at the next election on a radical left-wing manifesto. Was I the only person in the room who didn't think either of these things had the remotest chance of happening? I felt betrayed. I wanted to say, 'Oh, come on, Tony, do that other stuff you do. Do some of your early ones – that's what we want to hear. The bit about the Levellers and the Chartists, and the line about Henry VIII wanting a priest in every pulpit and Maggie Thatcher wanting to control the media today and how there's no difference between the two ...'

But after my initial disappointment he started to win me back over. I recognised some of the old numbers. 'Peace, Jobs and Freedom', that classic from '83: 'When the best leader's work is done the people will say "We did it ourselves".' We nearly held up our cigarette lighters for that one. And then, 'We want a fundamental and irreversible shift in the balance of power and wealth in favour of working people and their families . . .' This was his 'Stairway to Heaven'. By the end of the rally we were on our feet applauding and cheering.

The next morning I felt tricked. Was he brilliant or totally misguided? Many of Tony Benn's solutions may well have been the better choice for our society, but to adopt them would simply make it even more impossible for Labour to get elected. And getting elected, it seemed to me, was the whole point of a political party. An ideologically pure permanent opposition would achieve nothing. Labour was not a pressure group or a watchdog committee. It was there to get power, and Tony Benn was not the man to win over the nervous waverers.

The battle between socialist purity and electoral expediency is constantly being fought within the soul of every Labour Party activist. There are no emotional standing ovations at party conference for the pragmatic trimming of a socialist programme. But then there were no crowds of cheering activists who wanted to carry Michael Foot on their shoulders after 1983 for sticking with and losing with such a radical left-wing programme. There are those on the left who believe we can have our cake and nationalise it; that the British people really do want die-hard left-wing policies, it's just that we have never had a Labour Party with the political will or confidence to present them with sufficient vigour. These zealots have a different view of the British people to my own. My instinct tells me that a nation that puts little bits of carpet on top of its toilet seats is not yet ready for radical socialism.

Tony Benn had once been my political mentor. He

had persuaded me that since Thatcher had smashed the post-war consensus with an aggressive assault on all the Labour movement's achievements, the solution was for Labour to counter this with a dynamic programme of its own. It was the political equivalent of the head-teacher's advice: 'If a bully hits you, hit him back.' So we tried that and woke up from 1983 with a bleeding nose and two black eyes. After that nadir each successive defeat made us prepared to sacrifice more and more of our long-held beliefs. It was not 'power at any price', but ultimately it was 'power at any price that cost the country less dear than the Conservatives'.

As I went to cast my vote for the leadership my pen hovered nervously over the ballot paper. Benn would lose us the election. Kinnock would abandon our socialist policies (*and*, as it turned out, lose us the election). After much heart-wrenching I finally turned my back on Tony Benn, like Prince Hal to Falstaff. 'I know thee not, old man'. Out of all the NEC and shadow cabinet elections and votes on policies within the party, that was the first time I felt I was deliberately choosing the least left-wing of two options. 'There's nothing left-wing about keeping the Tories in power for ever,' I pleaded in my defence. But I knew I was a pragmatist at last.

Of course my soul-searching was completely academic, because Kinnock won the vote overwhelmingly and the policy review was unstoppable. A few months later Kinnock even announced that the Labour Party would drop unilateral nuclear disarmament. Labour was only a left-wing party for about five or six years really. When you consider just how right-wing Wilson and Callaghan's governments were, the idea that the Labour Party had always been some sort of pure bastion of ideological socialism until Kinnock and Blair came along is quite perverse. I don't know why they called it 'New Labour' – there's nothing new about Labour selling out and being right-wing. I couldn't bring myself to vote for Roy Hattersley as deputy and so voted for John Prescott as a guilty gesture towards my belief that I was still vaguely on the left. Many years later Roy Hattersley reviewed a TV show I had co-written and said it was quite the worse sit-com he had ever seen. Talk about bearing grudges.

Six months after Labour's final internal battle, the Conservatives won the last by-election victory of their whole eighteen years in power. And this achievement was only thanks to the very public rift in the Alliance. William Hague, the sixteen-year-old prat who had wowed them all at the 1977 Tory Party conference, resurfaced as their candidate in Richmond, Yorkshire, and was elected with 19,000 votes. The SDP got 16,000 votes and Liberal Democrats got 11,000 votes. If they had not stood against each other they would have easily beaten the Tories, and Hague would never have become a minister in time to eventually become Tory leader (so the Tories have David Owen's ego to thank for him). But the Alliance parties were fighting their battles in public, letting pride and personalities become more important than their effectiveness as a political force. They were attacking each other instead of the government, sinking into a downward spiral of internal warfare, alienating themselves from the voters and ultimately handing the Conservatives victory. After so many years it was such a pleasure to see it happening to someone else.

The road to Tiananmen Square

European Elections – 15 June 1989

Nineteen eighty-nine was the year that millions of Europeans threw off the yoke of dictatorship and spontaneously embraced democracy. Nineteen eighty-nine was the year that millions of Britons said, 'Euroelection? No, I don't think I'll bother voting, thanks.'

There will probably never be another year as politically exciting as 1989 for as long as we all live. The communist dictatorships of East Germany, Poland, Czechoslovakia, Hungary, Bulgaria and Romania all came crashing down and, in a symbolic climax, the Berlin Wall was finally breached, allowing thousands of East Germans to pour through in search of freedom, justice and a McDonald's chocolate milk shake. One East German border guard said on the television news, 'It is very bad – I will lose my job,' perhaps rather failing to see the broader implications of what was happening around him.

The political and economic changes that Mikhail Gorbachev was bringing to the Soviet Union sent ripples

211

in every direction. Inspired by the Russian leader's visit, thousands of Chinese students occupied Tiananmen Square. My mum and dad happened to visit Beijing at the same time and saw the students marching and singing and handing out leaflets. Mum and Dad took their photos, gave them the thumbs up and generally offered as much encouragement as a couple of miming Western tourists can. When they got home my mum framed the photos and put them up in the kitchen. The photos are still there, full of banners and smiles and optimism. Within a month of the pictures being taken, many of the students in them were probably dead.

The massacre of the students in Tiananmen Square took place on 9 June with an unknown number of executions continuing for many days after that. All the protesters had sought was a vote – the chance to live in a democracy. Six days later in Britain less than four people out of every ten could be bothered to wander down to the polling station to exercise their democratic right.

'I'm far too busy to bother with all that politics nonsense,' said one woman to me on election day.

'It only takes five minutes,' I pleaded.

'I haven't got five minutes.' And she closed the door in my face.

How can you be too busy to vote? I thought. Too busy just to go and put a cross on a bit of paper maybe once a year at most?

Another voter explained to me why she wasn't voting. 'Well I voted Labour last time but it didn't make any difference.' Well, no, because we lost. Everyone else has to vote Labour as well for it to make a difference. But more people voted for the other party and they got the result that they wanted. That's how democracy works.

Others would hear their doorbell then lean out of the window of their third-floor flat and shout down, 'No, thank you,' as if I was trying to sell them over-priced ironing-board covers. People said that voting never changed anything. Surely this is an argument to be more involved in politics, not less.

One rather dandy old man with a cravat told me he would not be voting because 'if you vote, it only encourages them'. Then he gave me a rather self-satisfied smile as if he'd just thought this line up there and then.

'No, surely not voting them out of office encourages them even more, doesn't it?' I replied.

'If voting changed anything, they'd abolish it!' he quipped back, with a smirk and a nod as if he was a panellist on *Call My Bluff*. By now my irritation with non-voters was reaching breaking point.

'Hundreds of people have just been murdered in Tiananmen Square because they wanted the right to vote.'

'Ah,' said the non-voter. 'But *that*, young man, was in China.'

'Erm, yes, yes, it was in China, you're right there.'

'And it wouldn't happen in England, because we already have a democracy. And *that's* my point.'

I didn't realise it was possible surgically to remove all logic from someone's brain. I didn't try any harder to persuade him to vote because I decided that the farther this person was kept from a ballot box the better it would be for all of us.

By 1989 thousands of voters had simply disappeared from the electoral register with the hope that they might avoid paying the poll tax. Many of them were young people, who, we were always being told, were 'just not

213

interested in politics these days'. Not voting was actually becoming something of a macho posture among some young people. 'They don't do nothing for me, so why should I do anything for them?' was a glib cliché I heard trotted out more than once. But there were some people that I could hardly blame for their indifference. They looked like life had knocked any hope or care out of them and they couldn't even get it together to get dressed in the morning, let alone get down to the polling station and vote for some sort of change. The poorer people get, the more alienated they become, and the less inclined they are to take part in the political process. That suited the Conservatives down to the ground.

Others had more curious reasons for not voting. The first time I saw the code JW against a voter's name, I thought I had better knock and find out what this meant.

> 'No, we won't be voting, because we are Jehovah's Witnesses. We believe that God will decide the future of our world, not politicians.'
>
> 'I see ... well, unless Judgement Day is before next Thursday, there will be a new member of the European Parliament for London South West, so do you not think it might be worth having your say as to who that should be?'
>
> 'God will cast my vote for me,' said the Jehovah's Witness smiling benignly.
>
> 'Well, he's not on the register in Queenstown ward.'

There is a perverse revenge in getting a Jehovah's Witness up from their armchair to answer the door, so I always canvassed them even if I knew I was completely wasting my time. The time in which I could have covered a whole street was spent pointlessly arguing that they ought to break with their religious beliefs and use their votes. Eventually their superior canvassing experience usually prevailed and I ended up pulling myself away politely before I succumbed to buying that month's copy of the *Watchtower*.

Other people told me they were not voting because 'they're all the same'. As if the party of Margaret Thatcher and Norman Tebbit and Nicholas Ridley was the same as the party of Neil Kinnock, John Prescott and Dennis Skinner. The idea that there's no point in voting because 'they're all the same' is just intellectually lazy. You don't have to wholly endorse everything one particular candidate stands for, you just have to consider one person as preferable to the other. If all of them are completely unacceptable, then stand for election yourself. Nothing gets my hackles up more than people who should know better copping out of the political system because they think they are above it. But I am just someone who feels very strongly that people should take part in *every* election: European elections, council by-elections — part of me even feels compelled to take part in the *Stars in Their Eyes* phone vote just because I have a right to do so.

The general public treated the vote as if it had always been there and always would be. It was only seventy years since the advent of universal suffrage, sixty years since women had got the right to vote on equal terms as men, and there are plenty of examples in history of people having had the vote and then losing it. I tried explaining to my bemused three-year-old that his helium balloon was like democracy. 'It's no good crying now. I told you if you let it go, you'd never get it back again.'

215

Was it just in Britain that we took democracy for granted like this? If the students of Tiananmen Square had got democracy, would that man in the white shirt who stood in front of the row of tanks end up thinking, 'I can't be bothered to vote because it looks like it might rain and *Last of the Summer Wine* is on after *EastEnders*?' Would the Romanians who had risked their lives to demonstrate against Ceauşescu end up saying, 'Well, I tried voting a couple of times but it didn't seem to make much difference'? Sometimes I worried that a British government could abolish the right to vote, the right to trial by jury, the right to free speech, and as long as they didn't change the theme tune to *The Archers* no one would protest very much.

The trouble with being a political animal in Britain was that the British are just not very interested in politics. In France the workers seemed to take to the streets in fury if the government so much as proposed to review a minor industrial subsidy. But Margaret Thatcher could lie to Parliament, ban GCHQ workers from joining a union, abolish local authorities, arrest civil servants under the Official Secrets Act, lose the log book to HMS *Conqueror* after it sank the *Belgrano*, and all the British people could muster was a long-suffering 'tut'. It was about the same level of irritation they'd express on discovering there was greenfly down on the allotment. Only in Britain are people criticised for attempting to make something 'a political issue', when surely *everything* is a political issue.

During this year Mark Burton and I moved a motion at our union's annual general meeting: that the Writers' Guild should not be promoting membership for the private health care company BUPA. Although we won the vote, the anger of those who considered themselves 'apolitical' was an education to behold. To quote a couple of the many bizarre letters from the Writers' Guild newsletter: 'To destroy others' rights . . . in the name of "union solidarity" is to take the first step along the road that led to Tiananmen Square.' Another angry correspondent wrote, 'This nibbling away at freedom of choice is a well-worn militant tactic, used to good effect, if memory serves, by the Bolsheviks and the Nazis.' All we proposed was that if people wanted to get a 10 per cent discount from BUPA, they should get it through the AA or Access or the National Trust instead of a TUC-affiliated union. The reason they were so angry with us was that we had brought 'politics' (gasp) into the affairs of the Writers' Guild. They genuinely believed that there was nothing political about supporting BUPA while ending that support was the 'sort of blanket and totalitarian compulsion currently being swept aside in Eastern Europe'. I don't know which depressed me the most, the fact the Executive decided to ignore our resolution on a technicality, the rabid reaction of those on the right, or the appalling standard of letter-writing by people who were supposed to be professional writers.

I resented the way 'politics' had become a dirty word. If people were discouraged from thinking about how their actions affected the rest of society, how could they be expected to understand that it was important that they should vote in the Euro-elections? Because the work done by their Members of the European Parliament really did matter. All right, I can't quite remember exactly how it mattered, but I can assure you it did. This was the trouble with these elections. Not only were the voters of Britain uninterested in or unaware of what went on in Strasbourg, so were most

217

Labour Party activists. As a result we just went round knocking on doors and asking people to vote Labour on the grounds that it was the best way to annoy Mrs Thatcher in Westminster. That occasionally did the trick.

Again I was responsible for running the campaign in my ward but this was now a much less significant corner of the huge Euro-constituency. Jackie had by now moved in with me and had loyally joined Queenstown Labour Party. She was herself a very political person – part of my initial attraction to her had been the way she led a strike in the BBC Radio Light Entertainment department. In an act of political flirting I had tried to get the *Week Ending* writers to join the strike, but the Broadcasting Union felt that this wouldn't be necessary – so a lucky escape for Thatcher on that occasion. It did the trick, though, and this beautiful radio production assistant and I were a couple within weeks. I think I realised that she must really love me when we went on holiday to the Pyrenees and she secretly smuggled a box of Trivial Pursuit questions into the car. As I drove south she sat in the passenger seat reading out the questions and enjoying the expression on my face as I went:

'Don't tell me – I know this – it's ... it's Bogotá!'

'No, it's Caracas.'

'Of course, Bogotá's the capital of Colombia. I knew that,' and before we knew it we were in Spain and secretly engaged to be married.

As if this level of devotion was not enough, Jackie even volunteered to go canvassing in the Euro-elections. It was the sort of gesture that might come up in arguments years later. 'You don't buy me little presents any more!' 'Well, you don't go canvassing for me any more!' Activists from Battersea were keen that she should not be too disappointed if we lost. In fact, so many people warned her not to get her hopes up too much that I started to wonder if I wasn't being rather cruel in encouraging her to go out on the doorstep at all. Secretly I thought our chances were virtually zero. Election day did not have the energy and adrenaline of previous occasions. Phil Green, who was running the other committee room in the ward, took the phone off the hook and went down the pub for a couple of hours at lunchtime. But we had done a thorough canvass, and even managed to get the turnout on the estates to exceed the national average.

After the polls had closed we went to a party in the next-door ward. Our host was in contact with the agent at the count and the first phone call suggested that the outcome might be closer than expected. The radio was bringing news of substantial Labour gains around the country, helped by a huge increase in the Green vote which had split the opposition. It looked as if Labour was going to win an election. All right, it was a Euro-election with a national turnout below 40 per cent, but this was the first national poll that Labour had won since 1974. The phone rang again and we knew it would probably be the agent with the result. Our host said, 'I'll just go and see if we need to open the champagne or not.' He spoke briefly and calmly, giving nothing away. 'I see. I see. OK. Bye-bye.' And then he put down the phone and calmly called through to the kitchen, 'Champagne!'

In previous elections I had not been able to believe our defeats. Now I disbelieved our victory even more. A Euro-constituency that included Epsom & Ewell, Kingston-upon-Thames, Surbiton, Wimbledon, Putney, and now even Conservative Battersea – to be represented in Europe by the Labour Party? It must be a

219

mistake. But, incredibly, we had done it. The official result had yet to be read out in Battersea Grand Hall and so we raced up there to enjoy one of the rarer experiences for Labour supporters during the Thatcher years.

A surprise win is the best sort and the excitement and delight of all the Labour activists in that room obviously added to the disgust of the shell-shocked Conservatives.

'Would you have the decency to keep quiet until the official result is read out?' said one angry old man to me.

'Oh, shut up,' I replied. 'You're not used to losing elections, are you? You better get used to it, mate, because this is the first of many,' I said, allowing hubris to get the better of me.

'Just be quiet,' he said crossly, but no amount of red-faced Tories were going to stop us savouring the moment. They were angry with us for taking the seat and having the impertinence to win an election.

From the very stage where I had heard Alf's result read out two years earlier came the official result for the Euro-constituency of London South West.

Anita Pollack, the Labour Party Candidate, 74,298.

Dame Sheila Roberts, the Conservative Party Candidate, 73,780.

We cheered like a football team who had scored their first goal in fifteen years. I thought about the night that Fiona Mactaggart had rung me up and said, 'I can't get to my ward meeting tonight, but could Queenstown ward nominate Anita Pollack as our Euro candidate, because she was very good last time.' On Fiona's recommendation we had done so, she had been selected, and I wondered whether our new MEP would be giving her victory speech now if Fiona hadn't made that call.

For people who had suffered as much as Battersea Labour Party members had suffered, there was now

220

perhaps a slight sense of indignation that a newcomer like Jackie should have had such a pleasant initiation. 'It's not usually like this, you know, we don't normally win elections,' people kept saying to her.

The next morning I learnt from the paper that our victorious candidate was Anita Turnoutack. During the campaign we had known her as Anita Pollack, but somebody at the *Guardian* had told their word processor to go through the election results and change the word 'poll' to 'turnout'. So the 'turnout' in London South West was 39 per cent and the winner was Anita 'Turnoutack'. It was great that the advent of modern technology had provided the *Grauniad* with a more imaginative way of producing typos. We snatched the seat by the narrowest majority in the country, 518 votes, fewer than the number of Labour supporters we had knocked up in Queenstown ward.

With the increase in British Labour MEPs the socialists became the largest group in the European Parliament, just as, it was noted by the right, the rest of Europe were rejecting socialist regimes. But of course the 'socialist' governments in Eastern Europe had as much to do with socialism as the Spanish Inquisition had to do with Christianity. The use of the word 'socialist' by the undemocratic governments of Eastern Europe had always rather undermined the left's cause in Britain. In fact, in pure public relations terms, the brand of 'socialism' had not had a very good sixty years. Pol Pot had murdered millions in the name of socialism, Stalin had murdered millions in the name of socialism, and even Hitler had murdered millions in the name of National Socialism. The latter seemed particularly unfair to me, that we should be occasionally tarred with the brush of the Nazis. When it was pointed out that Mrs

Thatcher had avoided joining the war effort when she turned eighteen in 1943, she replied, 'Members on this side of the House did everything that they could to defeat National *Socialism*.'

I had always tried to distance democratic socialism from the extremes of the regimes that had blackened the name of our cause. But there were still those on the left around me who did not tread so carefully. I remember going to the pub with a group of writers and a radio producer from Yorkshire who was rather curious to discover that my friend Pete Sinclair had spent some time in the Socialist Workers' Party. And as pint followed pint, Pete was probed further about his Trotskyist politics.

'So, Pete, if you did manage to bring about a revolution, would you, like, want to chop the Queen's head off and that?'

Pete was always one to pursue a political conversation on any level. 'Well, if the monarchy became figureheads for a counter-revolutionary movement, then it might be necessary to execute them, yes.'

The Yorkshireman looked worried. 'Not the Queen Mother though.'

'If she became a rallying point for those opposing a socialist state, then it might be unavoidable.'

'No, Pete, I'm all for socialism and all that, but you're going too far there, mate, if you think that people want the Queen Mother killed.'

'No, we wouldn't kill her as a matter of course,' said Pete, trying his best to sound moderate and reasonable.

222

'No, Pete,' slurred the northern royalist, 'You're a good bloke and that, but we definitely part company there, mate. Killing the Queen Mother, that's out of order that is.'

Socialists going around talking about who might and might not need to be executed did not, in my opinion, help distance British socialists from the despots of China, the Soviet Union and Liverpool City Council. Being a wishy-washy soft-left member of the Labour Party I really did not want to murder anyone. I had even suppressed my homicidal feelings towards Margaret Thatcher and resolved that she should be allowed to live as long as nature intended. Especially as by now she was having such a lousy time of it in government.

While we saw 1989 as the victory of people power over tyranny, our enemies saw this as a triumph of right over left. Socialism was less relevant than ever, we were told. Capitalism had won. What was more painful was that some people started to attribute the end of the Cold War to Margaret Thatcher. As ridiculous notions go, this is right up there with the idea that Michael Howard was ever fit to be Home Secretary. Margaret Thatcher *did not* win the Cold War. It is pure fantasy to imagine that a minor world power off the north-west corner of Europe even entered the thoughts of Mikhail Gorbachev when he was considering whether or not he should deregulate the Soviet economy. Yet according to her fans he sat in the Kremlin thinking, Hmmm, I could either bring in *glasnost* and *perestroika* or invade Western Europe. Ah, but they've got that Margaret Thatcher, haven't they, I'd better not mess with her . . .

1989 came to a close and the whole world had changed for ever. The Cold War was declared as officially over, the Berlin Wall was pulled down and on Christmas Day Ceaușescu was dragged out into a Romanian courtyard and shot by a firing squad. But, in England, Fergie had another baby, Torvill and Dean did a pageant on ice and Ken Barlow still had not got back with Deirdre. A few weeks later there was another tremendous event which brought new hope to the world. Nelson Mandela was released from prison. Perhaps this would be the event that would capture the imagination of the British people and stir the profound belief in freedom and political justice that lies buried deep within the British soul? The emotional occasion was shown live on television and hundreds of people spontaneously rang the BBC. But not to share in the joy of this historic moment. Not to ask if the footage could be repeated for those who had missed it. But to complain that coverage of his release had interrupted the *Antiques Roadshow*.

A brief note to activists: Sunday's Labour Party membership drive is cancelled, due to the realisation that there really is no point in carrying on.

The candidate

Wandsworth Council Elections
– Fairfield Ward, 3 May 1990

In the mid-1960s there was a famous film called *Up the Junction*, about how a middle-class girl copes with moving to Battersea and living among the working classes. By 1990 we were nearly ready to start filming *Up the Junction 2* – another gritty social drama, this time portraying the isolation of the last working-class person left in Battersea.

There had been two or three estate agents in Lavender Hill when I moved to the area. Now there were twenty-five. The old man who lived in the flat next door to me had no bath and no heating. When he died the flat was done up and I walked out of my front door to see Cecil Parkinson viewing it with one of his daughters. A Tory cabinet minister thinking of buying his daughter a flat in Battersea! What is wrong with Hampstead or Holland Park, for goodness' sake?

Cecil and his daughter were looking at all the Labour posters I had in my window for the local elections.

'Good morning,' he said with a smile.

'Blimey – I thought you were coming round to canvass me for a minute!'

'Well – I don't think I'd have much luck!' he quipped and we shared a good-natured laugh. *Damn!* I thought to myself as I walked off down the street, I was pleasant to him ...

I comforted myself with the thought that in a month's time Wandsworth might not seem the sort of place that he would want his daughter to live in. On the notice-board above my desk I had a map of the borough of Wandsworth, divided into all the electoral wards. In each ward I had stuck little red or blue dots to represent every Labour and Tory councillor that had been elected in 1986. For four years I looked at it, waiting for the day when I could stick on that extra red dot that would make the council Labour.

Wandsworth may have been seen as an efficient local authority (it grabbed the national headlines in March by setting the lowest poll tax in the country), but Margaret Thatcher was so fantastically unpopular by now that we were confident we could achieve at least the tiny swing needed to take control of her favourite council. In a Parliamentary by-election at the beginning of our campaign, Labour took the normally safe Tory seat of Mid Staffordshire with such a huge swing that I estimated even the Tory candidate must have voted Labour.

Phil (standing again as red dot for Queenstown ward) said he wanted to be there when I put the new stickers on my map, so I promised not to do it without him. I wasn't making any predictions about the result but I had quite a large sheet of red dots standing by. And one of the two little red dots in Fairfield ward would be me.

I had originally decided against standing for the council in May 1990, having been warned off it by the miserable time that all my friends had had in opposition. But when Fairfield ward were unable to find a suitable nominee, I suddenly saw a risk-free candidacy. The seat was, I was told, currently the most marginal in London, with a Labour majority of just four votes. I reckoned that if I was elected, Labour would be in power, and if Labour lost, I would be one of the casualties and so would avoid four dismal years being taunted by gloating Tories.

Fairfield were a nice crowd of people and I could easily take off a day a week to spend on council business. All this suddenly occurred to me almost spontaneously late one evening in the middle of a Scrabble game with Phil and Fiona. Fiona (who was by now the leader of the Labour opposition) was saying to Phil, 'What are we going to do about Fairfield?' Every person I suggested as a candidate was met with a depressed, 'They won't do it,' or, 'He's moving to Yorkshire,' or, 'He doesn't live in the borough and anyway he's already President of the Soviet Union.'

Eventually I cautiously ventured, 'Well, *I* could do it ...' and Fiona was so pleased that she rang the secretary of Fairfield ward before I had a chance to change my mind and then went on to beat us all at Scrabble. I sometimes wonder if I only volunteered to stand for the council to cheer Fiona up on that particular evening. However, I had been having second thoughts about my earlier decision not to be a candidate. Just about everyone I knew in the party was standing in some ward or other and I had begun to feel somewhat left out. I had to do something other than carry on as my local ward secretary. Every month when the time came to produce a ward notice I would become irritable and tired. A sort of pre-ward-meeting tension. As a councillor not only would I be doing something different, I would gain a little bit of kudos as well. For there were very important things I could do as a councillor. I could get my picture in the newspaper, I could get my name on a seat in the council chamber, I could get a free diary with all the dates of the committee meetings already printed inside. It was too much to resist.

There was still the formality of the selection meeting and this was held one evening in the local library in Fairfield ward. I had a brand new polo shirt which I thought made me look rather sort of casual smart and a dark jacket that made me feel responsible without being stuffy. The final touch was the little enamel Labour Party badge on my lapel (of the pre-red rose type – to show that I was not some Johnny-come-lately to the party). My opponent at the selection meeting did not, frankly, look like Fairfield material. Not only was she extremely left-wing, she had a northern accent to boot. This was the Labour Party, for goodness' sake.

I gave my short speech saying why I should be selected, although cheering up Fiona and getting a free diary were not given as reasons, and then I had to answer questions from the assembled party members. Unfortunately all the questions were about the minutiae of local government which was not my strongest subject. I may have known a little more than the average voter but, to be frank, if they'd allowed me to answer on The Albums of David Bowie 1969–83, I would have done a lot better. 'Wandsworth will, of course, be taking over the local schools with the forthcoming abolition of ILEA. In the light of this, what is the third track on side one of *Ziggy Stardust*?'

'That's easy – it's "Moonage Daydream".'

Some of my answers to their questions were vague and non-committal to disguise the fact that I didn't know the answers, so in this respect I thought I made quite a convincing young politician. I had been assured that the whole process was a formality so I felt confident enough as I waited outside during the vote. But while I sat making small talk with my rival in the children's book section, a heated debate was in progress in the next room. An older member of the ward, a former councillor no less, moved a motion that neither of the candidates be selected. The reason for my proposed rejection? That I had failed to wear a tie to the meeting. The irony was that I didn't have any aversion to wearing a tie and always wore one when I was canvassing. But I just liked my new shirt so much I thought I'd wear that. Since in Queenstown ward we had just re-selected Phil who had chosen to wear a pair of Lycra cycling shorts and chew on a licorice root for his selection, I thought I was pretty well above the line as far as personal smartness was concerned.

The secretary of Fairfield was so terrified that his year-long search for a candidate might be extended another few months that he threatened to resign there and then if they didn't choose anyone. It was nice to know that I was selected purely on my own merit. As this debate continued I sat in blissful ignorance amongst the pop-up Babar books thinking, They're taking a long time to count twelve ballot papers. And then I'd catch sight of my new open-necked shirt in the mirror and think how nice it looked. The dress-code motion was rejected and eventually the ward secretary came out to inform the other candidate that she had not been successful and to wish her the best of luck elsewhere, after which he turned to me to congratulate me for becoming the new prospective council candidate for Fairfield ward. I shook my competitor's hand and wished her the best of luck. I felt a bit embarrassed really. I knew most of the ward members pretty well and she did not know any of them, but you need to make it look as if there's a formal contest. She was like the team of white guys who play the Harlem Globe Trotters.

Fairfield would be a fine ward to represent. Handy for the attractive Arndale Centre, with a magnificent solid-waste transfer station, a 24-hour 'drive thru' McDonald's and above all the Wandsworth One-Way System made famous by Capital Gold traffic news. It was the Wandsworth bit of Wandsworth, with the town hall slap bang in the middle. I was already starting to feel a sense of parochial pride about the place. For the next six months I attempted to make my name synonymous with Fairfield ward. I wrote a letter to the *Wandsworth Borough News* every week. It didn't matter what the letter was about – my task was to get my name into the local press as often as possible.

> Dear Wandsworth Borough News,
>   My top tip for getting wax out of a carpet is to place kitchen roll over it and then apply a hot iron. Hey presto! The melted wax soaks into the paper! Works on curtains too!
>   Yours, John O'Farrell, Prospective Labour Candidate, Fairfield Ward

I joined the Wandsworth Society, a strictly 'non-political' organisation dedicated, as far as I could work out, to protecting house prices in the area. I spoke at public meetings on traffic problems. I joined one of the sitting councillors on his advice surgeries. I organised a petition about repairs on the largest estate in the ward. I didn't mind doing any of these things; if they helped to get me elected to represent the Labour Party it would all be worth it. But no one warned me about the other side of being a candidate. The 'being a good sport' bit.

In any other circumstances, if I was invited to an event that sounded as grim as a Labour Party Barn Dance I would explain that I'd rather stay at home and drill holes in my fingernails. But when you are The Candidate and the barn dance is being organised by the ward you are standing in, you don't have a great deal of choice. Not only are you expected to go, you are also expected to lead the dancing *and smile the whole night through as well*. London SW18 is a bit short of barns, so it was more of a Dusty Old Scout Hut Dance. As the first record ordered me to 'take your partner by the hand' I gamely accepted the arm of one of the older members who'd been out knocking on doors on my behalf, and then listened for the next set of instructions to be relayed via the speakers. Although the record wasn't quite this specific, my next move was supposed to be 'twirl around and take the arm of the ward membership secretary'. Pretty quickly I realised that I'd gone the wrong way and was twirling with the treasurer by mistake. What fun!

As far as I could work out, 'being a good sport' translated as 'being a prat'. Much to my disappointment, at no time did the record say, 'Walk out the door and go for a curry'. And, strangely, linking arms and dancing in circles with Labour Party activists while shouting 'Yi-haw!' did not become more fun the more hours I did it.

231

The square dance, the hoe-down, the hokey-cokey – none of them managed to unlock in me the joy that is country dancing. By eleven o'clock I was worried that I might have to go to St George's Hospital to have the fixed smile surgically removed from my face. Indeed I was wondering whether it might not be less painful just to have another Conservative council.

Being a candidate was different. I wasn't simply asking people to vote Labour, I was asking them to vote for *me*. Electors would look me up and down as if I were some old nag at Ballinasloe horse fair. I felt as if they were thinking, Hmm, you're sound enough on the issues, but what are your teeth like? And explaining that I was their Labour candidate was not always as straight-forward as I had hoped.

'Yes, I always vote for Alf Dubs,' said one woman seeing my red rosette.

'No, no,' I explained. 'This is for the council, not for Parliament. Your candidates are John Miller and me, John O'Farrell. You have *two* votes.'

'Two votes? Oh, yeah, there's my husband – but he votes for Alf Dubs as well.'

'No, no. *You* have two votes, *your husband* has two votes – two votes each for the local council elections and these are the people you have to vote for,' I pleaded, offering her a card with our names on. She thought about this while I attempted a responsible-candidate-type smile.

'No – I think I'll stick with Alf Dubs, thank you,' and she closed the door.

Occasionally I would pass a house with my name in its window, which was a rather surreal experience. Although I was flattered that people were prepared to trust me enough to display my surname publicly, deep down I thought it rather reckless of them. How did they know I was not some corrupt racketeer out to line my own pockets at their expense? But the words *O'Farrell* and *Labour* on the same poster did give me a warm glow inside, like there was something very official about it. There, I couldn't possibly be a Tory because my name was printed on a poster with the simple description 'Labour'. Unfortunately, because the poster had to have both candidates' names on, it actually said 'Miller O'Farrell'. Jackie said it sounded like a character from *Camberwick Green.*

The account of how I had nearly failed to be selected because of my unsuitable attire had rather stung me, given my insistence that Queenstown activists always look smart when representing the Labour Party. So I bought some more ties, a suit and another couple of jackets. These would all come in handy when I was a councillor, I thought. I was re-inventing myself in the mould of a smart local politician. I had an image of myself going to meetings at the town hall and speaking in the council chamber, and my tatty Levi jacket didn't quite fit with it. I polished my shoes, I ironed my shirts. I even bought myself a trouser press, for God's sake. I've still got the bloody thing, standing there in my bedroom, with lots of pairs of crumpled trousers piled on top of it.

To go with the smart new look, I took on this air of friendly yet concerned reliability. If voters wanted to chat I would take the trouble to chat. If an old lady took half an hour to tell me that her son had moved to Canada, I fought back the impulse to say, 'Well, I'm not bloody surprised'. One old lady was all in a fluster because her hoover had broken. So I stepped in and mended it. Then when I canvassed her neighbour she reported how helpful she'd heard I was and next thing I knew I was standing on a chair trying to loosen her kitchen window. Another very elderly woman I called on had been a Labour Party member all her life. Judging by the pile of junk mail that was pushed back as she opened her front door to me, she did not get many callers, so I accepted her offer to go in for a chat and something to drink. I was expecting a cup of tea but she shuffled back from the kitchen with a mug containing about two inches of Scotch. This was about eleven o'clock in the morning but it seemed rude to ask her to pour it back into the bottle.

She told of the battles she had fought when she was my age. Welcoming the Jarrow marchers, organising local pickets during the General Strike, witnessing the pitched street battles against Mosley's fascists. She still hadn't forgiven Ramsay MacDonald for the betrayal of 1931. I was genuinely in awe of her stories, and impressed that her anger had not diminished over the years.

'Our civilisation is going to collapse,' she told me with the gravitas and authority of someone who had fought for the Labour Movement from its infancy, 'for the same reason that all societies collapse,' she went on. This was getting better and better – Gibbon's *Decline and Fall of the Roman Empire* applied to Western Profit Capitalism. 'And do you know what will cause that collapse, young man?'

I racked my brains …

'Is it what Marx said, that capitalism will inevitably self-destruct?'

'No.'

'Is it that the progressive centralisation of power into the hands of a few multinationals will inevitably lead to world revolution?'

'No, dear,' and she leaned forward to share the secret. 'It's homosexuals.'

'I'm sorry?'

'Homosexuals. Queers. The Greeks had them, and look what happened to them. And now we've got them on the television and, you mark my word, it's the beginning of the end.'

I mumbled something about socialism meaning equality for all, and probably added 'and my girlfriend agrees with me on that' just to make sure I didn't lose her vote.

On top of the doorstep work, a good campaign should always have a few 'events'. On the Saturday before polling day we were all summoned to the Arndale Centre where twenty or thirty candidates were filmed as they gave out leaflets and helium-filled balloons. Fairly quickly I realised why the balloons were so popular. A group of kids were undoing the balloons and inhaling the helium so that they sounded like Woody Woodpecker. 'Oi, Mr Labour! Can I have another balloon?' they kept squeaking while their friends fell about in high-pitched hysterics. I could just see the headline: 'Labour in Gas-for-kids Vote-bribe Storm!'

The Tories organised the same event that they organised for every local election. They got a senior Tory politician to be filmed walking down the middle of a road that separates Wandsworth and Lambeth. This road is used so often for this purpose that I believe they're thinking of closing it permanently to traffic. A recent survey revealed that in a single day the cars using the road were easily outnumbered by the Tory politicians walking towards a TV camera saying, 'Contrast the good fortune of the lucky residents of Conservative Wandsworth with their poor neighbours on the other side of the road in Labour Lambeth.'

This time the visit was to be from Chris Patten, no less, the secretary of state for the environment, and the day before it I was rung up by Martin Linton who, as a journalist, had received prior notice of the stunt. The road was only fifty yards from where I lived and we spent that evening heavily canvassing the street, persuading even the Don't Knows that it would be worth putting up a Labour poster for the day just to annoy Chris Patten. The neighbouring ward in Lambeth did the same for their side of the street, with the result that virtually every other window on the Tories' impromptu filmset proclaimed, 'Vote Labour'. The next morning I arrived there just in time to see Chris Patten's minders anxiously walking up and down the road trying to find a bit in which they could film him. Finally they found a spot, and I watched as he started the now-familiar story of Tory efficiency versus loony Labour lefties. Martin was there, scribbling away on his notepad, and he leaned over to me and said, 'You *are* allowed to heckle, you know.'

'Oh, right,' I said, instantly realising the obvious. Up till then I had been treating Chris Patten rather like a member of the royal family, keeping out of his way and being considerate and quiet while the camera was rolling. 'You can't bribe the whole country!' I suddenly shouted, taking my place directly behind him.

'Would you mind keeping out of the way!' said a rather irritated Young Conservative.

'Yes, I would mind. VOTE LABOUR ON MAY THE THIRD!'

Chris Patten was far too seasoned a campaigner to let this put him off his stride so he carried on about value-for-money Wandsworth versus profligate Lambeth, while the local residents peered out of their net curtains, indifferent to the fact that there was another Tory minister standing in the middle of the street.

'Vote Labour! Vote Labour! Count the Labour posters in this street, Chris!' I continued.

'Would you like to have a talk about the issues over there?' said one Conservative to me, pointing to a spot that was nowhere near the camera. It was a clever ruse, but not quite clever enough. I realised *just in time* that he didn't want to talk to me about the issues at all, he just wanted me out of the way of the TV camera.

That night I watched the local news, hoping to catch a glimpse of myself on telly upstaging Chris Patten and generally being a pain in the arse. But the item didn't feature at all. I was most disappointed. I reported this fact to Martin who explained a possible reason. 'They probably decided they couldn't release the footage because *you* made it completely unusable.' I felt pretty smug after that. But it still would have been nice to be on the local news, so that everyone could see me making the film completely unusable.

Polling day was not wet. It was not raining on polling day. This is all you ever hope for. It was, however, about 120 degrees in the shade and by lunchtime our volunteers looked like John Mills in *Ice Cold in Alex*. 'Oh, no, it's far too hot to go out, dear,' said a couple of elderly Labour voters to me. I made a note to go back later that evening, preferably in the middle of *EastEnders*. We squeezed every last Labour vote out of that square mile. At about half past eight, one Labour supporter I had down on my list still had not voted. I called again at his house and his mother told me he'd gone to the Spread Eagle. So I walked into the Spread Eagle and shouted, 'Barry Johnson, is there a Barry Johnson in here?'

He looked rather surprised and faintly worried. 'Yeah, that's me, what is it?'

'The polls close in twenty minutes and you still haven't voted.'

All the mates he was drinking with thought this was hilarious. But nothing would persuade him to leave them and his pint for the short walk to the polling station. But then maybe I'd think twice about voting for someone who tried to drag me out of a pub.

During the last frenetic hour I had been in and out of the committee rooms and in the background I could hear this constant rhythmical running commentary. Jackie, who had loyally canvassed every night (though sensibly refused to go near the barn dance), had the job of crossing off our supporters' names as they voted. One person would read out the polling number and Jackie would say 'For' or 'Against' according to whether we had them down as Labour voters or not. There were lots of people in the room all saying different things and giving out different jobs, but underneath all this chaos I could pick out her voice in the background, replying 'against ... against ... against ...' to the numbers she was given. Like the patter of a bingo caller, there was a calming back-and-forth predictability to it, although the

reassuring timbre of the voice was in complete contrast
to the disastrous message it was sending out.

'Seven-four-six.'

'Against.'

'Five-four-three.'

'Against.'

'Three-four-five.'

'Against.'

'Seventy-six.'

'Against.'

Ten minutes after the polls closed I was lying back in a
foamy bath with a large can of beer to liven up the cocktail of adrenaline and anxiety that was already spinning
round my head. Soon Jackie and I were walking the
short distance down the hill to Wandsworth Town Hall.
Being as gentle as she could, she suggested that perhaps
there was just a possibility that I might not have actually
won. I was not quite ready to give up hope.

The Tories seemed to get more unpleasant at each
successive count. This time they brought along a man
wearing bright blue trousers that were even louder than
his laugh. David Mellor was there and John Bowis and,
needless to say, none of them deported themselves with
a great deal of humility. The Fairfield result was one of
the first to be counted. I stood behind the tellers
watching them separate the votes into piles. I couldn't
get used to seeing my name printed on all these bits of
paper. *There's my surname! Oh, of course, I'm a candidate. There's my surname again! Of course, it's on every
ballot paper ...*

The bundles of Labour votes, although not insubstan-
tial, were clearly slipping behind the Tory column.
Meanwhile worrying noises were coming in from other

239

rooms down the corridor. A Labour councillor lost in Earlsfield, an increased Tory majority in Parkside. But I couldn't take any of this in as I watched the votes pile up, many with crosses by John Miller's and my name, but more, it seemed, with crosses by the two Tories' names. There were lots of people who had not understood that they had two votes, or had simply chosen just to vote for John Miller. Some people had voted for one Tory and one Labour candidate — but I suppose that's what happens when the Liberals don't stand. Soon it was all over, and the result was announced by the same man who had announced Alf's defeat three years earlier.

Sarah Tracey Jane du Cann, Conservative Party, 1870 votes
Vanessa Graham, Conservative Party, 1952 votes
Sandra Joan Hewett, Green Party, 232 votes.
John Henry Miller, Labour Party, 1579 votes
John Peter O'Farrell, Labour Party, 1416 votes

Well, fourth out of five's not bad. There were loud Tory cheers, loudest of all from the man in the blue trousers. I went immediately to shake Vanessa Graham's hand, but she walked straight past me. So I shook the hand of Sarah du Cann, daughter of the rather dodgy Tory grandee, and then went after Vanessa Graham again and grabbed her hand firmly and coldly to offer her my congratulations.

It was a very, very bad result. I had transformed a Labour majority of four votes into a Tory majority of over 450. I had actually received more votes than the previous Labour councillor but what was remarkable was the enormous turnout in the ward. It was 65 per cent – nearly double what you might expect for an inner-city council election. All those extra votes were for the Conservatives. The headline-grabbing lowest poll tax in Britain had been enough to bring out all the normally disinterested and apathetic people who thought that saving themselves some money must be worth a trip to the polling station, even if nothing else was. And who was I to blame them for taking what they thought was the least expensive option?

In a rather strange reversal of our former roles, Alf Dubs came over and offered his consolation. He brought bad news of how the count was progressing from some of the other rooms. Labour councillors were losing their seats right across the borough, but worst of all in Battersea. Two lost in normally safe St John's ward, three in St Mary Park, and then the result that depressed me even more than my own defeat. 'Both seats in Queenstown!' proclaimed a satisfied Tory to his colleagues with the casual smug tone of someone who felt they had completed a job well done. *Queenstown was Tory.* Not only had I failed to get elected in one ward, but the place where I had put in so much energy and time over the previous five years, keeping up the Labour profile with petitions and newsletters and jumble sales, had just turned its back on my two friends and voted for two invisible Tories. I'd be surprised if the Tories even knew where the Patmore and Savona Estates were.

'All three in Shaftesbury!' proclaimed the man in blue trousers, and this excited them all much more. Fiona, the Labour leader, had consequently lost her seat and Labour were now wiped out in Battersea. We had gone from having seventeen councillors in the constituency down to a pathetic four. The Tories were cock-a-hoop.

241

We sat with Fiona in the office that had been hers as leader of the opposition but which would now have to be cleared out. The radio was telling a very different story. The Tories were having a terrible night everywhere else. A particularly unpleasant Tory regime in Bradford was ousted and I left the room to find someone I could share this good piece of news with. At the top of the great marble staircase I looked down on a sea of political activists, red and blue, and spontaneously shouted: 'Labour have taken Bradford!' Huge cheers came from the Labour supporters who badly needed a straw to cling to. Jackie said she was proud of me. To see the smile momentarily wiped from the Tories' faces made me feel so good that I kept going out and making more announcements, every time a new result came through on the radio.

Labour have gained Southampton! And the red-rosette wearers all cheered. *Labour have gained Basildon!* Even more cheers. *Shrewsbury and Atcham remains in no overall control, but Labour are now the largest party!* Hmmm – that one didn't seem to have quite the same impact.

But Labour's national showing was no consolation. I had been hoping that we would re-elect Alf as Battersea's MP within the next two years, and suddenly this looked like an impossible task. Fiona would have made such a good council leader, and I had so many friends I thought would be sitting on the council benches with me. But we had put in all that work for nothing and now Wandsworth's excesses would be unstoppable. I left the count as Fiona was getting a battering from the national press. She had been the focus of a fair bit of press attention during the campaign, coming as she did from a titled Tory family. The photographers were rather aggressively trying to get her to pose next to a bank of TV screens that showed all the Tory gains in blue and she was politely declining this kind suggestion. Then she got up on the stage and tried to give as dignified a speech as it is possible to make while Young Conservatives are looking up your skirt.

As Jackie drove me home and tried to keep my mind off the result, I sank into something of a gloomy martyred depression. For all my experience of elections and understanding of the wider political forces at work, I couldn't help feeling a sense of personal rejection. I had put my pride on the line, said to the voters, 'OK then, me or them?', and they had all said, 'Er, *them*, thank you very much.' I got it into my head that I was something of a political jinx. Starting out knocking on doors on Labour's worst ever day, fighting my first ever successful campaign to elect someone to an authority which then got abolished, researching for one of the half-dozen Labour MPs who lost their job in 1987, and then standing in the only borough that saw a Tory landslide on the night of 3 May 1990. If there was a wrong place and a wrong time to be in politics, it seemed you could count on me to be there then.

The next morning Phil came round and we went to my noticeboard. In a brief and private ceremony, we solemnly took a sheet of little blue dots and put seventeen of them over the red dots on my map. Then we stood in silence for a while and looked at it. It was like a map of the late twentieth-century British Empire – a few remaining red bits just to remind you what used to be. The Conservative majority had gone from one to thirty-five. And in the midst of all the Tory defeats across the country, this was the result the press focused on.

'Kinnock Poll Axed!' was the headline in that day's

243

Sun. Based on the Tories' success in Wandsworth (the Westminster result that mirrored Wandsworth was not counted till the Friday), the Conservative papers were trying to pretend the night had been a disaster for Labour because we had been wiped out in the Tories' flagship borough – despite the Conservatives having lost countless councils and hundreds of seats across the country.

The knock-on effect of this was that Margaret Thatcher's position as leader of the Conservative Party suddenly looked a lot more secure. This was the comfort I drew from it all. Wandsworth had deprived the Conservatives of the clear-cut disaster that would have precipitated her removal and now, lumbered with the most unpopular national leader since Vlad the Impaler, they would have to keep her until the general election when she would lead them to an ignominious defeat.

I philosophically reasoned that this scenario was worth losing Wandsworth for, that my sacrifice had been for the greater good and that all I had to do was wait a couple of years until I could enjoy the spectacle of Margaret Thatcher having to concede defeat to a triumphant Labour Party in the 1992 general election. Whenever anyone commiserated with me for the result in Wandsworth I cheerfully explained that politically it had actually turned out rather well. I just wish I'd explained it to Michael Heseltine.

The following week I went back to work as normal. A group of us were sitting round writing gags for the opening monologue on *Clive Anderson Talks Back.* I received a few commiserations and we got on with the job in hand. There was one news story I thought particularly uninspiring – a new museum of Labour history had just opened in London – but Mark wrote something down and put it at the bottom of the pile. At lunchtime all the jokes were read out by Clive to everyone in the office to see which got a chuckle and which didn't. By the time he had got to the bottom of the pile the jokes had helped me forget about the miserable events of the previous few days.

'And finally,' Clive said, 'in London, a new museum of Labour history has just opened. Its first exhibit will be John O'Farrell.'

How they all laughed.

Maggie Maggie Maggie –
gone gone gone

Conservative Party Leadership Election
– 20 & 27 November 1990

On the morning of my wedding day the postman rang. Jackie and I expected this to be a telegram of congratulations. It was a summons for non-payment of the poll tax. The best man read it out at the reception anyway.

Since she had quite enough to worry about on that day, Jackie wrote out a cheque there and then and got a dispatch rider to take it straight to Wandsworth Town Hall. I think she was worried that our marriage ceremony might be interrupted by council bailiffs bursting in and forcibly removing the gold ring from her finger. My own stand against the poll tax had been even less courageous. As a candidate in the local elections I was not really allowed not to pay, so in an attempt to get round this I sent in my cheque for £148 *but* – and this was the brave bit – I didn't date or sign it. Right, I thought, that'll put a spanner in the works – let's see how Wandsworth Council cope with that! They returned the cheque to me and said, 'Will you sign and date your cheque please?' and I went, 'Oh, all right then,' and sent it back to them.

Others were more radical. The day before the poll tax came into force, 300,000 people marched into Trafalgar Square, pitched battles were fought with mounted police and rioters turned over cars and looted shops as huge flames lapped up the side of South Africa House. And I wasn't there because I was helping at a Labour Party street stall outside Sainsbury's.

As I watched the footage of the riot, one part of me was annoyed with myself for not having been on the demonstration to witness such incredible sights, while another part of me was relieved to have been nowhere near any charging police horses or anarchists hurling scaffolding poles. As I returned to work on the Monday morning, the path of the rioters through central London was visible from the trail of broken shop windows. They had even looted the BBC shop outside Broadcasting House. I could just imagine the scene. Hundreds of Class War anarchists smashing the windows and running out with as many copies of Alan Titchmarsh's *Home Gardening Guide* as they could carry.

Margaret Thatcher made an uncharacteristic but ultimately fatal mistake with the poll tax. She allowed it to cost people more money. If it had cost people *less* money it would have been hugely popular. Council house sales, privatisations, tax cuts – these had all been a way of giving people free money and unsurprisingly people had consistently thought the idea of free money was an excellent one. Obviously they were paying for it elsewhere, but no one does any sums comparing the VAT they've paid on fish and chips with the cash they made on British Telecom shares. With the poll tax people felt betrayed. They had got all excited about getting rid of the rates (which they thought meant an end to those large cheques they had to write out every year), when suddenly the bill for this new tax arrived and, horror of horrors, it cost even more.

Of course if the real cost of local government had been levied on local ratepayers there would have been riots in Tunbridge Wells years ago, but central government had always subsidised it with the rate support grant. In the same way that no one could afford to stage an opera without a grant from the government or even go to university without a grant from the government, no authority could ever afford to run a local council without the chancellor writing out a huge cheque every year and saying over his half-moon glasses: 'There you go, but don't go spending it all on lesbian peace workshops.' The trouble with Margaret Thatcher was that she started reading the cheque stubs.

She decided that if the government was paying out all this money to local councils then surely she, and not the local people elected on the ground, should be deciding what all the money was spent on. So by the time I came to stand for the council in 1990, all that local councillors were permitted to do was turn up and eat the sandwiches. (Sandwiches whose fillings had been predetermined by The Local Government Sandwich (fillings) Act of 1988 – fish paste or cheese and pickle.) So much power was taken away from local government in the 1980s that I can only imagine the cabinet spent 90 per cent of its time debating whether or not Mr Johnson at number 42 St David's Hill should be allowed to put up a conservatory.

'Tom King, you've had your hand up for some time.'

'Well, Prime Minister, as minister for Northern Ireland I have to say that I am concerned about the security implications of this new conservatory.'

'I agree, Prime Minister, and as Minister for Agriculture I urge the cabinet also to consider the threat that Mr Johnson's new conservatory poses to our tomato-growing industry ...'

Eventually Mrs Thatcher got fed up with trying to run thousands of local authorities so she decided that, instead of her government having to foot the bill and then be criticised for all the cuts, she would let local people pay a bit more towards the real cost of local government and then see how many pensioners' day centres they *really* wanted to subsidise.

At the ideas stage the poll tax was a masterstroke. When I first heard about it, I remember being both terrified and awestruck by its right-wing political brilliance. A tax that would make poor people try to get themselves off the electoral register. A way to abolish the rates and keep Labour out of power for ever. Though it did have the effect of disenfranchising hundreds of thousands of people, the poll tax was a monumental cock-up because Mrs Thatcher attempted to save money at the same time. All she had to do was to subsidise it a bit more than the rates for a few years, maybe raise some extra money by selling off Scotland or something, and bingo! Two million Labour voters off the electoral roll and *Con Hold Battersea* for ever.

But the woman who had got elected by filling the

wallets of middle England was deposed for trying to take from the wallets of middle England. And once the poll tax was unpopular it was such a delight to watch the tabloid press start being as unfair to Margaret Thatcher as they had always been to us. For simplicity's sake they merged the two concepts: the fundamentally unjust tax and the administrative nightmare that the poll tax became. So every time someone was sent two bills (or not sent any bills in the case of a Labour authority where I now live), it was blamed on Mrs Thatcher. Family pets would be sent poll tax demands, babes in arms would be sent poll tax demands, and all of this combined to prove what a ridiculous idea the poll tax was. The reality was, of course, that dozens of people were too lazy to read the instructions on the community charge forms asking them to list everyone over the age of 18 who lived at that address. The form did not say: 'Please also write down the name of your border collie, your three-month-old baby and your imaginary friend.' But when poll tax demands arrived for these residents, the papers shrieked, 'How ludicrous – it's all Margaret Thatcher's fault!'

Her unpopularity, which had already been breaking all records, plummeted to new depths. However, four weeks before she was swept from office no one would have guessed she would be evicted quite so suddenly. Political commentators like to think that the grand issue of Europe is what brought Margaret Thatcher down, but actually Conservative MPs voted against her over a far more deeply held principle – that they should not lose their seats at the next election. If she had been ahead in the polls she could have taken Britain out of Europe and towed it to somewhere off the American coast and they wouldn't have minded. The reason that the Tory Party had been so successful for so long was because it was first and foremost devoted to the winning and keeping of political power. And when it looked like the woman who had won them three elections would not win them a fourth, they did not hesitate in abandoning her. This is not to say that it was inevitable. Nothing is inevitable in politics except Paddy Ashdown talking about proportional representation. But when the situation suddenly presented itself, the Tory Party seized the moment and dumped the woman to whom they owed so much. I doubt if the Labour Party could ever have been so ruthless, but then that was partly why they were in power and we were not.

The drama began with Geoffrey Howe's resignation speech. Thatcher had stabbed him in the back once too often and a man can tolerate being publicly humiliated for only so long. In Geoffrey's case eleven and a half years. It was a fantastic speech. It was the anger of the Sex Pistols conveyed in the voice of Eeyore. You could see the Conservative members behind him wincing at the damning invectives that the former deputy prime minister was unleashing against her, while Nigel Lawson gravely nodded in agreement with every word. Thank God for the televising of Parliament – it was worth paying my licence fee just to watch the expression on Margaret Thatcher's face. 'The time has come,' Howe concluded, 'for others to consider their own response to the tragic conflict of loyalties with which I have myself wrestled for perhaps too long.' And the House erupted. Heseltine now had almost no choice but to stand against her in a leadership contest.

In the bizarre way that the Conservative Party does these things, Heseltine raised his standard by writing a letter to his constituency chairman. This was front-page news the next day. If a Labour MP wrote to his or her constituency chair the letter would lie undiscovered under a pile of raffle-ticket stubs in the party offices for a month. To the embattled prime minister, Heseltine's challenge itself was damaging enough, but then he added that, if elected, he would undertake a fundamental review of the poll tax. You could almost feel her reeling from the double blow. He didn't even call it the 'community charge', bless him.

Mark and I were by this time writing for *Spitting Image*. I penned a short scene to go after the credits which featured Margaret Thatcher walking through an empty, shadowy House of Commons hearing the echoes of her former glorious speeches: 'This lady's not for turning! Just rejoice at that news! No, no, no!' and then there was just the sound of her gently sobbing to herself. I was told by a reliable source that two Conservative MPs were so moved by this they switched from abstaining to voting for her! Another triumph for political satire. How was it that I could never get people to vote Labour but I *could* get them to vote for Margaret Thatcher?

Although the nagging fear remained that if she was replaced her successor might go on to win the following general election, by this time the excitement of her imminent departure overtook us all and I was more than happy to watch the spectacle unfold. She was so totally confident of easy victory that she left all the sorting out to rather poorly chosen minions. Alan Clark describes in his diaries how he was so worried about Thatcher's lack-lustre campaign that he went to see its organiser on the most crucial day of the election and found him fast asleep in a leather armchair. Mrs Thatcher herself did not personally make a single telephone call to any of the waverers. When you consider that she was only four short of securing enough votes on the first ballot (i.e., that she would only have had to talk *two* people round to voting for her instead of Heseltine), it was in the end her blind arrogance that proved her undoing. While attending a summit of European leaders in Paris, she was told she had received 204 votes, with 152 for Michael Heseltine and only a handful of abstentions. John Sargeant stood outside the British Embassy in Paris and told BBC News that he had no idea when Mrs Thatcher would react to the result. While he was saying this, she was striding down the steps behind him, like Dick Emery in drag, and he was bundled off the microphone as she unilaterally declared that she would be fighting the next round. Back in London, the senior cabinet ministers who had been assured they would be consulted heard this pronouncement on the telly.

Having had 45 per cent of her Parliamentary party turn their back on her she was, of course, holed below the waterline. But being Margaret Thatcher the next day she declared, 'I fight on, I fight to win', and I rubbed my hands with glee at the prospect of a messy and ignominious end to her reign. It was the first time she had not referred to herself as 'we' for a long time. The trappings of her power were already slipping away from her.

As that Wednesday wore on, her campaign team had to inform her that support for Heseltine was increasing and that if she continued on her present course she would be ejected from office in the most humiliating and degrading way possible. Don't tell her! I thought. She decided to see her ministers individually to seek advice as to what she should do. Some were comforting. Some were harsh. Ken Clarke virtually said, 'Don't forget to switch the lights off on your way out.' John Gummer blubbed. But none of them tried to convince her she had any chance of beating Heseltine. 'It was treachery,' she said later, 'treachery with a smile on its face.' Good.

On the Thursday morning I was working at the London Weekend Television studios on the South Bank. My walk from Waterloo took me past the ramshackle squalor of cardboard city and I thought what a fitting monument that was to her final years in power. People didn't beg on the streets of London when I'd first moved there. I comforted myself with the thought that the woman who had taken their jobs and homes was about to lose hers.

But it came even sooner than any of us expected. An hour later I was sitting in an office when someone put his head round the corner and said, 'She's resigned', and went off to tell everyone else. That was it. I ran after him for more details, but there were none. What else did I need to know? We turned on the television which confirmed the news and then I walked out into the corridor in a daze looking for someone to tell. A technician was walking past with a toolbox so I said to him, 'She's gone!'

'You what, mate?' he replied, rather surprised to be addressed by a total stranger.

'Thatcher. She's resigned.'

He uttered an unimpressed 'Oh' and carried on down the corridor. I needed to speak to someone whose excitement would register the same on the Richter scale as my own, so I rang Jackie. She thought I was having her on. Eventually she was persuaded it was true and she excitedly broke the news to everyone in her office. I could hear their amazed reactions in the background.

'It's so fantastic!' I kept saying all morning. 'Eleven and a half years! Eleven and a half years! That evil woman has completely fucked up this country and at long last she's gone! Thank God!' And then I'd try to get on with some work and then I'd stop and say, 'It's fantastic! She's gone!' I'd get up and wander into the next-door office and say, 'She's gone! She's gone!' and everyone in the office smiled and said that they knew and wasn't it great. Then after a few hours they said, 'All right, John, shut up about it now.'

I had always told myself I would be there when she went. It was a scene I had fantasised about many times – thousands of people booing her as she was dragged kicking and screaming out of Downing Street. Pete Sinclair and I went down there that evening to join in the spontaneous party we hoped would by now have sprung up along the length of Whitehall. But there was no one there. It was all eerily quiet. Where were the people dancing in the street? Where were the steel drums and the bunting? Where was the Pickfords' van taking away all the empty Glenfiddich bottles? This was not how I had planned it all those nights when I couldn't get back to sleep at three in the morning.

We hung around for a while but nothing was happening. A black car drove out of the gates and we booed loudly but I didn't recognise the bloke sitting in the back seat. Some poor civil servant must have wondered what he had done to deserve such a barracking. A handful of socialist workers turned up and occasionally burst into chants of 'Maggie, Maggie, Maggie! Gone! Gone! Gone!' But apart from that it could have been any other Thursday night in Whitehall. Why out of 50 million oppressed subjects had only me, Pete and a few socialist workers turned up to celebrate her departure? This was my VE day but the British public at large didn't seem particularly bothered, as if nothing much had changed. The trouble was they were right of course.

The Tories were still in power. The spotlight shifted instantly from the departure of their former leader to speculation about their next. The choice was suddenly between Heseltine, Douglas Hurd and John Major. Major was first out of the trap. 'My Classless Society, by John Major' proclaimed the London *Evening Standard*. Hurd was thrown on the defensive because he had been to Eton and was therefore a bit posh. 'My father was a tenant farmer,' he said, and tried to drop his aitches. Finally he cracked: 'Look, this is the leadership of the Conservative Party, for goodness' sake, not some revolutionary left-wing organisation.' You had to feel sorry for him. He did sort of have a point.

Major was rapidly becoming the favourite, particularly after receiving the backing of Margaret Thatcher. The press pack caught him in Downing Street and asked him to pose. 'No,' he said, 'not with my back to Number 10.' This shook me. Humility in a Tory leader! Now that really would be a change. Shocking to admit it, but try as I did I just couldn't hate the bloke.

The political earthquake that had taken place left me rather indifferent as to who should succeed to the premiership. I decided I wanted Heseltine to lose because I thought he might be rather effective as Conservative leader and because I had never forgiven him for wearing a flak jacket to evict those hippies from RAF Molesworth. I was supposed to be sitting in a school governors' meeting on the evening of 27 November but the result of the second ballot was coming through as I drove there. I sat outside in the car park and listened to the car radio. *John Major 185, Michael Heseltine 131, Hurd 56*. Although Major was a few votes short of winning outright, Heseltine knew immediately that he could not win and emerged to announce that he was urging his supporters to vote for John Major in the next round. Standing on the steps of his home he exhibited all the dignity and self-possession of the consummate professional politician. Beside him his wife Anne betrayed with her face the real anger and disappointment that was felt inside the Heseltine household. Hurd also withdrew and consequently John Major didn't actually win the leadership with the required number of votes under the rules of the Tory Party. Margaret Thatcher magnanimously pointed out that Major had received fewer votes winning the party than she had received in losing it.

So John Major was suddenly prime minister. Eighteen months beforehand he had been nothing more prominent than chief secretary to the Treasury. For some reason Conservative Party leaders always pop up from nowhere. He opened his first cabinet meeting with a surprised, 'Well! Who'd have thought it!' Not him I imagine. But like every incoming prime minister before him, he had been in the right place at the right time. He became a councillor in 1968; the only year since the war when the Conservatives won control of Lambeth Council. Then he was elected to Parliament in 1979 at the beginning of the longest unbroken run of Conservative rule this century. He had only just risen to become chancellor by the time the Tories wanted to ditch Thatcher and replace her with someone other than Heseltine. So a complex series of circumstances (combined with a certain amount of his own political skill) meant that he, and no one else, got to rule the

257

country. And along the way countless potential prime ministers had fallen by the wayside.

The night he became PM *The Late Show* ended their programme with a quotation from *Catch-22*. 'Some men are born mediocre, some men achieve mediocrity, and some men have mediocrity thrust upon them. With Major Major it had been all three.' The result of the election suited me fine. The Conservatives had chosen a man of very little charisma or apparent verve. 'He's Alec Douglas Home,' I pronounced to my friends in the Labour Party. 'A caretaker prime minister who'll be swept out of office and completely forgotten. He'll end up as nothing more than the answer to a crafty Trivial Pursuit question. 'Who was prime minister after Margaret Thatcher?' 'Neil Kinnock!' everyone will shout, and then the questioner will go, 'No, actually the answer's John Major', and everyone will go, 'Oh, yes, I'd forgotten about him'. I think some people found my confidence reassuring. As a testament to my unerring political acumen, in the general election which followed eighteen months later John Major got the highest number of votes of any party leader in history.

April fool

General Election – 9 April 1992

The night before the 1992 general election, God appeared before millions of British television viewers. He said, 'Hello, I'm God. In this election I will be voting—' and then the screen went blank as if somebody somewhere had pulled a plug. It stayed like that for a few seconds, then the announcer apologised and said we would have to leave *Spitting Image* and go instead to an old episode of *Boon*, part of which was then broadcast in its place.

This was, of course, an elaborate joke designed to get round the fact that we had been forbidden to have God come out and declare his support for Labour the night before the general election. To stir up a bit of pre-show publicity we had let the press know that the Almighty would be declaring himself for Kinnock and, hungry for any new angle during the endless weeks of election coverage, the tabloids snapped this story up and ran it as one of those minor scandals that suit everyone, including the rentaquote MPs who were as desperate for free publicity as we were. From the moment the show began the duty office were busy with complaints. Reading the log of all the phone calls, one in particular stood out: 'It is outrageous that this programme should be allowed to be broadcast the night before a general election – I demand that it be taken off the air immediately. Oh, it just has been – thank you very much.'

Mark and I had become two of the lead writers on *Spitting Image* about a year before the departure of Margaret Thatcher. It had long been the show I most wanted to write for, and when I saw a confidential form lying on the producer's desk that said, 'Burton & O'Farrell – commissioned to write thirteen minutes a show', it felt like one of my lifetime's ambitions had been achieved. Because 'satire' is what I did, I had always tried to pretend to myself it was a worthy and important pursuit with tremendous political power. I had read a book entitled *Wit as Weapon* which described the importance of the Berlin cabaret as a form of opposition to the Nazis in the 1930s. At the back of my mind there was a niggling worry. If my historical knowledge served me right, weren't the Nazis in a fairly strong position by the end of the 1930s? Whoever said that the pen was mightier than the sword must have had a pretty crappy sword.

After a few years writing political satire (if a load of puppets whacking each other over the head can merit such a grand term), I gradually became aware of its limitations. Even so, I couldn't help but feel vaguely insulted when ITV decided it would be fine to allow us to broadcast an election special the night *before* polling day. 'They don't think we're really *that* impotent, do they?' I think, like us, they had realised that sketches and jokes never changed anyone's mind about anything.

We might occasionally crystallise a feeling that the public already had or we might influence the way that people saw an individual politician, but no more than that. A programme like *Spitting Image* was only important in as much as a democracy needs to be able to mock its leaders and remind everyone they are fallible and human. It is politically unhealthy for anyone to be so revered that we are not able to have a laugh at their expense. What I am claiming is that showing royalty on the toilet is an essential part of democracy and not at all a cheap botty gag.

With the rapid ascension of a new prime minister came a chance to define a new satirical characterisation almost from scratch. I tried to persuade the producer that John Major should be permanently grey, and although he said he thought this was 'a one-sketch idea', this was how the prime minister was eventually portrayed. It's strange the things that stick when you are caricaturing a politician. We wrote a sketch which opened with John and Norma sitting in an austere 1950s front room eating their dinner in embarrassed silence. The line 'More peas, John?' just made us all laugh and from then on every week we wrote another version of this excruciatingly awkward dinnertime where John and Norma ate nothing but peas. So John Major was grey, ate peas and later on had a crush on 'Ginny' Bottomley. Such was the savagery of our political satire.

But there has to be an element of truth to what you are saying. To have attempted to paint the new prime minister as an evil tyrant would never have worked. The unusual thing about John Major was that he came across as a disarmingly ordinary bloke, and after eleven years of hectoring from Margaret Thatcher the country was finding him rather a refreshing change. The

Conservatives' poll rating recovered and after he had posed with troops in the Gulf wearing what looked like a Marks and Spencer's khaki jumper he became the most popular prime minister since records began.

Two months into his premiership the Gulf War began and another piece of political good fortune had fallen into the Conservatives' lap. For years the Labour Party had been banging on about Saddam Hussein being an evil dictator to whom the Tory government should never have sold arms. Suddenly it seemed like the Conservatives had hijacked our baddie and were making political capital out of him. A lot of people on the left made the slightly glib point that we were only going to war over Kuwait because there was oil there. 'Why aren't Britain and America going to war to liberate Tibet?' lefties would say at meetings and everyone would agree and I'd think, Hang on – I don't want us to go to war against China, thank you very much – they've got nuclear missiles and 6,000 combat aircraft and a standing army of 2 million soldiers.

Saddam Hussein lost 'the mother of all battles' but was still in power long after George Bush had been sent packing, which is one of the many perks of being a fascist dictator. Like his ally across the Atlantic, John Major was legally obliged to face the electorate in 1992, and although he could have waited until the summer, the election was declared on 11 March and the next mother of all battles began. This was clearly going to be the closest-fought election since the 1970s and Labour started the campaign with a modest lead in the opinion polls. To be involved in an election in which Labour were the favourites was a new and very exciting experience.

In Battersea we were fighting to get Alf Dubs back into

the Commons, which was all the more reason to throw myself fully into the fray. On paper the arithmetic of Battersea looked promising. Labour would only need a tiny swing to overturn a majority of 857. But the gentrification had accelerated in the previous five years and now most of the skips in my road had made way for mud-splattered Golf GTis. Alf was not over-optimistic and Walworth Road, who last time round had refused to believe us when we said we were a Labour marginal, now wrote us off as a safe Tory seat. And yet, I thought, and yet – if Labour were ahead in the polls, surely we must have some chance of overturning a majority of 857? Perhaps my eternal optimism was a form of deliberate self-delusion: deep down I knew that I had to find motivation from somewhere and so I pretended to myself that we had a fair chance of victory.

The way the Labour Party fought elections was changing. The new computerised system of recording Labour voters was explained to Battersea party members who reacted with a great deal of grumbling and 'I don't like it' head-shaking. The Labour Party may be all for change in society, but in terms of how we like to organise ourselves or run election campaigns, no group could be more conservative. In the last week I was privately told we were not going to do it in Battersea. The canvass returns being typed into our new computer were falling well short in every ward, not enough people were saying they would vote for us. I gravely nodded and promised the agent that I would keep this to myself. For the last few days, I pushed people as hard as I could, sent them out in the rain and wind, gave them slightly more voters to canvass than they wanted, all in the knowledge that I was completely wasting their time. What else could I do?

Although I knew they were motivated by the same desire to improve the world as I was, I always felt incredibly grateful to the people who answered my pleas for helpers at election time, as if they were doing *me* a huge personal favour. For all the years that I organised elections in Queenstown ward, Liz Tomlinson didn't just leaflet her block or two or three blocks, she did the entire Savona Estate. It must have been nearly a whole day's leafleting which she unfailingly took off me for every election and every newsletter delivery in between. She never once said, 'Could I possibly *not* do five times more leaflets than everyone else this time?' I realised there must be thousands of Liz Tomlinsons all round the country, never letting the successive defeats stop them climbing the endless stairways, never even considering packing the whole thing in. My parents' local ward secretary ran their branch in Cookham for forty years. Forty years without even one little council by-election victory. No kudos or reward, no politician's ego or ambition, but like Liz Tomlinson just unfaltering commitment to the Labour Party. And while all these people were working so hard, in the middle of the general election campaign David Owen told everyone to vote Conservative – a man who owed his career in politics to the Labour Party then went and stabbed it in the back. David Owen, Liz Tomlinson put you to shame.

Although we didn't know it then, for the battle-weary foot-soldiers of Queenstown ward this would be the last election we fought together. It would have been nice to go out on a victory. Our hopes lay with the rest of the country. We were consistently if only marginally ahead in the polls and Labour's campaign was universally acclaimed as superior to the Tories'. The government went around proclaiming it had created hundreds of small businesses, although it neglected to add that these had previously been large businesses. The Tories also claimed that our spending plans would cost the country £35 billion, which was exactly the figure they had come up with in 1987 so somebody at central office must have gone, 'Ah, what the hell – it worked last time'. John Major, who had looked weak and ineffective throughout the campaign, laughably produced a soapbox to stand on which raised him just high enough above the heads of his minders for the egg throwers to score a direct hit every time. As the campaign reached a climax and I was driving with Mark past the hollow shell of County Hall the news came on the radio that three new polls gave Labour leads of 7 per cent, 6 per cent and 5 per cent.

'Yes!' said Mark triumphantly. We were on the way. It must have geed up Neil Kinnock as well. He was going to a rally in Sheffield.

Deep down if voters do not want to vote for you then any excuse will do: an embarrassing bit of rock-star posturing at a political rally in Sheffield, nonsense about the disintegration of the United Kingdom, or a few scare stories about tax. If these excuses not to vote Labour hadn't emerged then other reasons would have been found and endless post-election enquiries would have ensued into Glenys's hairdo or the hours that David Blunkett's dog was being made to work. But on that day we all believed that the country was finally going to turn its back on the Tories after thirteen miserable years. It was 1 April and it was the meanest April Fool anyone ever played on me.

The polls narrowed again in the last few days but I remained hopeful of victory on election day. As voting ended the poor bloody infantry who had worked so hard all day arrived back into my front room exhausted and excited. A strange chemical reaction happens on election day. The sweat of a whole day's knocking up mixed with adrenaline produces a ridiculous heady optimism that can only be neutralised by sitting down and watching *Election Special*. Phil arrived on his bike with a radio the size of a brazil nut stuck in his ear which I think he had bought especially for that five-minute cycle ride. 'The BBC exit poll is predicting a hung Parliament,' he said gloomily. 'But that would still be the end of thirteen years of Conservative rule,' I said and this cheered him up slightly.

We sat down to watch the results. People gratefully accepted pints of beer and glasses of wine and found what space they could on the floor or perched on the arms of sofas. I fussily adjusted the angle of the television, the colour and the volume, making sure that everything was absolutely perfect for the televisual treat we were about to enjoy. The BBC predicted that the Conservatives would be 25 seats short of an overall majority. Those words were such sweet music. It wasn't a Labour victory that I craved the most; it was a Conservative defeat. What would John Major say as he left Downing Street? I wondered. Which senior Tories would lose their seats as they were swept out of office? Jack Cunningham was interviewed from his count in Copeland and said that the Conservatives had suffered a humiliating defeat and been comprehensively rejected by the British people. In the studio David Mellor said that we should wait for the real results before making any judgements, but I thought he looked as if he knew the game was up.

Although the exit poll had shown only a 6 per cent swing to Labour, the swing had been estimated at 8 per cent in the marginals, which I noticed from Peter

Snow's swingometer would be just enough to give Labour an overall majority. Fourteen thousand people had taken part in the most sophisticated exit poll ever. Rather than simply ask them what they had just voted, the BBC had got them to put a cross on a duplicate ballot paper and place it in a BBC ballot box in total secrecy. No one was going to lie in a secret ballot, were they?

Reports from the various counts around the country started to come in. The SDP were about to be completely wiped out as Labour looked set to regain Greenwich, Woolwich and Devonport. The Tories were looking vulnerable in many of the key battleground areas, London, the West Midlands and the north west. It was accurately predicted that junior ministers Lynda Chalker and Christopher Chope would lose their seats, the latter getting a particular cheer in my front room since 'Chopper' Chope was a former leader of Wandsworth Council. The Tories would be reduced from ten to only three seats in Scotland, we were told, with Ian Lang and Michael Forsythe both set to be ejected. It was tantalising viewing. Occasionally the producer cut to Rory Bremner for some light relief, not realising that the show already had one of the country's top comedy performers in Peter Snow.

At around ten past eleven the first two results came in, both showing small swings to Labour. Snow's gangly frame leapt around the election battleground, his arms waving and his excited voice extrapolating these two results onto the 649 that had yet to come in. There were columns of blue bars behind him listing all the seats that Labour needed to win from the Conservatives. He told us that on the basis of the exit poll combined with the results in so far *this* was what was going to happen – a little pause while we held our breath – and then he pressed his little button and the wall turned a joyous shade of deep red behind him. The first column went red, the second column went red and halfway down the third column – after about eighty projected Labour gains, a few Tory seats stayed blue. Battersea, only eleventh in the first column, looked a Labour certainty. Our hearts were racing. It was a sort of political pornography, exciting us with the unattainable. For although we didn't know it, watching these imaginary Labour victories was to be the high point of our evening.

In the pit of my stomach was a growing knot of anxiety. The first results had not really been emphatic enough – a mere 2 per cent swing to Labour. Perhaps the swing might improve as the evening wore on. Then at twenty-five past eleven we cut to Basildon. A really thumping Labour majority here would see us well on course. Of the 97 seats that Labour needed to gain power, Basildon was thirty-third on our list. Something wasn't right. The Labour candidate on the platform wasn't smiling. The Tory was. The figures washed over me and suddenly Conservative MP David Amess was holding his arms aloft in victory. *Con Hold Basildon* flashed up on the screen, as if it wasn't obvious enough. Thank you, BBC, we can see that the Conservatives have held bloody bastard Basildon.

Basildon wasn't an especially good result for the Tories. It was just the time of the evening at which it came and the kind of electorate which it represented that left the name of Basildon permanently seared on the heart of every Labour supporter. It certainly wasn't the Tory seat that saw the greatest swing against Labour. The Great Election God was saving that particular honour for the constituency of Battersea. But the results from Basildon onwards confirmed Labour's failure. The

BBC had spent £20,000 on a huge 16-foot swing-ometer and it hardly swung at all. Tories held on by the skin of their buck teeth in dozens of key seats and regained all seven of their by-election defeats from the previous Parliament. *Con Hold Battersea* finally flashed up on the screen to confirm our agent's pessimistic prediction. It seemed to me that Alf's political career was effectively over. He had consistently said he was not optimistic but I realised, seeing this result flash up on the television, that he must have hoped deep down that he would get back into the House of Commons. I wished I'd gone to the count now, to be there to offer some words of consolation.

At half past twelve the BBC flashed up the caption *Conservatives Gain Overall Majority*. It felt like having the inside of your stomach kicked out. From bright optimism to total despair in two hours. The Tories were back in. I was totally disgusted with the British people. Peter Snow pressed his little button again and we saw the scale of Labour's failure as column after column of Tory marginals stayed blue. They looked like the lists of the dead from the First World War. Some party members left then. A seventeen-year-old boy and his friend walked home and somewhere between my house and his put a brick through a window with a Tory poster.

Still I clung to straws. An overall Tory majority of two or three seats might give us the chance to fight them again soon, but even that pathetic defeatist hope slipped away as Basildon was repeated again and again around the country, with the Tories even gaining the odd seat here and there. Watching Chris Patten lose in Bath was small consolation, although I felt at least there was some sort of cosmic justice at work; that the man who had organised this undeserved victory should pay with his own seat – perishing at his moment of victory like Nelson at Trafalgar.

In the early hours of the morning Neil and Glenys Kinnock arrived at Labour's headquarters in Walworth Road. Only a hundred or so people were left to hear him concede defeat. He came to the balcony ready to make a dignified speech but they couldn't find a working microphone. If he needed confirmation that he wasn't prime minister then this was it. Standing in front of a straggling band of dejected supporters in a god-awful street in south-east London waiting for somebody to fix the microphone.

When the Tory majority reached eighteen somebody in my front room said, 'Well, that's easily enough to see them through for five years!'

'Five years?' I said. 'Five years? You don't think they're just in power for five years, do you? That's it for ever. Today was our last chance. Like Wandsworth in '86 – we had our chance but we blew it and now we'll never get another chance again.'

Nobody could muster the optimism to disagree with me. If we couldn't turf out a government when the country was deep in recession, when interest rates were high, when millions were suffering from negative equity and businesses were folding at 1,200 a week, when the government looked weak and accident-prone, and when the Tories had run such a widely vilified election campaign, when exactly were we likely to beat them? Never, was the simple answer. Never, ever, ever.

The next morning I had to get up at about six o'clock to go and write the *Spitting Image* topicals which had been postponed from the usual Thursday. I had watched

Labour lose their fourth successive election, had a couple of hours' sleep, woken up with a hangover and then was supposed to go off and be funny. Great. One of the younger volunteers had been sick right across the kitchen floor and again into the sinkful of washing-up. I don't know whether he had drunk too much or whether he had just been watching the Young Conservatives celebrating outside Tory Party head-quarters. In the front room, sheets of paper and lists of voters were scattered everywhere. Glasses lay on their sides as stale beer soaked into the carpet. If we had won the night before this would have looked like the after-math of a fantastic victory party where wine was spilt and cigarettes were dropped all in the joyous cel-ebration of a new dawn for Britain. But of course it didn't look like that at all. The election had done to my front room what it had done to the country.

When I arrived at the *Spitting Image* studios I had no stomach for writing jokes or sketches and the five of us – three other writers and the producer – sat around in depressed disbelief, picking over the entrails of the defeat. We knew that by lunchtime they needed to start filming what we had written, but people who have suffered a major trauma need time just to talk it through. We talked and talked and talked, and then we realised that we had a lot to get off our chests and that we were in the unique position of being able to do this in front of millions of people. With emotions running high in the country and with so much anger coursing through our veins I think we ended up writing the best *Spitting Image* ever out of all the nine series I worked on. The producer Bill Dare had the idea of ending the show with Neil Kinnock going up to the attic and, on a dusty old piano, mournfully singing 'Everything's Coming Up

Roses'. More than one person told me they cried when they watched that.

With the topical portion of the show written, Mark, Pete and I sat outside a pub somewhere in Bayswater and talked about the prospect of living under perpetual Conservative rule. Positive Pete tried to raise our spirits. 'It's not just about elections. There are lots of ways to fight the Tories. Strikes, demonstrations, civil disobedience. If the Tories were all-powerful they wouldn't have got rid of Mrs Thatcher and abandoned the poll tax.' I wrote something along these lines in a letter to everyone who had helped in Queenstown ward, but I'm not sure I believed any of it.

On the Saturday I went to watch Fulham. Immersed in the game I temporarily forgot the disaster that had unfolded 36 hours earlier. We beat Bury 4–2 and as the supporters streamed out along Bishops Park Road a man playing tennis bounded up to the fence and in the poshest voice I had ever heard cheerfully shouted across to us, 'What was the score?' Normally, if your team has won, this is information you're keen to volunteer. But his accent brought the crowd back to the grim reality of what had happened. Somebody behind me said to him, 'Oh, fuck off, Tory!' Then somebody else further ahead of me said, 'Yeah, fuck off, Tory', and everyone in the passing throng murmured agreement. I've never seen anyone look so completely dumbstruck.

A couple of weeks later I had everyone round for a party. We were all about to go our separate ways. Phil and Eileen had originally got their flats on the Patmore Estate as GLC 'hard to let' properties when they were in their twenties. By now they were both ready to move somewhere nicer. Phil had got fed up with having his front door regularly smashed down and having the burglar go straight to the drawer where he kept his dope. Our chair bought his first home in another part of Battersea. Jackie and I bought a house in Clapham. When middle-class Labour activists reach their thirties they move to streets where most of the other residents vote Conservative. Although this gathering was really intended for old friends to commiserate together in private I thought it might be a good idea to invite along a couple of the new members that we had picked up during the election campaign. The more they were involved, I thought, the more likely they were to take over the reins of running the party. It was not one of my better ideas. The new couple arrived pissed and grew increasingly offensive as the evening wore on. Eventually a shouting match developed between one of our long-standing members and the woman I had taken it upon myself to invite. As it got louder and increasingly personal and abusive, more and more people tiptoed out of the room and into the kitchen where we attempted to make casual chit-chat and pretend we couldn't hear the sound of shouting and swearing coming down the hallway. It was the last time we were all together. It was supposed to be a fond farewell, but fate was against us till the last. A year or two later I heard that Queenstown ward Labour Party had ceased to operate as an organisation.

As I left the borough and surveyed the political landscape that I left behind, I couldn't help asking myself what had been the point of being a Labour Party activist. What had I achieved? My mum threw her energy into Amnesty International. She organised flag days, wrote letters and sent telegrams. Sometimes a prisoner of conscience was released. An innocent person who'd been arrested and possibly tortured in some faraway country was returned to their family. Now that is something worth giving up your evenings for. I walked away from my corner of Battersea leaving it with two Tory councillors, a secure Tory MP and no functioning ward Labour Party to take our place. For all the years that I had been an active member of the party, could I honestly point to a single human being and say that I had made that person's life tangibly better? For all my efforts, all my ward notices and dreary meetings in draughty halls and Sunday mornings spent walking up smelly stairwells, no job was ever saved, no eviction was prevented, no school or hospital kept open, and certainly no Tory government ever voted out of office. Had it all been worth it? How could the answer be anything but no?

Bacon is delicious

Labour Leadership Election – 18 July 1992

I used to really love bacon before I was a vegetarian. Sizzling smoked streaky bacon, fresh from the frying pan, with a fried egg and a couple of fried tomatoes. Perfect. But of course my commitment to the Church of Labour Party Activists involved a certain amount of self-denial, which for my particular sect included not eating our dear comrades from the animal kingdom. Mark would regularly come into work with a bacon and tomato roll and my mouth would water as the smell wafted across the room. Sometimes he would leave a bit and I would observe him with the same forlorn expression that my dog wore as she watched me scrape my leftovers into the bin. I would have loved some bacon, but I had worked out long ago that eating meat simply could not be justified on political grounds.

But strange things started to happen to me after Labour's defeat in 1992. The little enamel Labour Party badge that I had always worn on the top left-hand pocket of my Levi's jacket was replaced with a badge for

Fulham FC. I started to turn straight to the sports pages of the paper instead of the politics. My subscriptions to *Tribune* and *New Statesman* lapsed. And then one day I walked out of my front door, into the café and ordered bacon and egg. Without any hesitation or sense of guilt I cut off a little slice of bacon, dipped it in the egg yolk and popped it in my mouth. It was delicious. Ten years I had denied myself this pleasure. Ten long years of adding vindaloo curry paste to baked beans in a vain attempt to make them less insufferably dreary. I was never one of life's natural vegetarians. It's not as if I particularly like vegetables.

The arguments had not changed. I still understood that meat production was an inefficient use of agricultural resources which contributed to Third World poverty and that the cereal it took to produce one steak could produce x hundred loaves of bread, that factory farming was cruel, that eating meat increased your chances of heart disease, and that meat was often unhygienically stored and transported and harboured all sorts of dangerous forms of food poisoning. But ranged against all these valid arguments was the incontrovertible fact that bacon was delicious. And so was chicken tikka masala and roast lamb with mint sauce and Peking duck wrapped in those little pancakes with the sliced spring onions and hoisin sauce. By the end of the week I had feasted upon all of them. Big Macs remained beyond the pale of political correctness and fortunately for me they were still disgusting as well.

I had always known it was impossible for one person to change the world on their own. But I felt so bitter about the outcome of the 1992 election that I stopped particularly trying. The Conservatives had won. Pathetic to admit, but with that final blow of John

Major's 21-seat majority they had beaten me. I just didn't have the stomach to keep throwing so much hope and passion into fights that I kept losing. Shame on me, really. Demonstrations always seemed to clash with planned expeditions to Sainsbury's Homebase to get bunny wallpaper for baby's bedroom. Answerphone messages from my new local Labour Party asking for leaflet deliverers must have somehow wiped themselves. Then when my weekly five-a-side football game was moved to the same night as ward meetings, I had to choose one or the other. After not very much soul-searching I didn't do what I *ought* to do, I did what I *wanted* to do. To be honest it felt rather liberating.

I was quite open about my surrender to the Tories. I still knew that they had to be fought every day by every means possible. I just wouldn't be taking part myself any more that's all. Jackie and I had our first child and were decorating our new house, and I was more pre-occupied than ever with my work, but I am not going to lie and pretend that I had become too busy to carry on helping the Labour Party. I was still a member but I stopped being a die-hard activist because I was made of weaker stuff than all those thousands of valiant souls who continued to fight the good fight.

And so for a couple of years after 9 April 1992 I didn't knock on a single door or deliver a single leaflet. During the campaign the Tories had described Labour's tax plans as Labour's 'double whammy'. But the real double whammy of the 1992 election was the result. Not only did the electorate unexpectedly return a Tory government, but by destroying the credibility of opinion polls, they also denied me the hope that used to keep me going between Conservative election victories. In the dark days of the 1980s and early 1990s the *Guardian* and

Observer used to regularly cheer me up by printing polls declaring that the government was now less popular than scabies. Now every such survey was dismissed with a contemptuous tut. The maths of converting Labour's poll leads into projected Parliamentary majorities had been proved to be a spiritual exercise rather than a scientific one.

Of course lying to opinion pollsters was nothing new. The results of every opinion poll that I could remember went like this:

> What do you currently consider to be the most important political issue?
> Answer 1) Unemployment 2) The Health Service 3) Education.
> Which party do you consider has the best policy on those issues?
> Answer 1) Labour 2) Labour 3) Labour.

And then they regularly went out and voted Conservative. For some reason, when people were asked what they considered to be the most important issues, no one volunteered the true answer, 'my wallet', or 'how rich I am' or 'keeping an extra few pence back from the tax man and living in a shitty run-down country as a result'. People felt so guilty about the way they were voting that they lied to pollsters *and even lied to themselves* in the secret ballot at the exit polls. They did not vote for any positive national interest or grand social plan – there was no exciting vision of Britain that the intellectually exhausted Tories could offer them. Yet 14 million people went out and voted JM 4 PM. That's more people than ever voted for Clem Attlee or Lloyd George or Mrs Thatcher or Winston Churchill. All

278

that seemed to matter was money – and in the kingdom of accountants, John Major was king.

Despite the amazing feat he pulled off in winning the 1992 election, Major still came across as a man who would have been over-promoted if he'd been made manager of a motorway service station. His big idea was a Citizens' Charter which said that public officials should have little badges with their names on. This provision had been carelessly left out of the Magna Carta and the Bill of Rights in 1689. John Major's other supposed greatest triumph was that he negotiated an opt-out from the European social chapter. We were supposed to be patriotic about the fact that we were the only country in the EC that did not have a minimum wage or the right to join a union. Hurrah! Wave that plastic Union Jack – we've got the lowest-paid workers in Western Europe!

That was the level to which our country had sunk. A place where the establishment attempted to revive our fading patriotism with damaging anti-Europeanism, the preservation of self-conscious royal pageantry and contrived anniversaries of events in the Second World War. Our future lay in our past. Meanwhile in the real Britain people were grubbing out a living making Japanese cars or serving up American fast food. That summer I went into a branch of McDonald's when they were doing a special promotion on some sort of Chinese McFood. Everyone behind the counter had to wear cardboard Chinese hats except for the manager who happened to be the only white person there. It was a sort of surreal vision of twentieth-century multinational imperialism: a white man in a shirt and tie shouting, 'Faster, work faster, come on!' at a lot of black people in overalls and cardboard Chinese hats. It was John Major's Britain.

After the 1992 election Neil Kinnock did what I did not have the courage to do and left this depressing cowardly country altogether. He resigned the leadership to become an EC commissioner and he suddenly had the air of a man with a huge burden lifted off his shoulders. He appeared on *Have I Got News For You* and for once he was on the winning side. He was confident and relaxed and I remember wishing that he could have come across so well before the election.

John Smith seemed the automatic choice to inherit the party leadership. His profile had been deliberately raised in the run-up to the 1992 campaign to try to attract some of the flak away from Neil Kinnock. As Labour's luck would have it, a poll was commissioned to show that we would gain enough support to win the election if Kinnock resigned in favour of John Smith, so our leader was made to look even more of a liability. Some commentators suggested that it was Smith's shadow budget that had exposed Labour to criticism of its spending plans. But I still voted for John Smith because the papers that were making this claim were the same ones that had lied so shamelessly about his tax proposals during the election campaign. No doubt they were already 'gathering evidence' of hundreds of sex scandals involving him. After all, 'John Smith' was written in the register of every dodgy hotel in the country. I knew that Smith was slightly older than Kinnock, but when I heard that he had been a minister in the last Labour government I couldn't quite believe it. By my reckoning that made him about 112. There were one or two rumblings about the wisdom of choosing a leader with a heart condition but these were dismissed out of hand. Smith won the ballot with 86 per cent of the vote. Bryan Gould took his overwhelming defeat very well apart from resigning his seat and going to live in New Zealand.

Smith inherited a party which was totally demoralised and unsure what else it could possibly do to try to win elections. But of course the general rule is that oppositions don't win elections, governments lose them. Fortunately this government set out in a very determined fashion to lose the next election in some style. They wasted no time – on 16 September 1992, 'Black Wednesday', Norman Lamont spent £15 billion of Britain's reserves trying to bolster the level of sterling artificially. As if buying millions of ten-pound notes at £20 each would make the ten-pound notes worth more. Those were the billions we had been told we did not have to spend on hospitals, schools and training. Suddenly it was all thrown away in a day. This was apparently not a serious enough mistake for him to feel that he ought to perhaps resign. If he had been caught releasing deadly poisonous gas on tube trains he would not have felt it was a resigning issue. There are some people whose genius allows you to forgive their arrogance. Norman Lamont was not one of them.

Such was the strength of feeling that Lamont should be dismissed that the issue refused to go away and a full nine months later he was eventually sacked. This was the pattern of Tory resignations throughout this Parliament. First the scandal, then blind refusal to walk, some dithering from John Major apparently unsure whether he should sack one of his ministers or not, then increasing pressure and then finally the resignation. They all ended up doing the honourable thing without any honour whatsoever. David Mellor, Neil Hamilton, Tim Smith, Stephen Norris, Michael Mates, David Willets ... each looking shabbier than the last and reinforcing the impeccable trustworthy image of John Smith. Only one minister managed to escape this pattern. In May 1994 Nicholas Scott admitted that he had misled Parliament but refused to step down. What's more he had misled Parliament over a shameful attempt by his department to block a bill that would outlaw discrimination against disabled people. The pressure grew. John Major initially stood by him but then went ominously quiet and even Scott's daughter (who worked for a charity for the disabled) said her father should resign. I reckoned it would be about 24 hours before he was gone. Nothing would deflect the media from this scandal. John Smith was said to be really fired up about it. But twenty-four hours later Nicholas Scott was not gone. John Smith was. It was the morning of 12 May 1994. One hour after having a heart attack in the bath John Smith was declared dead.

Deaths of famous people are announced on the news on a regular basis. Sometimes you are briefly saddened but usually their passing does not seem particularly inappropriate. Sometimes you're even surprised they hadn't died ages ago. But John Smith's death was sudden, unexpected and somehow just *wrong*. I felt as if I had lost a favourite relative. His life was cut short before his best work could be done and when the Labour victory for which he had worked for so long was finally within our grasp. Everyone was shocked and deeply saddened (except secretly, perhaps, Nicholas Scott, who must have been glancing around wondering what happened to the baying media pack that had been closing in on him).

As a leader Smith had given us hope. For the first time in my adult life Labour had a leader who really looked like a future prime minister. Though Neil Kinnock had done so much to make the party electable (and Blair conceded his own victory could never have been achieved without him), it had always been hard to imagine Neil waving on the steps of Downing Street. Smith had a certain unflappable solidity that made you want to trust him with the nation's finances. Now it seemed our greatest asset had been taken from us.

Inappropriately, but unavoidably, my thoughts turned to the succession. However, my concern now was not just as an ordinary Labour Party member but as a courtier to one of the claimants to the throne. I could not help but be excited that the man I thought could well become the next Labour leader was someone Mark and I had got to know quite well in the previous few years. Someone we regularly met up with, someone who rang up to run his speeches past me, someone who sent me a Christmas card every year. Was the next prime minister really going to be a man *I* wrote jokes for?

My party, right or left

Lambeth Council Elections – 5 May 1994

I have never played football with Gary Lineker or had a game of chess with Nigel Short. However, I did once attempt to discuss economics with Gordon Brown. Fairly quickly I realised that Gordon has a brain roughly the size of Canada. He told me of the complex and inter-locking difficulties that modern high-technology economies face in an ever more open marketplace and about the need for supply-side measures to stimulate investment in the regions. And I gave him the same nod of earnest concentration that I used to give my maths teacher when she explained quadratic equations. I understood what each of the words meant individually, it was just when I heard them all in a row that I was struggling a bit. I tried to come up with my own criti-cism of the government's economic policies, but I decided that Gordon would not be over-impressed with my observation that the new five-pence coin was much too small and fiddly. If you ever happen to find yourself in the situation where you are discussing economics with the next Labour chancellor of the exchequer, I would recommend that if he is drinking mineral water you should avoid having several pints of lager because this gives him an even more unfair advantage.

This meeting had been the idea of Geoff Mulgan who worked in Gordon Brown's office. My friend and local councillor Phil was going out with Geoff's sister (before Phil decided it would be more right-on to become gay). Geoff had thought that as a Labour supporter I might be up for donating the occasional gag to pep up a speech or two. Before you could say 'tragic political groupies', Mark and I were sitting on the terrace of the House of Commons chatting with Gordon about what sort of jokes he might be looking for. An old face from Battersea Labour Party happened to walk past and looked rather surprised to see me sitting there having a beer with Labour's Trade and Industry spokesman. If she hadn't spotted me I probably would have stood on the table, shouted her name and waved my arms until she did.

We gave Gordon some new jokes and one or two that had been rejected by Clive Anderson or the *Spitting Image* producer. We were always careful to type them out again in case we got careless and he ended up opening a conference speech with the lines, 'Hello and welcome to *Clive Anderson Talks Back* ...' Every few months after that we would meet up with Labour's fastest-rising star to bounce ideas and soundbites back and forth while Mark and I inhaled the scent of approaching power. He would make us feel valued and then he'd tell us some of the jokes he and his assistants had written and we'd realise that most of the time we were pretty surplus to requirements. I suppose it was precisely because he had a creative sense of humour that he appreciated that he might be able to use a couple of experienced comedy hacks to polish the gags he'd written or add a few jokes of our own. But he was always fulsome in his thanks and generous with the bottles of House of Commons whisky, and we were more than happy to turn up in the vain hope that we might get a sneak preview of an important policy announcement or witness a heated telephone conversation with some shadow minister who had carelessly made a rash spending promise. On one occasion Tony Blair wandered in and said hello, and we said hello back, then Gordon and Tony exchanged a few words about a policy matter that went completely over our heads before Tony said goodbye to us and left again. Since that meeting I've always felt that Tony Blair and I have a special sort of friendship.

I was impressed that Gordon generally telephoned us himself, rather than getting some minion to track us down and announce that they had Gordon Brown on the line for us. Once Mark's daughter answered the telephone and Gordon did his best to pursue a conversation with a three-year-old girl before she dropped the receiver on the floor and told her dad that 'Gordy Bran' was on the phone. After our meetings or chats on the phone we might fax him a few more lines, which we would always end with the line 'My name's Gordon Brown – thank you, good night!' I'm sure Gordon would have preferred it had we never told anyone that we wrote the occasional joke for him, but what's the point of writing gags for a top politician if you can't brag about it to fellow comedy writers and give your mum and dad something to be proud about? After a recording of *Have I Got News For You* I introduced my father to Ian Hislop. Dad's opener was: 'Have you told Ian that you write jokes for Gordon Brown?'

'No, Dad, when somebody prefers me to be discreet about something, I tend not to tell the editor of *Private Eye.*'

Because he wasn't paying us and because we were krazy komedy writers we were somehow allowed to be a little less respectful than most of the people he had around him. When he commented that *Spitting Image* was being very cruel in its depiction of Gerald Kaufman, I said, 'You wait till next week, Gordon – we're doing *you* as a serial killer.' His face froze in terror until Mark's laughter made him realise I was winding him up. Our sessions with him were always light-hearted and convivial, but if he was rung up with a problem he would switch directly into the mode of fierce and combative operator. He struck me as intelligent, personable, witty, dedicated and driven. Part man, part machine – all politician.

At the beginning of the 1992 election campaign we turned up at his temporary office just as it was being swept for bugs. We talked for a while about the themes of Labour's line of attack upon the Tories and gave him a few jokes about Norman Lamont's tax-cutting budget. ('Norman Lamont tells British industry, 2p off!' – © *Benny Hill 1971* – I can't imagine why Gordon didn't use it.) On the way out I handed one of his researchers details of the Tories' planned advertising assault upon the Labour Party, which I had persuaded someone I knew at Saatchi and Saatchi's to spy out for me. The researcher later told me that my friend and I were the only source of information the Labour Party had about the Tories' poster campaign. It felt quite exciting to be the central link in a spy network.

Despite the major setback that it must have been to his own hopes, Gordon took the disappointment of the 1992 defeat far better than I did. Then came Black Wednesday and he seemed fired up with genuine anger at the government's incompetence. He told me that they were looking for a phrase that would tie Major and Lamont together, that said they were *both* responsible for this monumental fiasco so Major wouldn't get off the hook when Lamont was inevitably sacked. At the Labour Party conference that month I faxed him a line about Major and Lamont being 'the Laurel and Hardy of British politics' and the soundbite was passed on to John Smith's speech writers. Suddenly the phrase was on every news bulletin and conference report. The *Daily Mirror* did a front-page photo-montage of Major and Lamont as Laurel and Hardy and they sent a couple of Laurel and Hardy look-alikes down to the Tory Party conference. I felt so proud. I framed the front cover of the *Daily Mirror* for my office but stopped short of putting it up because I wondered if this might be perhaps a little bit naff. Especially as I later heard that someone else claimed credit for this soundbite so it's quite possible that we both came up with it. 'Success has many fathers but failure is an orphan.' (About a dozen writers claim that line as well.)

From Black Wednesday onwards John Major's government lurched from crisis to crisis. One neutral observer suggested I must at least concede that Mrs Thatcher was better than this lot. I replied that I'd still rather have John Major's policy of drifting hopelessly towards the rocks than Thatcher's policy of heading towards them at full speed. But it was comforting that somebody who might have voted Conservative a few years back was convinced that we badly needed a change of government. Once again I was letting my optimism get the better of me. The Conservatives were scoring own goals on a regular basis. Not just 'deflect it into the net' own goals, but spectacular 'dribble past three defenders and cannon in it into the top left-hand corner' own goals.

The Tories' local-election base had been whittled away every year until by 1994 'base' was perhaps too generous a word for what remained. It was more a crumbling toehold. When you heard that the Conservatives had lost control of Tunbridge Wells in the local elections in May of that year you got the warm feeling that they were in deep trouble. Other true-blue bastions like Epping Forest, Hertsmere, Basingstoke and Southend also fell. However, there was one exception to Labour's excellent set of results that night. It seems wretchedly appropriate that the last Labour wipe-out of its eighteen years in opposition should occur in the borough where I was working.

Somehow I had managed to move from the most famous Conservative borough to the most infamous Labour borough. I had thought that by quietly slipping across the border I might now be able to keep out of local politics. But like any religious cult, the Church of Labour Party Activists does not let you go that easily. Eileen Hogan, my former councillor in Queenstown ward, had also moved to Clapham and she told her new party, 'John O'Farrell? Oh yeah, he's been ward secretary, chair, membership secretary, election organiser, everything ... He'll do something for the local elections.'

And mainly because I was too embarrased to say no, I was on the doorstep again. Only now when people said, 'Why should I vote Labour in Lambeth after the mess they've left things in?', I could only shrug my shoulders and say that I completely understood why

289

they should feel like that. If they hadn't already slammed the door, I might apologetically add that if we got back in there would be a new Labour team running the borough and that I could personally vouch for the character of the candidates in Clapham Town ward. But nothing damages a political party as much as the whiff of corruption – except perhaps having me working for them. 'It's meltdown in Lambeth' was how the jubilant Liberals described the result on the television on the night of 5 May. Labour lost over a third of its council seats. Fortunately the Tories gained only one seat off us in the whole borough. Unfortunately it was the ward in which I was running the committee rooms.

Early in the morning I had spent a couple of hours sitting outside a polling station collecting voters' numbers. There are not many occasions when you sit for two hours on a plastic chair in the middle of an empty school playground with a complete stranger. If I could choose the sort of person that I'd like to do this with, Conservative Party activists would be fairly near the bottom of the list. Why do they imagine I could possibly want to discuss politics with them?

> 'You have to admit that the leader of the Labour Party is always going to have to do whatever the union bosses tell him.'
> 'Oh really? Gosh, I had never thought about it before, thank you for putting me straight on that – do you have an application form to join the Conservative Party?'

A few days later this fascinating man passed me in the street and I was forced to smile and nod politely as he said, 'Ha! We nicked a seat off you in this ward, didn't we!' Thankfully in every part of Britain except Clapham, the Tories had very little to feel pleased about.

Labour scored their most crushing defeat over the Tories in any local elections since the war. The Tories' share of the vote was down to 27 per cent, level pegging with the Liberal Democrats. One Conservative MP offered himself as a stalking horse to stand against the accident-prone John Major. In comforting contrast, John Smith looked like such a safe pair of hands.

Then one week later, on 12 May, all was uncertainty again. The political situation was in flux, Labour's fortunes could go either way. And given Labour's propensity to snatch defeat from the jaws of victory, I wouldn't have been surprised if we had chosen Fred West as our next leader.

It seemed disrespectful to think about who would succeed John Smith, but it was so important I couldn't help it. No doubt the same thing was happening to the leading candidates. While mourning their friend and colleague, they had simultaneously to manoeuvre for political advantage against one another in the imminent race to replace him. It takes an especially strange mind to get to the very top in politics.

My immediate reaction was that Gordon must be the next in line. The man Mark and I occasionally met up with, the man to whom I had thrown questions in preparation for a *Newsnight* interview, the man who got us tickets for Labour Party conference and bought me drinks and introduced me to senior Labour MPs would quite likely be the next prime minister. I had this vision of sitting by the fire in Downing Street, making him chuckle with our pithy put-downs of the leading Tories. But much to my amazement the papers were all talking about Tony Blair. It seemed to be obvious to everyone except me who was going to win this election. Much like any other election really.

For years Gordon Brown and Tony Blair had been inseparable. So much so that I had once even suggested to the producer of *Spitting Image* that we make one puppet with their two heads on it. Fortunately for my later hobnobbing, this idea was never taken up. I didn't speak to Gordon during that month, but it is well documented that he wrestled with the possibility of standing against his friend and even made a speech to test the media and party reaction to a possible Brown leadership bid. In the end he took Tony Blair out to a restaurant in Islington where he told his oldest political ally (who had very much risen in Gordon's shadow) that he would stand aside for him. I hope Tony paid for the dinner.

The media had crowned Blair leader before Labour Party members had even received their ballot papers. John Smith's legacy had been 'one member one vote', but when it came to exercising the right on which he had staked his leadership it felt like that decision had already been taken for me. I rather resented this *fait accompli* and sulkily ignored my ballot paper until true to form I missed the deadline by which it had to be returned.

In 1963 Wilson had won the leadership of the Labour Party on the sudden death of Hugh Gaitskell and became prime minister on the wave of optimism on the left which rapidly evaporated once they saw him in office. Tony Blair was not going to make the same mistake – he was getting his disillusionment in early. At his first Labour conference he told the party (albeit in code) that he intended to do what Gaitskell had failed to do – abolish Clause Four, Part IV of the Labour Party's constitution. This was written on the back of every Labour

Party membership card that I had received down the years (and, tragically, I had kept them all). *To secure for the workers by hand or by brain the full fruits of their industry and the most equitable distribution thereof that may be possible upon the basis of the common ownership of the means of production, distribution and exchange, and the best obtainable system of popular administration and control of each industry or service.* OK, so it didn't read too well, but he didn't have to abolish it. Mark and I would have been more than happy to gag it up a bit.

The era of Labour as the party of state intervention was over. Labour was now openly committed to a compassionate management of capitalism, if such a thing is possible. Not just because Tony Blair was determined that it should be this way, but because the rank and file of the Labour Party were so exhausted and demoralised at losing so many elections that we were prepared to let him do it. I was not against changing the Labour Party *per se*, in fact I used to get annoyed with the knee-jerk hostility that greeted every new idea. But abandoning Clause Four was not some cosmetic re-packaging exercise – this was a major wrench for the Labour Party. For the teachers and local government workers who populated the party in London, this was the most disorientating betrayal since Bob Dylan went electric. I suppose the proposition should have made me angry but to do that it would have had to have been surprising. The Parliamentary road to socialism had been closed off years ago, and anyway four successive election defeats had already left me with the distinct feeling that the nationalisation of the banks was not around the corner. I was attached to Clause Four for its nostalgic, symbolic value – it proclaimed to the world that, once upon a time at least, we were a left-wing party.

At a special conference at Westminster Hall in April 1995 delegates voted on the leader's proposal for a new mission statement for the people's party. In my bones was the worry that however many concessions we made to the right it would never be enough. Next we would be declared unelectable because of our links with the unions or because of our support for a minimum wage, and one by one each worthwhile commitment that we stood for would be chipped away. I avoided reading about the ongoing debate in the papers and once again bottled out of voting on the issue. I wasn't sure enough that Tony Blair was wrong to oppose the change openly. I suppose deep down I was really saying, If you think that's what it will take to get rid of this lot then so be it. Do what you have to do, Tony; I'll pretend I wasn't looking.

And soon it wasn't the Labour Party any more, it was *New Labour*. Every few weeks Tony Blair would shock us with another even more audacious abandonment of Labour baggage. He seemed to place no value in Labour's traditions. It was traditional that conference decided policy, it was traditional that the leader went to the Durham Miners gala, it was traditional that we, er, lost general elections. None of this meant anything to Tony Blair. Even *I* had better Labour credentials than he did. We had both stood as candidates in school mock elections, but at least I had stood for the Labour Party. I bet he'd never even thrown darts at a picture of Margaret Thatcher.

A few people I know resigned from the Labour Party during this period, but I never even contemplated it – Labour was my party, right or left. I still believed that it represented the best hope of improving the lives of the people of this country. But beyond that there is a tribalism to British politics which bound me to Labour whether I cheered Tony Benn or Tony Blair. I had hated the SDP and the betrayal I thought they stood for. But now that we had moved into the centre and I was a member of what was effectively a social democratic party, I celebrated our every by-election triumph. That summer I got chatting to an old man in a pub in the west of Ireland about politics. 'Tell me,' I asked him, 'what exactly is the difference between Fine Gael and Fianna Fail?'

'Ah, well, that's easy,' he said. 'It's the difference between shit and shite.'

His cynicism reminded me of a country not a million miles away.

By now Mark and I had left *Spitting Image* and were writing for *Have I Got News For You*. *Spitting Image*'s power to shock and surprise diminished with each passing year and after nine exhausting series we felt it was time to move on. A couple of series later the show was axed altogether. I was bequeathed a Maggie Thatcher puppet which stares at me every morning as I come down the stairs. When small children visit we have to lock it away because it frightens them. They're lucky they never experienced the real thing.

Working in television brought with it the questionable perk of meeting all sorts of politicians over the years. After recordings of *Clive Anderson Talks Back* I'd attempted small talk with Ted Heath, Nicholas Ridley and even Norman Tebbit – and I was struck how they all had an air of bitterness about them. I once appeared on a TV debate show opposite John Prescott who wanted us to justify our portrayal of him on *Spitting Image*. It's a bit hard to say to someone's face on live television, 'Let's face it, John, you're not exactly Lord Snooty are you?' We had a good-natured drink with Prescott afterwards, but when I commented that Bryan Gould had come up with an excellent joke about Heseltine's relationship with Major ('the blond leading the bland'), Prescott's face froze over. In an instant I thought how much politicians were like so many of the TV celebrities I'd met – fine as long as they were the centre of attention, but never keen to hear praise for any of their contemporaries.

In 1996, as John Major's disastrous government entered its final year, we had another election in Clapham Town ward. A test of the political winds on my own doorstep. One of our councillors resigned to return to his native Ireland and Eileen was persuaded to stand in his place. Ten years after I had fought to get her on to the council in Wandsworth, here she was prepared to do it all again. Would the Tories capitalise on their recent gain in the ward? Would the Liberals add another Labour scalp to their Lambeth collection? Having phoned Eileen to encourage her to stand, I then loyally failed to do much more than a little bit of leafleting and a couple of nights' canvassing. Ten years ago she and Phil had bought me a personal stereo for all my hard work in getting them elected. If she failed now, she would be more than entitled to ask for it back.

But by now I was the father of two children: a boy aged three and a half and a girl of eighteen months. And if ever a clearer indication were needed of where my deepest loyalties now lay, I had to stop knocking up on the night of the by-election because our youngest child was falling rather frighteningly ill. All thoughts of local elections were long gone by the time the doctor diagnosed her as having pneumonia. The only political thought that went through my head in the entire three days that she was recovering in St Thomas's Hospital was: I've spent years saying the NHS is in a terrible state and actually, it's fantastic.

When my family life had returned to normal I learnt that Eileen had won the by-election and done so very convincingly. Even in Lambeth the voters were coming to Tony Blair's remarketed party in droves. New Labour, New Lambeth, Same Councillor I had in Wandsworth. With no party in overall control, Labour and the Liberals were running the council in a sort of unofficial pact. It had always been very easy to be in opposition – not to have to justify anything that was happening in Westminster or in the town hall, just to assure voters that you would do it a lot better. But now that I had a friend in power I found myself nervous of criticising some of the things she had to oversee. The concerts on Clapham Common were leaving broken glass everywhere, the library at the bottom of my road was facing cuts, the consultation on residents' parking was a shambles – and I would bump into her and feel embarrassed at mentioning some of these things. It was all so much easier when the Tories had control of everything. I realised I had only been programmed for opposition. I was like one of those long-term prisoners who can't cope with their new-found freedom. A terrifying thought went through my head as we entered election year. If John Major somehow achieved another miracle and won it for the Conservatives, was there a little part of me that would be more comfortable with that?

It's a wonderful life

Halifax Building Society Conversion Ballot
– 23 February 1997

The last vote I cast during Labour's eighteen years of
opposition was in the Perfect Election. Somehow it
symbolised everything that had gone before. Obviously
I was on the losing side, that was by now a given, but
the defeat of the left's position meant that from a purely
personal point of view I ended up substantially better
off.

The Halifax Building Society was balloting its
members on its proposed conversion into a bank, a
process which would mean large windfall payments to
all its members if it went ahead. Ever since Jimmy
Stewart had tried to save the 'Buildings & Loans' in *It's
a Wonderful Life* I had had rather a romantic idea about
building societies. Now it seemed that they wanted
to turn them into banks so they could lend money to
fascist dictatorships and charge people £20 for letters
telling them they were £10 overdrawn. The moral path
was clear. With a Paddy Ashdown-type sanctimonious

sneer I cast my vote *against* the mercenary route of conversion. I did this safe in the knowledge that a huge majority of the other members would eagerly vote for the free money, and that a large cheque would soon be winging its way towards my bank account. I never checked the small print but I thought it unlikely there'd be a clause stating that anybody making a hopeless principled stand against conversion will not of course get any free Halifax shares. It was the best of both worlds, the archetype middle-class left-winger's election: I occupied the moral high ground and then waited for a cheque to arrive.

It was like railing against Wandsworth's zero poll tax, or Lawson's tax-cutting budget. You knew there must be a greater cost for someone down the line, but you secretly comforted yourself with your own personal good fortune in the meantime. When I was in my twenties my friends and I agreed that the answer to Britain's social problems was to tax high earners. Now when I had the same conversation with my contemporaries, we would still agree that the government should tax the better off, but this assertion would be followed by a nervous pause, after which we would agree that 'better off' meant about five grand a year more than we were currently earning.

I could not pretend that I had personally suffered under the Tories. In fact as a would-be political satirist it seemed that John Major's government had consistently gone out of its way to assist me. In oppressive dictatorships they locked up and tortured people who mocked the government. In Britain, they paid them more than they deserved, gave them big lunches and cars home until they were as bloated and comfortable as the establishment they were supposed to despise. The latter approach was surely a far cleverer way of neutering criticism.

And what had my years as a Labour Party activist left me with? A few old badges, some stubs for the 1991 Christmas raffle that I still hadn't sent back, and a thorough knowledge of the parts of Battersea and Clapham that I would never visit through choice. I also had a large book which listed thousands of Iranian names. I had once proposed a motion on behalf of the exiled Iranian opposition which became Battersea Labour Party's motion to the party conference that year. As a token of their thanks the Iranian delegation presented me with a book that listed all the people who had been murdered by the Ayatollah's regime. As if that wasn't grim enough, every few pages between the unrelenting columns of names were pictures of young men hanging by their necks from hydraulic cranes that had been quickly converted into temporary gallows. I thanked them for the book and told them they shouldn't have. Really, a small box of chocolates would have been fine. The book did not stay long on my coffee table. Neither did it really look right on the shelf next to the redundant vegetarian cookery books. Now it lives in a special drawer for things that I can't throw away but I will never ever need again, between a bag of foreign coins and the presentation box that my wrist-watch came in.

I suppose the important things I have taken from my years as a Labour Party activist are not tangible. Experience in managing and motivating people, an understanding of political procedures, tolerance of seemingly pointless meetings, an awareness of the limitations of how much we can individually achieve – these are all now part of my psychological make-up.

More significantly I am left with the certain knowledge that other people's lives can be improved through the existing political system, whether on a local or national level, and that we all have a moral obligation to try to make this happen. Just voting is not enough. Buying the *Big Issue* is not enough. However foreboding it may seem, all of us have a duty actively to do *something* to help other people – whether it's spending a night answering the phones for the Samaritans or taking part in a fancy-dress charity fun run (personally I think I'd find the latter more depressing).

I have also made some lasting friendships. When I moved to London aged 22 and became active in the Labour Party I suddenly got to know lots of like-minded people who lived in my area. Some had moved on, some had fallen out of politics and some now shamed me with their unwavering commitment. Others were about to become MPs. Fiona was selected to fight Slough, a couple of miles from where I grew up. Martin Linton had the slightly harder task of winning back Battersea, and the chances of this were regularly discussed on the terraces at Craven Cottage. I think he was the only person in Britain more interested in psephology than me. When Fulham were playing Mansfield once I said to him, 'Where *is* Mansfield exactly?'

'Mansfield? It's in the Nottinghamshire coalfields. It was a stronghold of the Union of Democratic Miners in the pit strike and in the 1987 general election the Labour candidate lost a lot of votes due to his support for the NUM. When these votes came back to Labour in 1992, Mansfield represented one of the biggest swings to Labour in the whole country.'

The old bloke with the Fulham scarf in front of us turned round and gave us a very strange look.

With all being well, soon I would know (or have known at some point) half a dozen people in the House of Commons – and all sitting on the side of the House that mattered. Because just as I, in my own way, had grown into part of the new establishment, my party was at last deemed grown-up enough to become the party of government. Power was coming – I could feel the difference. I know I've said before that I knew Labour would win the election, but this time I really *knew* that Labour would win the election. In previous contests I had never understood what more experienced party members meant when they claimed they could sense that we were *not* heading for victory. I realised now that this was because I had never experienced a feeling like the last year of John Major's government. It was a national mood: reactions in pubs when the Tories came on the telly, conversations overheard, the accumulation of comments from people you would have expected to be natural Conservative supporters. Gradually I realised that even our age-old enemies had come round to thinking that perhaps we might be worth a try.

The government were behaving like an opposition and Tony Blair was exuding far more authority than the prime minister was. Michael Heseltine was desperate that his pet project of the millennium dome should not be abandoned by an incoming Labour government, so he magnanimously agreed to discuss the plans with the opposition. But the leader of the opposition didn't go to him. The government minister had to go to Tony Blair's office. That was where anyone who wanted to be near the centre of long-term decision-making had to go. I hope Tony kept the deputy prime minister waiting in reception for a few minutes for good measure.

Apart from my brief hello to Tony Blair when he had

wandered into Gordon Brown's office I had given up any
hope of exchanging a few pleasantries with the man who
would soon be prime minister. He was the man of the
moment, as thousands of votes for the *Today* programme's *Man of the Year* poll (albeit on Labour Party
Campaign HQ headed notepaper) clearly testified. I
know I should have known better than to fall for the cult
of the personality, but I really did want to meet the man
who personified the hopes of millions up and down the
country. Then suddenly my opportunity came.

He was going to be at a Guy Fawkes party to which I
was invited. Clive Anderson had known Tony and
Cherie since the days when they had all been mere bar-
risters. Clive's new house overlooked Highbury Fields
and the public fireworks display there was reputed to be
very impressive so the event was combined with a
house-warming party. In truth, of course, nobody would
be watching the fireworks – everyone would be watching Tony Blair. 'Ooooh! Look at all the different blues in
that tie!' 'Aaaah! Look at the bright sparkle of that smile.'

I tried to imagine it – myself and the prime minister-
in-waiting, exchanging views on Labour's first hundred
days in office over a couple of glasses of mulled wine
and a jacket potato.

> 'So you see, Tony, it's not enough to be tough
> on crime, you have to be tough on the causes
> of crime as well.'
> 'Hmm, yes, I see what you're saying, John.
> Maybe I could work that into a soundbite.'
> 'If ever you need any gags, Tony, you know,
> for your speeches like, I'd be more than happy
> – I mean – we could still do them for Gordon
> and that.'

> 'Well, that would be fantastic, John – would
> you like to be Minister for the Arts as well?'

However, by the time my wife and I abandoned our car one mile short of our destination we realised that we were not the only people headed for Highbury Fields. The crowd was only slightly smaller than Woodstock. It was not even possible to get into the roads approaching the display, and the house we were headed for was at the epicentre of this crush. It wasn't fair – they were only there to see some fireworks, not meet the next prime minister. As the display began everyone was already very densely packed together and they had all grudgingly accepted the restricted views from which they were forced to watch the show. They did not appreciate a couple going, 'Excuse me, excuse me, please, sorry, excuse me!' as if we were attempting to barge our way to the front. I tried to justify our apparent pushiness by occasionally holding up my bottle of wine and saying, 'Sorry, we're going to a party, excuse me please, sorry ...' Really I wanted to shout out, 'Get out of my way! I'm going to meet Tony Blair!' Every inch of ground had to be fought for against a scrum of tightly packed north Londoners, who alternately tutted at us or just pretended not to hear our pleas for them to move. Parents with toddlers on their shoulders, dangerous-looking youths in Arsenal shirts, couples with their arms resolutely locked together preventing any way through; every obstacle had to be overcome before we realised we had battled 100 yards in the wrong direction. Tony Blair must be at one of those houses way over on the other side of the green. We finally got to the road where I had worked out we would be able to cut through and were met by 10-foot-high crash barriers with a row

304

of police on horseback. I considered explaining to them that they ought to let me through because I wanted to get to a private party which would be my only chance ever to meet Tony Blair, but they did not look like they would be very interested.

It would take us another hour to fight our way round to the other side, by which time Jackie's crowd phobia – which up until now I had pretended not to notice – would have sent her into terrified flashbacks of being trampled underfoot by hundreds of flag-waving old ladies at the Silver Jubilee celebrations. We forced our way back out again and sat exhausted in a pub. I attempted to quiz Jackie on what she would most want to achieve if she became prime minister but somehow the answers did not have the same thrilling immediacy. Anyway, abolishing mass fireworks displays was not even Labour policy.

That was my chance to chat to Tony Blair. The next day friends were saying, 'Oh, yes, he was very approachable,' or, 'We chatted for a while but he was rather guarded'. Not one of them said that he kept looking at his watch and saying, 'Where's John O'Farrell?'

As winter dragged on, the prime-minister-in-waiting looked like he was going to have to wait and wait and wait. Previously talked-about election dates in January and February came and went as it became clear that John Major was going to call the election as late as possible in the hope that Labour would somehow blow it. The Conservatives had been trailing Labour in the polls by around twenty points for more than four years now. Tony Blair's situation had been likened to a man carrying a very valuable vase down a long slippery corridor. But in truth the longer the prime minister delayed the more time there was to expose the shambles the government had become. The Tories lost their Parliamentary majority when a Tory MP died and then gained it again when a Labour MP died a few days later. They lost a division in the House of Commons by one vote and then won it again when it was discovered that a government whip had miscounted.

My confidence that Labour were going to win by a landslide was not shared by any professional pundits nor even the bookmakers – who are normally the best guide there is. Looking at the various odds for projected Labour majorities I noticed in the paper that Ladbrokes were offering 12–1 for any Labour majority over 121. This seemed to me to be very generous considering it was the result the polls had been predicting for four years, and I was obviously not the only person to think so because by the time I got to the bookies the odds had shrunk to 6–1 (although the man behind the counter still gave me the impression that I would be wasting my money). I forgot all about it until Cheltenham Gold Cup week when I went into Corals to collect 50 pence' worth of winnings from £10's worth of bets. I nonchalantly asked what odds they were offering on Labour getting a majority of over 121. She rang up the race room and reported back the odds. They were 100–1.

'Are you sure?'

'Yes, one hundred to one.'

My heart started racing.

'It's just that Ladbrokes are offering odds of six to one'.

She passed this information on to the head office and still the odds were confirmed to me as 100–1. I opened my wallet – only £25 in there, but I put it all on. Some loose change in my pocket so I paid the tax in advance as well. Occasionally you get the feeling that bookies have been too generous with their odds; you place a bet and they prove you wrong when they keep your money. But a Labour landslide at 100–1? What could they be thinking! When I got into work I reported these bizarre odds to everyone in the office. I was working on *Room 101* and Nick Hancock pulled out a wad of notes and said to the people rushing down to the betting shop, 'I'll have a hundred quid on that as well.' Pretty soon a queue was forming at the window. This rush alerted Corals to their mistake. As well as refusing to take any of these bets they gave my colleagues the message that my bet was void and that I would get my stake back if I went in that day. They must be joking, I thought. I didn't even risk walking past the front of the shop. I had thought the Halifax Conversion Ballot to be a perfect election. But now it seemed I had a good chance of receiving a windfall *and* being on the winning side! I couldn't wait for the day.

Finally on 17 March John Major came out into Downing Street and proclaimed that the election was going to be on 1 May. Labour day – how perfectly appropriate. The next morning the *Sun* announced it was backing Tony Blair. I have always said what a fine paper the *Sun* was. Almost immediately the cash-for-questions scandal resurfaced and Tim Smith resigned as the Conservative candidate for Beaconsfield. Neil Hamilton promised to make the issue run and run by refusing to follow his lead. A couple of sex scandals were published for good measure and within the first few days the Tories' campaign looked in total disarray. I had a feeling that these were going to be the most enjoyable six weeks of my life.

Things can only get better

General Election – 1 May 1997

After flopping drunkenly down onto my bed at about eight in the morning, I have a vague memory of Jackie pulling off my shoes. After that, the date 2 May 1997 does not appear as a day in my life.

A body can only take so much alcohol and cheering and jumping up and down and a brain can only take so much euphoria and astonishment. After ten hours of this a siren suddenly went off inside my head followed by a public address announcement: This body is closing down in one minute – repeat: total shutdown, one minute ... and then I was gone. Which is a shame because by all accounts 2 May 1997 was a very happy day in the history of this country. Jackie said that everybody on the streets was smiling from ear to ear. A passing bus driver gave her a cheery wave, cars stopped to let her pass with the buggy, love was all around. I would have liked to walk around the streets of England to soak up the euphoria on that scorching spring morning. It was the day I had waited eighteen years for.

It was a shame that I didn't manage to be conscious for it.

It was especially wonderful for all those people who after so many successive defeats had completely given up believing that it was ever going to happen. The disappointment of 1992 had etched itself so deeply into the souls of every Labour supporter that hardly anyone dared believe what the polls were clearly telling us – that the Labour Party was heading for a landslide. I had found myself going around trying to share my enjoyment of the Tories' disarray, only to find everyone else with their heads held low saying, 'They're going to get back in – I just know it – everyone's going to bottle out and vote Conservative again.' Like brides that have been abandoned at the altar and can never let themselves fall in love again, Labour's supporters spent the month of April in despondent denial.

A general election campaign is the one period every five years in which the political parties can really focus on their vision of what Britain should be. It is the time when they set out their policies and ask the voters to trust them upon that basis. With this in mind the Conservatives began the campaign by organising a man in a giant chicken costume to run around flapping his wings behind Tony Blair. The *Daily Mirror* then countered this argument by hiring a man in a fox costume to chase the chicken. Then, for reasons that were never made clear, a couple of pantomime rhinos joined the scene. Perhaps they represented the 'Don't Knows'. Some of the newer democracies from Eastern Europe had sent observers to see how it should be done. I can't lip-read Romanian but I think he was probably saying, 'For *this* our brothers laid down their lives?'

The Tory campaign was gratifyingly appalling. Their poster campaign started with the phrase 'New Labour,

New Danger' but they decided that this wasn't quite catchy enough so they changed it to 'New Labour, Euro Job Losses'. Then, pursuing the animal motif that they had begun with the giant chicken, they unveiled a poster which featured a lion with a tear falling down his cheek. It looked like the lion was crying because he'd been press-ganged into such a crappy advert. It was like he was thinking, Look, my agent made me do it. I wanted to be in *Daktari*.

Lady Thatcher asked where she could be of most use, and was promptly sent to Hong Kong to open their new suspension bridge. Her power and influence had withered away, and now she did not even have a vote. (Those without a vote are royalty, peers of the realm and certified lunatics — which by my reckoning ruled Thatcher out on all three counts.) But there were plenty of other loose canons in the Tory Party ready to contradict the government line at every turn. One commentator predicted that the issue of Europe would be a thorn in the side of the Tory campaign. In reality it was more a sword between the ribs going through the heart and right out of the other side again. Over a hundred MPs issued election addresses which contradicted government policy. John Major tore up the script for his party political broadcast and used the slot as a direct plea to his Parliamentary candidates not to bind his hands on Europe. He clasped his hands together to illustrate what bound hands looked like. They looked very similar to praying hands. He claimed he was making this broadcast to talk directly to the British people, which was a bit unfortunate because they were all watching the Coca-Cola cup final replay on another channel.

As if the Tories didn't have enough to embarrass

them, every other day we cut across to watch the unfolding sideshow in Tatton. A plot had been hatched at Labour's HQ to field an independent candidate against Neil Hamilton, with Labour and the Liberals standing aside in a seat which neither stood a chance of winning. Martin Bell, the earnest former war correspondent, was persuaded to stand. Despite having ducked snipers in Beirut and been hit by shrapnel in Bosnia, nothing had prepared him for being harangued by Neil Hamilton's wife Christine. She was such a phenomenon that someone had the bright idea of inviting her on to *Have I Got News For You*. This was arranged during the campaign, although she said she would not have time until after polling day.

'And you'd still be prepared to come on even if your husband loses?' asked the researcher.

'I can assure you there is absolutely no possibility of that happening!'

Once Hamilton was turfed out, we thought we might as well ask him on as well. Their immediate reaction was, 'Will it mean another appearance fee?' It did and we gave them the money in brown envelopes at the end of the show.

I chatted briefly to them in hospitality afterwards. She was quite the most charming, terrifying and frankly bonkers woman I had ever met – a sort of cross between Joyce Grenfell and Lady Macbeth. I was also struck with wonderment at how a man quite as dim as Neil Hamilton ever got to become a government minister. It was a fitting reflection of the dearth of talent in the Tory Party in its final years.

In 1992 we had been allowed to broadcast a *Spitting Image* special the night before the general election, and mainly because of the way that we portrayed Neil

Kinnock some commentators felt we may have actually helped the Tories. I was anxious that this charge should not be levied against us now that I was writing for *Have I Got News For You* in the run-up to polling day. I wrote a little link along the following lines: 'And with the scores at four-all, the teams are as evenly balanced as the BBC's election coverage,' and then the words *Vote Labour* were to flash up on the screen. The producer and Mark thought this was a funny enough gag, but both said it would be far more surprising if we put up the caption *Vote Conservative*. No, no, we can't possibly say that, I laughed, hoping that they were joking. No, they said with a determined look of mischief in their eyes. Let's say *Vote Conservative* – that'll really put the cat among the pigeons. How could Mark do this to me? A fellow party member? I tried a different tack. 'Our audience will enjoy the joke much more if it goes along with what the majority of them want us to say.' But nothing could pull it back. 'I withdraw my joke!' I protested, but it was too late, it had escaped and was out of my control, a Frankenstein's monster of a joke. I winced as I saw the words *Vote Conservative* flash up on the screen because of a set-up I'd written. It is rare to get more than two or three complaints about a line in a show. There were more than two hundred complaints about that one. The anger of many of the callers was remarkable. They really believed the BBC was taking instructions from Tory central office. Who were all these stupid paranoid people? Then it struck me – they were *me,* fifteen years ago.

On the doorstepping front there were two campaigns that I could help with. My own constituency, the rock-solid Labour Vauxhall, or my former constituency of Battersea just down the road. Having the choice meant that I could always give the impression that I was being frightfully busy elsewhere every time an election organiser rang me up. Having worked so hard in all of Labour's defeats down the years I did very little to help them win their greatest ever victory. I couldn't help thinking there might be some link between these two facts.

At long, long last it was polling day. I had the same sort of excited spring in my step as on the day I got married. This was the day, the day I had waited for. Six thousand five hundred and seventy-two days after Margaret Thatcher had swept to power and I had been publicly humiliated in my school's mock election – at last it was our turn to take control. I tried to wait until after I had had my breakfast, but it was no good. I went out and voted about ten minutes after the polls opened.

Although we have a secret ballot in this country, I am prepared to reveal at this point that I put my cross next to the name of the Labour candidate. Then I folded the paper and popped it in the battered old ballot box. I still love doing that. It was like releasing a champion racing pigeon – it was just a question of waiting fifteen hours to see it come in first. Soon I was walking the half-mile to Queenstown ward to volunteer my services. My old empire had been revived and was now in capable hands. I had to keep stopping myself suggesting things or telling volunteers where the various blocks were. I was just a foot-soldier now. I was given a bundle of *Vote Today* leaflets to deliver to the Labour promise and as I walked round the Patmore it felt like a very different place to the cold scowling estate that I had canvassed so many times before. People saw my red rosette and gave me a friendly wave and thumbs up. Some builders shouted, 'Yeah! Labour! All right!' I had never experienced such enthusiasm from the electorate at large. I wondered whether those builders who had so mercilessly baited me all those years ago would be voting Labour for the first time today. With all my leaflets delivered I spent a couple of hours sitting on a polling station out under the blazing sun, feeling my forehead turning as red as the electoral map of Britain.

The rosette pinned to my lapel had been worn in every campaign I had ever fought. It was a sort of lucky mascot – although it's hard to see what had ever been lucky about it. It had extra frills and was a deeper red than the flimsy standard-issue things that were being given out these days. To be honest I was rather proud of it. But when I'd been sitting there a few minutes, an officer from the council came out of the polling station and told me I would have to remove the sticker from the middle. Apparently it's fine to sit there with a red rosette on, but to sit there with a red rosette that says *Vote Labour* is an attempt to persuade people on the way into the polling station. After six weeks of poster campaigns, party political broadcasts, leaflets through their letter boxes and advertisements in their newspapers, members of the public were going to see my little *Vote Labour* sticker and finally be persuaded to abandon a lifetime of voting Tory. Although I had never encountered this objection before I reluctantly pulled off the thick collection of stickers that had accumulated over the years to leave a tatty piece of cardboard. The council officer was satisfied and my vintage rosette was ruined.

I sat there in the sun and with growing amazement I peeled the stickers apart and remembered all the different campaigns they represented. Under two ordinary *Vote Labour* stickers from recent Lambeth Council elections was a sticker that said *Alf Dubs* – that was from our defeat in Battersea in 1992. Under that was *Wandsworth May 5* from my personal council defeat in 1990. I could still see the Conservatives leaping with ecstatic amazement as each Labour ward after another turned blue. Under that *Anita Pollack,* the surprise victory in the Euro-elections in 1989. I remembered Anita had said how fantastic that result had been for the Labour Party in the south-western corner of her constituency out in Epsom – they had never even had a Labour councillor before. A few more ordinary *Vote Labour* stickers from a couple of hopeless Wandsworth by-elections and then another that said *Alf Dubs* – from the 1987 general election campaign when we had first lost Battersea, perhaps my personal all-time political low point. Under that was a sticker that said *Wandsworth and ILEA – May 8.* I'd forgotten that we had had an elected education authority, let alone that I'd campaigned for a Labour candidate for it. That was from 1986. Beneath that was a sticker that said *Nick Raynsford*, from the false dawn of the Fulham by-election, then some more *Vote Labour* stickers with the old red flag logo, then *Vote Labour GLC & ILEA,* and finally at the bottom of the pile *Vote Labour – June 9* – that was from 1983, the first election I ever helped in and the worst day in the Labour Party's history. It felt a very long time ago. On what was to be Labour's greatest ever day, I peeled away the defeats of the past, seeing how every campaign had tried to paper over the disappointment of the last.

I had to lend my rosette to the person who replaced me on the polling station. I told him it had a lot of sentimental value but I never saw it again. I suppose its mission was now accomplished.

1 May 1997 was my dad's 78th birthday. He had been 59 when the last Labour government had fallen. Now he was going to get the best birthday present he could have wanted. Like the last two general elections I spent the evening in Battersea but this time I spent it in a very nice restaurant. It seemed like the New Labour thing to do. I gave Dad his present wrapped in a Labour Party poster. By now we all felt that Labour would probably win, but nobody shared my unbounded fate-tempting confidence. 'It'll be bigger than 1945!' I declared and my prediction was greeted with cautious scepticism. 'A Labour majority of thirty,' predicted Dad, who had often described to me how they had jumped up and down with delight when the news of Labour's 1945 landslide had reached the troops in India.

My brother Pat, I was relieved to discover, had heard that there was a general election earlier in the day. He had rung me to ask if he should tactically vote Lib Dem in Richmond Park. I had always persuaded him that he should vote Labour even where they were guaranteed to finish a poor third, but this time I told him to go for it and that night the Liberals duly took the seat on a tactical anti-Tory vote. Mum and Dad came back to Clapham to watch the results and Pat, incredibly, went home to bed. I sometimes wonder whether we are really related. As Big Ben struck ten o'clock David Dimbleby announced the results of the BBC exit poll. Labour were 18 points ahead of the Tories. A landslide really was on the cards. Jackie would still not believe it – as if to count electoral chickens before they hatched would cause the result to go the other way.

My confidence was not as impenetrable as I thought because soon after came a couple of scares that made my heart miss more than a few beats. First Anthony King said that for Labour's result to be in line with the exit poll we should expect Chris Mullin's vote (in Sunderland South – the first seat to declare) to be around 34,000. I heard the returning officer announce the figure of 27,000 and the nightmare of Basildon '92 flashed before me. Jackie said, 'That's bad, isn't it?'

'Erm, no, look, they're saying it's a big swing to Labour,' I said unconvincingly. Then almost in a throw-away comment David Dimbleby said that it was looking like a close call in Mitcham & Morden. I knew this was a seat that we had to win well, a seat we had held even when Thatcher was first elected, so to lose it would be to lose the election. No further mention was made of Mitcham until we took it with over a 13,000 majority, so I don't know how they contrived to give us such a fright.

There were two hours of speculation and uncertainty before the Tory dam really burst and the Labour gains poured in. If there had been a power cut at Birmingham's National Indoor Arena, the smile of Gisela Stuart beaming from the stage would have lit up the whole hall. It was a warm, measured, yet ecstatic smile that finally washed all my anxieties away. Neville Chamberlain's old seat of Birmingham Edgbaston had never been Labour and now we took it with a majority of nearly 5,000. 'That's Labour's Basildon!' said David Dimbleby. Now even Jackie believed we were on our way.

This was the first seat to change from Conservative to Labour on television. But fifteen minutes earlier Labour had taken Crosby – such a safe Tory seat that no one had bothered to put television cameras there. But on a monumental 18 per cent swing Clare Curtis-Thomas became the first of 100 women Labour MPs elected that

317

night. The seat was 120th on Labour's list of winnables. It was looking distinctly promising, but even then I did not dare hope for some of the delights that were still in store.

I knew that the first minister to go would be a particular treat. Just how gratifying it would turn out to be I could never have imagined. The television cameras cut to Battersea. *John Bowis, Conservative, 18,687. Martin Linton, Labour, 24,047* ... The other figures were drowned out in the cheers from the town hall and my front room. That afternoon I had shaken hands with John Bowis when he visited the polling station on which I had been sitting. His driver just parked in the middle of the road and allowed a huge queue to build up behind him. Typical inconsiderate Tory, I had thought. Now the man who had deposed Alf had himself been cast aside. Martin smiled his modest smile at the result and we cheered some more as Battersea was returned to its rightful owners.

At one a.m. the ghost of Basildon was laid to rest – we took it with a majority of 13,000. David Mellor then lost with particularly bad grace in Putney and laid into James Goldsmith's Referendum Party for attempting to 'buy the British political system'. As if the £20 million that the Tories had just spent had all been raised by old ladies making jam. All three Wandsworth constituencies were now Labour – that gave me a particularly warm glow inside. Many more ministers were to follow. Forsythe went in Stirling. Peter Snow got particularly excited about the electoral map north of the Border: 'We are forecasting that John Major's Conservative Party will be down to an all-time low of ... three seats in Scotland.' Ha! No chance. The final tally would of course be three less than that. It seemed that John Major's warning of the break-up of the United Kingdom had rather failed to strike a chord. No seats in Scotland or Wales. By now the red bars were flashing up on the screen faster than we could count them. All sorts of places that sounded far too nice to have Labour MPs: Cleethorpes, Kingswood, Bedford, Vale of Glamorgan, Falmouth & Cambourne, Gloucester ... ah, Gloucester! That was the seat that we had to win if Labour were to have an overall majority. We took it with 8,000 votes to spare. By the end of the evening the Tories would have lost more seats than they held.

The gathering of Labour supporters in my front room was sitting there with fingers crossed for good luck at every result, and legs crossed because they had drunk too much beer and didn't want to miss a single moment of it. It's strange the people you end up watching elections with: old party friends who ring you up, someone from down the road, a bloke you met in the pub that night, a few friends and relations – all brought together and suddenly behaving like intimate friends through a common desire to see a Labour victory.

When Labour had lost previous general elections it had always skilfully combined abject failure with a sprinkling of bad luck on top: losing seats by less than a hundred votes but never holding them by such tiny margins. Now this was happening to the Tories. The counting in Winchester went on until the next day when the Liberals took it by a disputed two votes. In the meantime Rupert Allason held the record by losing by 12 votes in Torbay. This was particularly pleasing since he was suing *Have I Got News For You* about a joke we had written about him. I later learnt that during the campaign he had had lunch in a hotel in his constituency and had failed to leave a tip. All the

319

waiters and kitchen staff agreed to vote Lib Dem as a result and the Liberals took it with those dozen votes. Perhaps there is a God.

Lamont went, although the cameras didn't dwell on this for nearly long enough for my liking. Lady Olga Maitland was ejected from Sutton and Cheam. She had become a particular un-favourite of mine back in my CND days when she had set up an organisation called something like 'Women and Families for Total Nuclear Annihilation', if memory serves. Sir Marcus Fox was particularly disgusted to lose his seat to some twenty-four-year-old I think I recognised as the lad who did the photocopying in Gordon Brown's office. Rhodes Boyson was ousted in Brent and even Mrs Thatcher's old seat of Finchley turned red. If only she'd still been there to lose it.

Then we cut to Tatton. Martin Bell had taken on the monumental task of overturning a Tory majority that with boundary changes was reckoned to be about 22,000. He won the seat with a majority of 11,000 and became the first independent MP in the House of Commons since 1950. In a humble and sincere speech Bell quoted G. K. Chesterton while fairy lights on the extended nipples of a seven-foot transvestite candidate flashed on and off either side of his ears.

Still the biggest treat was yet to come. They had started to whisper that even Michael Portillo might lose his seat. This truly would be a catastrophe for the Tories. In case I should feel any pangs of sympathy I remembered how he had stood up at the Tory Party conference and said that there were three letters that struck terror into the heart of our enemies: 'S–A–S. They spell out the message: "Don't mess with Britain"' and all the sheep had cheered and the observers had looked at each other in horrified disbelief. Now the arrogant standard-bearer of the Tory right was to get his come-uppance from quite the most unlikely hero of the election.

A young man called Stephen Twigg had been given the job of secretary of the Fabian Society on the understanding that he was not going to become a Labour MP in the near future. Alf Dubs, who was on the society's interviewing panel, recounted to me that when Twigg said he was fighting Portillo's seat, they were quite confident they would not be losing him to the House of Commons. And here he was swaying slightly nervously on the stage behind the defence secretary waiting for the most memorable result of the whole election. *Portillo, Michael Denzil Xavier* (a few chuckles just to warm us up), *19,137. Twigg, Stephen, 20,570.* At that moment Twigg's face went through a series of expressions that took us through his mental journey from astonishment to exhausted elation. There was a relieved sigh, then a coy smile, and then he rolled his eyes heavenwards in a look that said 'Ooh-er, gosh!' like Miss Albania being crowned Miss World against all expectations. I was rather disappointed he didn't cap it all by fainting. Portillo's humiliation was total. The returning officer had not even been able to pronounce his middle name correctly. 'Xavier' became 'ex-saviour' which, for the Tory Party, was exactly what he had just become. It was about half past three in the morning and Jackie had just gone to bed. I went and woke her up again to tell her what had happened and for this she did not mind. Then I got a mini-cab to the only place to be.

As I arrived at the Royal Festival Hall, D:ream were on stage playing 'Things Can Only Get Better'. At long last they had. I met Mark and he seemed almost as drunk as me. Then I spotted Alf and together we watched more Labour gains pour in on one of the screens. Alf had entered the Commons as Labour began its years in opposition and as we cheered every Labour gain I couldn't help wondering if he was now wishing he could be part of the new era. They interviewed Robin Cook on the telly, and then I looked across and saw them doing it for real a few yards behind me. I wandered round greeting a few friends I had not seen for years. I bumped into Martin Linton, the new MP for Battersea, and I congratulated him. I had thought that there was no swing or turnout that could ever surprise this walking encyclopaedia of electoral facts. 'You know we've taken Hove,' I said to him.

'Hove?!' he said in utter disbelief.

Well, no result that could surprise him until now.

'Yes,' I said, rather pleased to be the bearer of this news.

'Hove?' he just repeated, in a tone of voice that said, 'Are you sure you haven't been hallucinating?'

'Yes, Hove.'

'Hove!' he said again and again in amazement.

It has to be said that 'Labour', 'Gain' and 'Hove' are not three words you would normally expect to find in the same sentence. The name conjures up images of old ladies sitting in tearooms reading the *Sunday Express*. But there were plenty of other unlikely recruits that night. Wimbledon, Hastings & Rye, Norfolk North West, Stroud – places where Labour had come a resounding third in my *Times Guide to the House of Commons 1983*. When Michael Portillo had first won Enfield Southgate in the 1984 by-election we only got 11 per cent of the vote. Suddenly I was shaking the hand and congratulating the man who had just taken the seat for

Labour on a 17 per cent swing. I told him I thought his speech had been great – when he had thanked all the people who voted for us 'consistently through the difficult years as well as the good years for Labour; their loyalty and consistency has been repaid with this result'. Those lines had been for people like me.

There was some commotion at one of the doors and I saw that Gordon Brown had arrived. There were lights on him and camera crews buzzing, and lots of people were patting him on the back, so I thought I wouldn't trouble him now. Then it occurred to me that I might never speak to him again – so I went over and shook his hand and he thanked me profusely for all the stuff I'd sent him during the campaign. He struck me as a very happy man that night, released at last from the sterile futility of opposition. But the whole room was packed with elated MPs, jubilant party activists and the occasional bemused celebrity who wasn't quite sure why they were there. Word spread that Tony and Cherie would soon be arriving and I joined the crowds pouring outside to stand before the stage where *He* would speak.

Behind us was a huge bank of photographers and cameramen, like the auditorium at a theatre, which of course is exactly what it was. We the crowd were the chorus and Tony and Cherie would be the stars. The crowd grew thicker as we waited for about half an hour, listening to and singing along to 'Things Can Only Get Better' by D:ream. After that the DJ chose to play 'Things Can Only Get Better' by D:ream, and then he flicked through his extensive record collection and dug out 'Things Can Only Get Better' by D:ream (the specially extended singalong 'Labour-have-just-won-a-landslide' mix). The lights swung over us and we clapped our hands in the air chanting 'Tony! Tony!' Once I had whistled and cheered right in the front of the stage at Bracknell Leisure Centre waiting for the Boomtown Rats to do an encore. Now I was behaving in exactly the same way, waiting for the new prime minister.

A passing train hooted and we gave a huge cheer, hoping this noise signalled his arrival. I looked up at the sky. In the half-hour that we had waited there dawn had risen over the Royal Festival Hall. Like May Day had been, it was another beautiful day. Did a strategy meeting plan for Tony to arrive there at the dawn of this glad confident morning or did it just work out that way? Either way it was perfect. A projection above the stage said 'New Government'. They managed to get that made quickly, I thought.

Finally he came – a gleaming car sped up from the right between a path of crash barriers and Tony and Cherie were carried right to the edge of the stage. A surge in the crowd as we leaned forward for our first glance. Tony, calm and collected, touched his cuffs as he always does when he knows he's being filmed and then continued the night's handshaking marathon. Dozens of hands reached out and some were grasped and others were missed. The vast majority of the crowd were now total converts to his mission and those that were not still stretched their arms out as if to say, 'Please touch me, leader, and cure me of this Old Labour cynicism'. He stood behind the lectern and the cheering went on long enough almost to embarrass him, until he signalled for us to allow him to speak.

I cheered in all the gaps where we were supposed to cheer and clapped when everyone else clapped, although I can't remember exactly what Tony said. I think he used the word 'new' once or twice. I saw myself on television afterwards. While everyone else was cheering and gazing up at Tony, I was on tiptoes looking around at everyone else cheering and gazing up at Tony.

I would have liked to live that event ten times over. Once to listen to Tony Blair's speech to take in the words he was saying. Once to watch Cherie looking at him and applauding and laughing at the distant football-like chants of 'Tony Blair, Tony Blair, Tony Blair!' Once to look at the faces of all the supporters in the crowd, young and old, former MPs and new MPs, activists and celebrities. I would have liked to watch Neil Kinnock, standing beside the stage, looking up, applauding and grinning with no trace of envy or regret. The crowd chanted his name and he waved and smiled, but he knew this was not his moment. I think Cherie suggested to Tony 'what about getting Neil up?' but Tony had learnt the script off by heart and was not going to let a spontaneous urge to clasp hands with a man who had lost two elections become the front page on the next day's newspapers. I would have liked to watch the photographers, picking out all the celebrities and ordinary activists for the perfect image of the perfect day. I would have liked to watch the people who couldn't get into the party – crowded on every distant balcony and terrace of the South Bank, like Beatles fans waiting at Heathrow airport. And finally I would have liked to do what I actually did do another ten times over, which was to watch them all in little bits, not wanting to miss any of it and trying to take in the scale of the event, the size of our victory, and the sheer volume of happiness. The Tories never had a victory party like this one, because they never waited eighteen years for one. We were drunk on victory, adrenaline, and – well – alcohol. I hoped John Smith was looking down from heaven.

When all the waving and cheering had finished, I

raced round to the side of the stage where Tony and Cherie were leaving and suddenly I was right at the front of the crash barrier. He'd seen me, he was coming towards me. Tony Blair grasped my outstretched hand and shook it, and in my drunken emotional state I blurted out, 'We've waited so long! We've waited so long!' and he smiled and gave me an affirmative nod which sort of said, I know what you mean but I'd better not chat with you 'cos you look a bit pissed. Cherie shook my hand too – both of them had learnt to clasp the back of people's hands so they could be the ones to let go.

They stayed at the party a while and then they were gone. And after the bride and groom have headed home it is time for all the guests to leave as well. I floated back along the South Bank towards Westminster. With the dawn sun shining on the Houses of Parliament, the new gold paint glistening and reflecting in the Thames, it really did look like a completely different place. It was ours. I wouldn't have been surprised if a giant rainbow had sprung out of the top of Big Ben and sprinkled fairy dust as it formed a giant shimmering arc with the Royal Festival Hall. A solitary car came over Westminster Bridge. There were red balloons and Labour posters all over it and it tooted at me and I waved. There would never be a greater day to be a Labour supporter. Or a greater place to have been one.

The British people had finally come good. The Conservatives had tried to frighten them with horror stories of high taxation, immigration, German domination and the break-up of the United Kingdom, but at long last hope had triumphed over fear. In the town where I had joined the Labour Party, an openly gay Labour candidate had fought a particularly unpleasant

326

homophobe. The Tory described his opponent's homo-sexuality as a 'disease-ridden, sterile and God-forsaken occupation' and had issued a leaflet saying that if the Labour candidate won 'schoolchildren would be in danger'. But the people of Exeter, God bless them, voted with a 12 per cent swing, higher than the national average, for Labour's Ben Bradshaw. In his victory speech he said that they 'had rejected bigotry and chosen reason, and for that,' he spoke with the emotion that revealed the very real fear he had had of defeat, 'I want to thank them from the bottom of my heart.'

I wanted to thank them as well. I wanted to go straight to Exeter and walk around Cathedral Yard and shake the hand of everyone I met. I wanted to thank everyone in the whole country who had voted for us – the 13.5 million people who had the courage and decency to put their trust in us. I wanted to say well done to the tube driver who drove me home, to the passengers who were setting off early to go to work, to the newsagent who was putting out his historic first editions. We did it! We should be proud of ourselves. Bliss was it to be alive in that dawn.

An hour later I was out cold. Though I would not be conscious for most of the day, the business of getting on with life continued. People took the kids to school, went to work, opened their shops. Jackie took our little girl to playgroup and started chatting about the previous night's events.

'I've only had a couple of hours' sleep,' she said.

'How do you think I feel?' replied the other mum. 'My husband got elected MP for Hornchurch last night. We weren't expecting it at all.'

At some point in the evening I came round and flopped in front of the telly to watch every news programme back to back. John Major resigning and going off to watch the cricket. The new prime minister going to the Palace. Then the model family arriving in Downing Street and a lump in my throat as I saw his kids standing there, excited yet bemused.

'How are they going to get to school?' asked Jackie, homing in on one of the toughest problems to face an incoming Labour government. The smiling hand-picked Labour supporters were arranged in order of height and each had been given a Union flag to wave. Even though I knew this I was still moved by the sight of it.

On the Saturday morning I listened alone in my kitchen as Radio 4 played the edited highlights of the Conservatives' eighteen years in power – a sort of Rock 'n' Roll Tory years. For some reason when they played an archive recording of a miner during the pit strike and then cut straight to a burst of '99 Red Balloons' by Nena I started to cry. What had become of me? Reduced to tears by '99 Red Balloons'! Somehow the huge sensation of relief and the end of months of subconscious anxiety, mingled in with the sense of a lost youth and great happiness at the result, all overwhelmed me. It was all over.

During the next few days the new cabinet were called to Downing Street. John Prescott stood on the steps of Number 10 waving and said, 'I've always wanted to do this.' Harriet Harman's daughter took the call from Number 10 Downing Street while her mum was gardening.

'Someone's on the phone, Mum. It's Number 10, down the street.'

Mo Mowlam was asked what position she had got and she replied, 'Shadow Northern Ireland. Oh, no, not shadow, *minister* for Northern Ireland.' Over and over again the new Labour ministers talked about mistakes by 'this Tory government – sorry – the last Tory government'. It would take a while to change the habits of eighteen years.

Then I read that Alf, Lord Dubs of Battersea, had been made under-secretary of state for Northern Ireland. I was so delighted for him; a member of the government after all. I sent him an illustrated history of Ulster. As I lay in bed that night I suddenly feared I had made a very stupid mistake. 'Oh, no – I've just sent a parcel to the home address of the new junior minister for Northern Ireland. It'll probably be blown up in a controlled explosion.'

On the Saturday night, as if to welcome us back into the European fold, the juries of Europe voted us overwhelming winners of the Eurovision Song Contest. As each country said '*Royaume Uni – douze points*' it was like a surreal repeat of election night – you wanted Peter Snow to have a graphic for demonstrating landslide Eurovision victories. 'There's Abba in '73, there's Ireland all the way through the early 1990s, now *look* what happens to Katrina and the Waves in 1997.'

With the temperature in the seventies it already felt like a bright optimistic new country. Some friends of mine have an old lady living next door to them, and on the Sunday morning they chatted over the fence.

'Isn't it brilliant?'

'Yes, it makes you proud, doesn't it?'

'Did you watch it all?'

'Ooh, yes,' said the old lady. 'All of it. I was sure Ireland were going to win again.'

On the Tuesday I went into Coral's with my betting slip and a racing heart. I had already spoken to several people who had worked in betting shops and they were all agreed I would not get any money. If a member of staff makes a 'palpable mistake', then the bookmakers do not have to pay. They had been expecting me. True to form they said they could not pay up because the odds on my betting slip were a mistake, and so I said that obviously I would have to take this further. I wrote to the man who deals with complaints and set out exactly what had happened. How I had made them check the odds twice and how they had still accepted my money. Then I'm afraid I shamelessly exploited my job. I had already written the letter on the headed notepaper of the TV production company I was working for. The final paragraph of my letter said that if the money was not paid I would be contacting the press, using what I claimed were my 'extensive contacts in the print and television media'. Ahem. 'Having made millions out of the election,' I went on, 'Corals must decide if they think that £2,500 is worth that much bad publicity.' The next day I got a phone call telling me to go back to the betting shop to collect my winnings. This is what I hoped life would be like for everyone under New Labour. As I left the bookies with two and a half grand stuffed in my pocket, the lady called me back. A moment of fear – like the escaped prisoner of war having his ticket double-checked at Colditz railway station. She explained that when I'd originally placed the bet I'd paid 10 per cent tax instead of the new rate of 9 per cent. She gave me the 25 pence difference. I should bloody well hope so.

I spent some of the money from my bet having the front of the house redecorated and the front door painted bright red. Once I declared my politics with a spray can and clichéd slogans. Now my political colours were proclaimed on a big front door in a leafy street in Clapham. And now every day the Tory Party activist who lives opposite me is reminded who won on 1 May 1997. He had a word with our decorator to ask him for a quote to get his house done. 'But we'll be keeping our door blue,' he said. I was so pleased he'd noticed.

Gordon Brown's office rang up a few days later. 'Hello,' they said. 'We are having a party here in Downing Street for all the leading people in the media.' Here it comes, we thought, payback time. The reason we had written Gordon all those jokes for free – so that we could rub shoulders with the rich and famous in Downing Street once Labour were in power.

'Yes, all the leading people in the media, yes,' said Mark expectantly.

'Well, Gordon was wondering if you could write some gags for his speech.'

As compensation, I invited myself to the House of Commons to have a bite to eat with Fiona. As I sat in the central lobby watching people come and go it felt a very different place. Ten years earlier it had been packed with Conservative MPs doing deals with smug-looking businessmen. Now it was bustling with young and *normal* people – women MPs who had employed women researchers, lots of people who, basically, looked a bit like me and my friends.

Then one week after the Tories' greatest ever rout they were reduced from 165 MPs to 164 with the death of the MP for the seat of Uxbridge. As a consequence of this I had a rather disturbing dream – that the Labour Party high command wanted me to stand. My reaction in the dream shifted from flattered excitement to depressed foreboding. If elected I would have to work every hour of the day and never see my kids, I would always be getting in trouble for saying the wrong thing and I knew I'd panic at the faintest prospect of any real political responsibility. I rapidly realised that the last thing I ever wanted to be was an MP. I woke up with a huge sense of relief and realised that I could never be a politician and that the days when politics was all I cared about were far behind me.

In my mid-thirties I was part of the new establishment, a member of the safe and tepid middle classes. Part of a whole generation of former angry young men and women who had grown into mellow middle age. Toyah Wilcox used to dye her hair bright colours and sing, 'I'm going to turn this world inside out, I'm going to turn suburbia upside down'. Now she was doing the voices for Teletubbies. A friend told me he had got hold of some really excellent grass – and I knew he was referring to the problems I'd been having reseeding my lawn. Pete said it was just as well we didn't all go on demonstrations any more because the chants would have changed somewhat. *What do we want? A winter-flowering clematis! When do we want it? Before we lay the patio!* We were no longer a threat. I think this had been confirmed to me a few years earlier on the last demonstration I ever went on. The charming young chaps from Class War were throwing bits of sticks and empty beer cans at a row of riot police. The police charged and with their usual care started lashing out at everybody. Suddenly a policeman came running up to me. He raised his truncheon in the air to strike me and I stood there with an expression of such indignant disbelief that he was completely thrown. So he turned to an ageing punk who was trying to clamber up a statue beside me and started whacking him round the legs instead. In a split second my face must have said to him,

332

You can't hit me – I'm middle-class. I never really felt in danger again after that. The policeman had seen it in my eyes. I was a mortgage-paying, pension-planning, pram-pushing, respectable conformist.

In its eighteen years of opposition the Labour Party had come of age, and I had grown up with it. But just because I was more left-wing when I was younger does not mean I'll admit to having moved to the right in my old age. I just stayed in the Labour Party, that's all. The membership card's still there in my wallet. It's between the one for the National Trust and the Marks & Spencer chargecard. All right, so I've got a nice house and a four-door family saloon and bottles of wine that I didn't drink on the day I bought them. And all right I don't go to Labour Party meetings any more, or eat beanburgers or wear T-shirts with slogans on. And all right I used to rail against my parents for having money and calling themselves left-wing. But the day after my dream someone from the local Labour Party came round and asked me if I would deliver some leaflets. If I'd changed that much I would have said no. If I'd changed that much I would have said I couldn't be bothered. But I took the leaflets and two weeks later they were all delivered. Every single one. I paid our au pair a fiver to do them for me.

J O'F – May–Oct 1997

The long-awaited follow-up to the classic bestseller THINGS CAN ONLY GET BETTER . . .

Coming Autumn 2017
Bringing you the very latest on Brexit,
Trump and Theresa May's snap election . . .

'As the Labour candidate I prepared for every possible question on the local radio Election Phone-In. What I had not prepared for was my mum ringing up to say that she agreed with John O'Farrell. On EVERYTHING.'

Things Can Only Get Worse is the personal story of one political activist helping Labour progress from its 1997 landslide to the unassailable position it enjoys today.

Along the way, John O'Farrell stood for Parliament against Theresa May but failed to step into her shoes; he was dropped from Tony and Cherie's Christmas card list after he revealed he always sent their card on to a friend from the SWP; and he campaigned for a new non-selective inner-city state school, then realized this meant he had to send his kids to a non-selective inner-city state school.

The long-awaited sequel to the best-selling *Things Can Only Get Better* is for everyone who could use a good laugh in the face of Brexit, Trump and Britain's ever-changing political landscape. A roller-coaster ride through the last two decades, via the very best political jokes (excluding the ones that keep getting elected).